£11.95

Social Semiotics

Social Semiotics

Robert Hodge
and
Gunther Kress

Polity Press

First published 1988 by Polity Press in association with Basil Blackwell.

Editorial Office:
Polity Press, Dales Brewery, Gwydir Street, Cambridge CB1 2LJ, UK

Basil Blackwell Ltd
108 Cowley Road, Oxford OX4 1JF, UK

British Library Cataloguing in Publication Data
Hodge, Robert
   Social semiotics.
   1. Nonverbal communication 2. Social psychology
   I. Title II. Kress, Gunther

302.2'22 HM258

ISBN 0-7456-0253-3
ISBN 0-7456-0373-4 Pbk

Typeset in Ehrhardt in 10½ on 12 pt by
Photo·graphics, Honiton, Devon
Printed in Great Britain by TJ Press, Padstow, Cornwall

Contents

Preface

This book represents a stage in a project that has been under way for over a decade. In 1979 we published a book entitled *Language as Ideology*, which was the culmination of six years' work in developing what we called variously a 'usable linguistics', or 'critical linguistics'. This was a theory of language whose aim was to provide an illuminating account of verbal language as a social phenomenon, especially for the use of critical theorists in a range of disciplines – history, literary and media studies, education, sociology – who wanted to explore social and political forces and processes as they act through and on texts and forms of discourse. The theory has been well received by those whom we had hoped to reach. However, there are a number of intrinsic limitations in the scope of that theory. We have felt the need to redress these, in order to fulfil our initial aim for a usable, critical theory of language. Some of these limitations we take up later in the book. Here we stress the two premises that constitute the basis for our present enterprise. The first is the primacy of the social dimension in understanding language structures and processes. In *Language as Ideology* we had recognized and assumed the importance of the social dimension, but even so we had accepted texts and the structure of language as the normal starting point for analysis. We now see social structures and processes, messages and meanings as the proper standpoint from which to attempt the analysis of meaning systems. Secondly, we see the limitation to verbal language in our earlier work as a major inconvenience in terms of our own main purpose. Meaning resides so strongly and pervasively in other systems of meaning, in a multiplicity of visual, aural, behavioural and other codes, that a concentration on words alone is not enough. Hence we were led, inevitably, to our second premise, namely that no single code can be successfully studied or fully understood in isolation. So, a theory of verbal language has to be seen in the context of a theory of all sign systems as socially constituted, and treated as social practices. That led us to this extension of our earlier enterprise, and hence the title of this present book: *Social Semiotics*.

In fact *Language as Ideology* grew out of general semiotic considerations which were left implicit because at that stage we felt unable to theorize them adequately. It seemed valid to us at that time to focus intensively on a part of semiosis, on structures and functions of verbal language, leaving the wider framework to be taken for granted. An oscillation between part and whole has proven its value in many other fields of enquiry. Our present book has a complementary movement to that of *Language as Ideology*, and both have for us been essential moments in a single enterprise. Without our intensive grappling with verbal language and with various traditions of linguistic theory, our ventures into semiotics would have been liable to vague vacuity. Without a confrontation with the problems of general semiotics, our modes of analysis, even of verbal language, would have been of less practical benefit to other students of ideology and culture. We continue to stress the potential value of linguistic theories, when released from their often restrictive formulations, and the need for linguistics and the study of verbal language to be thoroughly assimilated into a general theory of the social processes through which meaning is constituted and has its effects.

We hope our book will have a practical value for people working on different problems, perhaps in different institutional settings, but needing to trace in precise ways the transactions of meaning in sets of texts, whether those texts are verbal or visual, or embedded in specific objects, actions, practices or behaviours. But though we see its value as consisting in its contribution to various analytic practices over a range of disciplines, that is not to say we offer it as a box of tricks that anyone can make use of, whatever their orientation and purpose. We base our work on a number of premises in a theory of communication and society. We see communication essentially as a process, not as a disembodied set of meanings or texts. Meaning is produced and reproduced under specific social conditions, through specific material forms and agencies. It exists in relationship to concrete subjects and objects, and is inexplicable except in terms of this set of relationships. Society is typically constituted by structures and relations of power, exercised or resisted; it is characterized by conflict as well as cohesion, so that the structures of meaning at all levels, from dominant ideological forms to local acts of meaning will show traces of contradiction, ambiguity, polysemy in various proportions, by various means. So for us, texts and contexts, agents and objects of meaning, social structures and forces and their complex interrelationships together constitute the minimal and irreducible object of semiotic analysis. This is undoubtedly a complex and demanding object of analysis. However, the seemingly simpler assumption, which considers codes, texts and meanings in isolation, turns out to have its own complexities, no less difficult and ultimately far less adequate to the task.

Many people have contributed ideas, criticism and materials at various stages in the slow gestation of this book, whose help we gratefully acknowledge. Of many writers who have influenced us who are mentioned in references, we would like to single out M. A. K. Halliday, not only for his theoretical texts such as *Language as Social Semiotic*, but for his inspiring example as a researcher, teacher and explorer of the social functions of language. A number of scholars have published criticisms of our earlier work which we have found stimulating and useful, even if we have not agreed with every suggestion. We would especially like to mention here Pierre Achard, John Frow, Richard Helgerson and John Thompson. John Thompson also read and commented with acuity and generosity on an earlier draft of this text, which benefited very greatly from his criticisms. Some colleagues have been especially helpful with ideas or discussion. Of special note are Stephen Muecke of the University of Technology, Sydney, Noel King of Curtin University of Technology, and Alan Mansfield, Horst Ruthrof and Michael O'Toole of Murdoch University. Materials, comments and discussions have been contributed by Arnie Goldman, Steve Sinclair, Anne Cranny-Francis, Rachel Kress, Jonathan Kress and Cathy Mitson. We thank these and all the many others who have permitted us to use their texts and discourse.

The scale of the contribution of Pam Hodge and Jill Brewster is too great to be merely acknowledged. Most of the chapters in this book were tested on them in such close debate that many ideas in it owe as much to them as to us; though we remain responsible for all errors and misunderstandings it still contains.

Finally our thanks to Cynthia Baker, under whose magic hand what was lost was found, and a chaos of illegible fragments came together in a single beautiful typescript.

Acknowledgements

The authors and publishers are grateful to the following for permission to reproduce material already published elsewhere: Patrick Cook, *The Bulletin* (for plate 6.1); D.C. Comics Inc. (for plate 6.2; *Wonder woman* is a trademark of D.C. Comics Inc. Illustration © 1983 used with permission); D.C. Thomson and Co. Ltd (for plate 5.1); Harper & Row (for the text of the poem 'Child', from *The Collected Poems of Sylvia Plath* edited by Ted Hughes. Copyright © 1972 by Ted Hughes. Reprinted by permission of Harper & Row, Publishers, Inc.); Olwyn Hughes (for the text of the poem 'Child', from *Collected Poems* by Sylvia Plath, published by Faber & Faber, London, copyright Ted Hughes 1965 and 1981, published by permission of Olwyn Hughes, and for plate 4.3 of the manuscript at Smith College, copyright Ted Hughes and published by permission of Olwyn Hughes); Michael Joseph Ltd (for plates 7.2, 7.3, from *Only One Woof* by James Herriot, illustrated by Peter Barrett, published by Michael Joseph); The Mansell Collection (for plates 3.1, 4.2, 6.3, 6.4); Marvel Comics Limited (for plate 5.2 © 1981 BBC); Bill Mitchell/*The Australian* newspaper (for plate 4.1); *The Star* (for plate 5.6); *The Sun* (for plate 5.7); The Telegraph Colour Library (for plate 3.2).

1

Social Semiotics

The term 'semiotics' is relatively new for many people, and a number of conceptual difficulties continue to attach to its use. Semiotics has been defined as 'the science of the life of signs in society' (Saussure 1974). So defined it has a scope which is breathtaking in its simplicity and in its comprehensiveness. In its terms, everything in a culture can be seen as a form of communication, organized in ways akin to verbal language, to be understood in terms of a common set of fundamental rules or principles. In academic institutions today the study of such phenomena is often fragmented and parcelled out amongst a multitude of disciplines: psychology (in its many competing schools), sociology, anthropology, history, philosophy, linguistics, literature, art and film studies, to name only some of the most prominent. Semiotics offers the promise of a systematic, comprehensive and coherent study of communications phenomena as a whole, not just instances of it.

However, we must acknowledge from the outset an uneasiness and ambivalence towards semiotics, in so far as it has come to establish itself as a single discipline, which for good or ill it has not yet done. Semiotics has impressive achievements to its credit, enough to demand that its claims be taken seriously. Yet it has also been subjected to a series of critiques which have a cumulative force in challenging the validity of its assumptions and its practices. The central premise of this critique argues that the social dimensions of semiotic systems are so intrinsic to their nature and function that the systems cannot be studied in isolation. 'Mainstream semiotics' emphasizes structures and codes, at the expense of functions and social uses of semiotic systems, the complex interrelations of semiotic systems in social practice, all of the factors which provide their motivation, their origins and destinations, their form and substance. It stresses system and product, rather than speakers and writers or other participants in semiotic activity as connected and inter*acting* in a variety of ways in concrete social contexts.

It attributes power to meaning, instead of meaning to power. It dissolves boundaries within the field of semiotics, but tacitly accepts an impenetrable wall cutting off semiosis from society, and semiotics from social and political thought.

Many colleagues whose views we respect have rejected semiotics itself because of such objections. They see these defects as so fundamental and so interwoven with the field of study that they regard semiotics as beyond redemption, a snare and a delusion. We have adopted a less drastic stance. We see it not only as possible but as necessary to attempt a reconstitution of semiotics: one which recognizes the force of many of these critiques and goes beyond them, incorporating the strengths of existing forms of semiotics, taking the risk that we will not entirely avoid some of its limitations. This has to be done because the critiques, however sound in their own terms, lack a convincing analytic practice. It is semiotics, some kind of semiotics, that must provide this possibility of analytic practice, for the many people in different disciplines who deal with different problems of social meaning and need ways of describing and explaining the processes and structures through which meaning is constituted. Much of semiotics has not been conceived with this kind of use in view. But it remains the most obvious site for such an enterprise; and it is that task that this book addresses.

Ideological complexes and logonomic systems

Social semiotics cannot but rest on some general assumptions about society and meaning. Our own starting point derives from Marx's famous formulation:

Men are the producers of their conceptions, ideas, etc., that is, real, active men, as they are conditioned by a definite development of their productive forces, and of the intercourse corresponding to these up to its furthest forms. Consciousness (*das Bewusstsein*) can never be anything else than conscious being (*das bewusste Sein*), and the being of men is their actual life-process. If in all ideology men and their relations appear upside down as in a *camera obscura*, this phenomenon arises just as much from their historical life-process as the inversion of objects on the retina does from their physical life-process. (Marx and Engels 1970: 42)

This formulation emphasizes concrete individuals, acting on each other and the material world, as the basis and source of *Bewusstsein*, here translated as 'consciousness', but referring to the full set of semiotic processes with agents, objects and forces derived from the material and social world and only to be understood from that basis. Forms of intercourse (*verkehr*: communication, systems of exchange) correspond to particular forms of social organization and are necessary to their very existence.

In contemporary capitalist societies as in most other social formations there are inequalities in the distribution of power and other goods. As a result there are divisions in the social fabric between rulers and ruled, exploiters and exploited: such societies exhibit characteristic structures of domination. In order to sustain these structures of domination the dominant groups attempt to represent the world in forms that reflect their own interests, the interests of their power. But they also need to sustain the bonds of solidarity that are the condition of their dominance. Dominated groups are not always and everywhere blinded to the operations of these structures – as they have been portrayed in certain Marxist accounts. They in their turn attempt to resist the effects of domination, often succeeding, in countlessly many social encounters within social structures.

From this double and contradictory necessity of the dominant groups and the resistant or oppositional portion of dominated groups, arises the ambiguous category of ideology. Ideology viewed as false consciousness represents the world 'upside down' and in inverted form. But it also displays an image of the world as it ought to be, as seen from the vantage point of the dominant, or as it is, from the vantage point of the dominated group. To capture the contradiction characteristic of ideological forms, we will talk of ideological complexes, a functionally related set of contradictory versions of the world, coercively imposed by one social group on another on behalf of its own distinctive interests or subversively offered by another social group in attempts at resistance in its own interests. An ideological complex exists to sustain relationships of both power and solidarity, and it represents the social order as simultaneously serving the interests of both dominant and subordinate. It is the actual opposition of interests which creates the necessity for contradiction within the complex. The components of the complex will consist of two kinds of model: relational models (classifications of kinds of social agent, action, object, etc.) and actional models (specifications of actions and behaviours required of, permitted or forbidden to kinds of social agent). This indicates the sense in which we will use the terms 'ideology' and 'ideological (content)', to refer to a level of social meaning with distinctive functions, orientations and content for a social class or group. We are aware that others use this term in different senses, with equal validity. This variety of usages may be unfortuante and confusing, but it cannot easily be overcome, and the term is too important to be renounced by social semiotics.

Ideological complexes are constructed in order to constrain behaviour by structuring the versions of reality on which social action is based, in particular ways. Since ideological complexes exploit contradictory semiotic forms as a means of resolving contradictions in attitudes and behaviours, they cannot function successfully on their own. The different halves of their contradictions would cancel each other out. We need, therefore, to invoke a second level of messages which regulates the functioning of ideological complexes, a level which is directly concerned with the production and reception of meanings.

Each producer of a message relies on its recipients for it to function as intended. This requires these recipients to have knowledge of a set of messages on another level, messages that provide specific information about how to read the message. A simple example is a 'joke', a statement which might by itself prove offensive to the recipient. The message-maker however relies on the fact that the reader knows that such a statement, perhaps with other signals of 'joke' attached, is 'not to be taken seriously'. The recipient of course may not have knowledge of that level of message – a situation common in cross-cultural interaction – or may choose to reject the message of that level – as when a member of an ethnic or racial minority chooses not to treat an offensive statement as 'a joke'. The operation of irony is another well-understood case of a second-level message regulating the function of a message. We will call this higher-level control mechanism a *logonomic system* from the Greek *logos*, which means a thought or system of thought, and also the words or discourse through which the thought is presented, and *nomos*, a control or ordering mechanism. A logonomic system is a set of rules prescribing the conditions for production and reception of meanings; which specify who can claim to initiate (produce, communicate) or know (receive, understand) meanings about what topics under what circumstances and with what modalities (how, when, why.) Logonomic systems prescribe social semiotic behaviours at points of production and reception, so that we can distinguish between *production regimes* (rules constraining production) and *reception regimes* (rules constraining reception).

A logonomic system is itself a set of messages, part of an ideological complex but serving to make it unambiguous in practice. Where structures of domination are unchallenged, a logonomic system serves the dominant by ensuring that acts of semiosis ultimately assure their dominance. Where structures of domination are under challenge, logonomic systems are likely areas of contestation. The logonomic rules are specifically taught and policed by concrete social agents (parents, teachers, employers) coercing concrete individuals in specific situations by processes which are in principle open to study and analysis. They are challenged by social agents – e.g., children, students, employees. Logonomic systems cannot be invisible or obscure, or they would not work. They become highly visible in politeness conventions, etiquette, industrial relations, legislation, and so on.

Logonomic rules rest on a set of classifications of people, topics and circumstances which are the result of contestation over long periods, but which ultimately derive from the ruling ideas of the dominant group. The logonomic system necessarily codes a set of messages which arises out of a process of interaction, and thus indicates the status of relations of dominant and dominated groups. For instance, when a logonomic system allows a statement offensive to women to be read as 'a joke', this signifies a particular structure of gender relations, one in which males are dominant as a group in relation to females but need to mask their hostility and aggression towards them.

Thus logonomic systems imply a theory of society, an epistemology and a theory of social modalities. Logonomic systems like ideological complexes reflect contradictions and conflicts in the social formations. They typically have an overall structure consisting of general rules (expressing the dominance of the dominant) plus alternatives or exceptions (acknowledging though circumscribing the opposition of the subordinate). Thus, ideological complexes and logonomic systems are related in function and content, with logonomic systems expressing ideological content by controlling one category of behaviour (semiosis), while the ideological complex as a whole projects a set of contradictions which both legitimate and ameliorate the premises of domination.

Message, text and discourse

In analysing semiotic structures and processes, social semiotics draws extensively on terms and concepts from mainstream semiotics. But semiotics has not arrived at a single agreed set of terms and concepts. Even if it had, social semiotics would need to redefine some of them, to reflect its emphasis on social action, context and use. In what follows, we give an outline of how we will understand the key terms we use.

The smallest semiotic form that has concrete existence is the *message*. The message has directionality – it has a source and a goal, a social context and purpose. It is oriented to the semiosic process, the social process by which meaning is constructed and exchanged, which takes place in what we will call the *semiosic plane*. The message is about something, which supposedly exists outside itself. It is connected to a world to which it refers in some way, and its meaning derives from this representative or mimetic function it performs. We will call the plane in which representation occurs the *mimetic plane*.

But the field of semiosis does not consist simply of an accumulation of messages. Messages pass in clusters back and forth between participants in a semiotic act. In the study of verbal communication two words are generally used for this larger unit of semiotics, 'text' and 'discourse'. We will use 'text' in an extended semiotic sense to refer to a structure of messages or message traces which has a socially ascribed unity. 'Text' comes from the Latin word *textus*, which means 'something woven together'. 'Discourse' is often used for the same kind of object as text but we will distinguish the two, keeping discourse to refer to the social process in which texts are embedded, while text is the concrete material object produced in discourse. 'Text' has a different orientation to 'discourse'. Its primary orientation is to the mimetic plane, where it has meaning insofar as it projects a version of reality. 'Discourse' refers more directly to the semiosic plane.

'Text' is also opposed to another important concept, 'system'. Mainstream semiotics has developed the notion of a system of signs as an abstract structure which is realized or instantiated in text. It tends to treat such systems as static, as a social fact which is not, however, implicated in social processes of development or change. We would emphasize in contrast that every system of signs is the product of processes of semiosis, and documents the history of its own constitution. Terms in a system have value by virtue of their place in that system. At the same time, a system is constantly being reproduced and reconstituted in texts. Otherwise it would cease to exist. So texts are both the material realization of systems of signs, and also the site where change continually takes place.

This dialectic between text and system always occurs in specific semiosic acts, that is, in discourse. Discourse in this sense is the site where social forms of organization engage with systems of signs in the production of texts, thus reproducing or changing the sets of meanings and values which make up a culture. So for instance the institution of medicine defines a specific set of meanings which are constantly involved in the social processes which are appropriate to that institution, and engaged in by significant classes of participant, such as patient, surgeon, researcher and so on. In these interactions and the texts that they produce, the set of meanings is constantly deployed, and in being deployed is at risk of disruption. For social semiotics, the two terms 'text' and 'discourse' represent complementary perspectives on the same level of phenomenon. But although discourse is emphatically a social category, this does not mean that text and message are asocial terms. Both text and message signify the specific social relationships at the moment of their production or reproduction.

Genre, conformity and resistance

In order to trace the relationship of micro to macro structures we need some mediating categories. Logonomic systems have rules that constrain the general forms of text and discourse. Such systems often operate by specifying *genres* of texts (typical forms of text which link kinds of producer, consumer, topic, medium, manner and occasion). These control the behaviour of producers of such texts, and the expectations of potential consumers. Genre-rules are exemplary instances of logonomic systems, and are a major vehicle for their operation and transmission. Like the category of text, genres are socially ascribed classifications of semiotic form.

Genres only exist in so far as a social group declares and enforces the rules that constitute them. For instance, there are clear rules which regulate the interactions among participants that are called a committee-meeting. That is, a particular kind of social occasion is established, recognized and named by a social group, and practices are delineated which govern the actions of participants on such occasions. The texts which are formed in the process of a committee meeting therefore have a form which codes the set of practices, relations of participants, their expectations and purposes. The form of such texts – whether as 'full transcript', or as 'minutes of the meeting' – themselves become recognized as 'genres', and become potent as a semiotic category. Other instances come readily to mind: interview, lecture, feature article, chat, novel. Each such genre codes 'particular' relationships among sets of social participants. The rule systems at issue are clearer to see in some instances ('interview') than in others ('novel'), but are no less operative for that. The 'Rise of the Novel', so called, is a history that traces a set of historically specific relationships that involves the position of classes, definitions (and discourses) of gender, the state of technology, leisure and education, class-based notions of the family, and so on. The history of the genre of 'novel' since its 'rise' equally traces shifts in these relations, the appearance as salient factors of new discourses and of shifts in existent discourses. Genre therefore represents one semiotic category that codes the effects of social change, of social struggle.

An excessive concentration on normative systems (logonomic systems, genres, ideology) contains an inbuilt distortion and reinforces the ideas of their dominance. These systems only constrain the behaviour and beliefs of the non-dominant in so far as they have been effectively imposed and have not been effectively resisted. Attention to the detail of semiosic process reveals countless instances of contestation, where smaller-level shifts in power have significant effects, leading to modification in the structures of domination, at times tracing the success of dominated groups, at times the success of the dominant. This process is well described in Gramsci's work on hegemonic structures and their establishment. Processes of struggle and resistance are themselves decisive aspects of social formations, and affect every level of semiotic systems. At the micro level, power is put to the test in every exchange, and the logonomic system typically is a record of this by classifying large areas of semiosis as 'private', to be treated as beyond the reach of the 'public'/social. The ideological complex similarly attempts to pre-empt opposition by incorporating contradictory images into its coercive forms; even so, they continue to exist there, silently declaring the limits of dominant power. So the meanings and the interests of both dominant and non-dominant act together in proportions that are not predetermined, to constitute the forms and possibilities of meaning at every level. We do not assume that resistance is always successful or potent: but nor do we take it for granted, as many theorists of social meaning seem to do, that resistance is always effortlessly incorporated and rendered non-significant.

Social semiotics and the analysis of texts

We will illustrate this basic account of social semiotics by analysing a billboard advertisement for Marlboro cigarettes, to which the BUGAUP group (Billboard Using Graffitists Against Unhealthy Promotions) has added some amendments (plate 1.1).

We will begin our description with an account of the logonomic system, that is, the set of social messages which govern the normal production and reception of this text. By starting with the semiosic plane, with the conditions surrounding the production of this text, we wish to show that a social semiotic account cannot proceed with a naïve text–context dichotomy, but rather, that context has to be theorized and understood as another set of texts.

Plate 1.1 'New. Mild. and Marlboro.' Amended

The original advertisement is a text on a large scale, displayed on a billboard, which is itself mounted on a brick wall in a public space. This indicates one set of logonomic rules immediately: the right to erect a billboard of this size is explicitly controlled by local government laws, and there are agencies which control the appearance of messages in a 'public' space such as this. By its appearance here the text receives too different kinds of institutional legitimation. Here we have one social determinant of this genre: local council by-laws or discretionary powers can determine both whether a text may appear here, and what kind of text may appear. Access to the space is further regulated by an agency which hires the space to advertisers. From a spectator/viewer's point of view this has significant effects for reception, even if these go seemingly unnoticed by the reader. The text has an institutionalized legitimacy and authority. This effect can readily be tested by imagining other texts appearing there: perhaps a message encouraging the use of heroin, or advocating the release of a prisoner alleged to have been framed by the police. The appearance of such a text in that place would seem 'shocking'.

The text itself is of a scale and kind which implies the use of significant material resources. The availability of such resources is understood by a reader to be a precondition of the production of such a text and that gives the text a particular status, and places readers in a particular position. In this instance, the text is one of a series of texts which appeared as part of a 'campaign', so that readers/viewers were likely to have seen other texts of a very similar kind in a cinema, or on their television, or in a magazine.

These are indications of some aspects of the logonomic systems which enter into the production, appearance and reception of this text. They project a particular relation of producer and consumer for the text. Readers/viewers are placed in a particular way: they are participants, but cannot participate in any public act of meaning-making. That possibility is expressly ruled out: there are laws against 'interference' with billboards. They can only look, read, and respond *privately*. Because of the generic structure of this text they are addressed as (potential) consumers. If readers permit themselves to be constructed as consumers then this gives them a kind of power. So as readers they are powerless; as consumers they are powerful, though that power is in the gift of the makers of the text. This question of the placing/construction of the reader/consumer brings us to the ideological structure of the mimetic content. The original picture shows a silhouetted horseman and a large packet of cigarettes. The words say 'New. Mild. And Marlboro.' The full stops are important. These are not merely words, or elliptical sentences: these are 'statements'. As readers we are meant to accept that each statement contains vast areas of significance, even if we have to read that into each statement. So we are expected to perform a significant amount of semiotic work, and yet we are also treated as readers who are already members of the group that is thoroughly inward with the significance of these statements. Hence the text operates through a tension around the position of the viewer/reader in an active reading/engagement with a text whose meanings are already entirely familiar. This is one aspect or effect of the position inherent in ideological complexes. If we perform the reading we will be forced to attempt to retrace a path already constructed in previous advertising texts, where 'New' is an essential quality of modern human beings, a requirement they (are told to) make of themselves, of others, and of all objects. But 'New' also stands in tension with the nostalgic and self-consciously romanticized image of the cowboy, who is very much 'old', unless he is the 'new' urban man who is equally at home in the anti-urban outdoors. 'Mild' stands in contradiction with the tough masculinity portayed by the man and his way of life. But its appearance here also points to a suppression/negation of other discourses: of discourses around health (the anti-smoking campaign), but also discourses around gender, perhaps constructed as a response to feminist critiques of traditional notions of the masculine, so that mild/gentle can come to signify the 'new' kind of male toughness. It is important here to insist that reading positions, and readings, are gendered. The makers of this text may have intended, quite deliberately, to appeal to a 'feminine' audience here, an audience which is traditionally thought to have affinity with values such as are indicated by 'mild', rather than by 'tough'. In this context it is relevant to note that in Australia young women constitute the fastest-growing segment of the cigarette market.

Some oppositions of this ideological complex are there by absence: women are absent, and yet they are 'included' not only by the effect of 'mild', but also by an assumption that at least certain female readers/viewers will 'identify' with the hypothetical partner of this new, old fashioned, mild, tough male. The cowboy is a worker who is here shown as having no boss, as being his own boss; and notions of the unfettered individual, alone 'against' or in nature forms a potent opposition and contradiction with the structure of the lives of most of the viewers/readers of the text.

These, then, are some features of the ideological complex that constitutes this text. It is clear how aspects of quite immediately adjacent and contingent social structures and practices, many in the form of (series of) texts, have their effect in the formation of this text: the barely covert response to texts of the anti-smoking campaign, and feminist deconstructions of traditional versions of masculinity; the pressure of other, similar texts, by other promoters of the same product, signalled by the appearance of 'New'. and 'Marlboro'. Above all, of course, there is the need by the producers of this commodity to maintain or, if possible, improve their market share, their profits. The structure of texts is in all aspects always an indicator of complexes of social factors at work.

On to this text intrudes one particular reading, a reading which carefully exploits some of the contradictions in the ideological complex of this text, the reading/rewriting performed by BUGAUP. That reading/ rewriting resists the meanings of both the ideological complex, and the logonomic system. Where the latter positions the pliable, acquiescent reader in a passive role in the act of communication, the BUGAUP reading attacks that system in a radical fashion. An individual could deface this advertisement in exactly the same way in a magazine; as a private act it would cause no ripple. By 'defacing' a billboard the BUGA UP readers/authors are inserting themselves into a forbidden semiotic role, as communicators of subversive meanings presented publicly, in a public space. They are challenging the right of the company, and implicitly the right of the state as delegated to a local authority, to control authorship and content of 'public' texts. In doing so they are operating on yet another contradiction, namely that of the state which insists on the publication of a health warning on every packet of cigarettes, which controls or prohibits advertising of tobacco in certain media, and which depends on revenue generated from tobacco taxes.

At the ideological level, the BUGAUP authors exploit some of the contradictions we have already mentioned. The complex of meanings around masculinity/femininity and health carried in 'Mild.' is negated by the change to 'Vile.' The implied unity of rider and horse (one aspect of the unity of human nature) is undermined: the horse is given words which suggest a feminist critique of this construction of maleness, and which also undercuts any possibility of a female identification with this kind of man. That is, the rewriting writes in aspects of the suppressed discourses, writes in at least the echo of a female voice.

Just as the effect of the original advertisement depended on the combined effects of ideological and logonomic messages, so this challenge derives its potency from both levels. By both exposing and subverting a logonomic rule it co-opts those who are normally passively constrained by such rules, and the release of pleasure co-opts them against such advertising. Conversely, those who align themselves with the right of the state to control meanings might reject the message as 'childish', 'in poor taste', even if they disapprove of smoking.

Finally, we need to consider the level of discourse, understood as the ongoing flow of semiosis. The original advertisement as a text gained meaning from an intertextual relationship with other texts, including TV advertisements which included a fuller narrative, as well as a multitude of other texts, authored both by Marlboro (or its advertising agency) and others. The comments by BUGAUP could have occurred in the flow of discourse of innumerable private readers, in which the meanings of the billboard could be negotiated and assimilated or contested, in a continuous chain of acts of discourse. In that case the meanings of the text would have been greatly changed in the process, and an analysis of it would have been very misleading as to its overall effectivity. The BUGAUP additions constitute a specifically dialogic text, in which one reading of the original text is reclaimed and incorporated into the text itself. However, even after this interaction the flow of discourses will still continue, situating the new text in relation to other agents of discourse and their interests. The notion of text needs to be retained and contrasted to the notion of discourse as process, precisely because a text is so limited and partial an object of analysis. Text is only a trace of discourses, frozen and preserved, more or less reliable or misleading. Yet discourse disappears too rapidly, surrounding a flow of texts. Analysis needs to be able to take account of both.

In making oppositional readings visible, this particular text is not a typical one. Instead of eliding opposition and suppressing the possibility of counter-readings (as the original advertisement did) the text brings these to the surface, so that their presence cannot be ignored. In illustrating the processes involved in any reading, the text shows what is entirely typical, but typically invisible. Social semiotics cannot restrict its analysis to texts with commentaries by BUGAUP or similar groups. What it does need to do is to acknowledge the importance of the flow of discourse in constructing meanings around texts, and find ways of turning this process itself into kinds of text. Meaning is always negotiated in the semiotic process, never simply imposed inexorably from above by an omnipotent author through an absolute code. Traditional semiotics likes to assume that the relevant meanings are frozen and fixed in the text itself, to be extracted and decoded by the analyst by reference to a coding system that is impersonal and neutral, and universal for users of the code. Social semiotics cannot assume that texts produce exactly the meanings and effects that their authors hope for: it is precisely the struggles and their uncertain outcomes that must be studied at the level of social action, and their effects in the production of meaning.

2

The Founding Fathers Revisited

In this book we offer a specific conception of what semiotics can and ought to be. Yet inevitably our version of semiotics is positioned in relation to other kinds of semiotics, and we have drawn extensively on the work of others for our own purposes. Social semiotics as we propose it is not an autonomous project. It has developed out of an intensive critical reading of earlier work from a particular standpoint, rejecting some parts, incorporating, reordering or transforming other parts into a theory which aims to be coherent and powerful in its own right, to be judged not for its novelty or derivativeness but for its validity and usefulness to those with a similar orientation. So in this chapter we sketch out in broad terms where we stand, and give a critical reading of some of the founding fathers and founding concepts of modern semiotics from this point of view.

Like any social activity semiotics has a past which acts on its present and its future, and which is also constructed in histories which make the contingencies of the past and present seem inevitable and unchallengeable. We want to contest one particular version of history which underpins a specific and limiting conception of what semiotics was and is, and should be and do. We will refer to this as the dominant tradition without implying either that it is all of a piece or continuous with itself as it reached back to claim its past. What we want to do is neither to break with the past (if that were possible) nor to reunite it and appropriate its potency. Instead we will try to restore to it some possibilities that have been foreclosed, emphasizing some fissures and contradictions that were prematurely and illicitly resolved. We have talked of 'traditional semiotics' so far as though it could be neatly opposed to 'social semiotics', but that is an oversimplification. In practice the 'tradition' of traditional semiotics is not monolithic or even an agreed body of theories and concepts, and it by no means repudiates the social dimension unequivocally. In coming to terms with so amorphous and shifting an entity, we will not try to offer a tidy survey, which would be superficial and tendentious at best. Instead, we will look critically at the work of some key figures who were producing their ideas at a crucial stage in the formulation of the semiotics project.

One figure we cannot ignore in such an approach is Ferdinand de Saussure, who in all accounts of semiotics is named as a founding father of the discipline. Sometimes his name is bracketed with that of C. S. Peirce, but his thought was undoubtedly far more influential. As professor of general linguistics at Geneva University, with pupils later occupying chairs in prestigious universities in Europe, he was ideally placed to exert influence, even posthumously. His legacy shaped modern structural linguistics as well as structuralist semiotics. Peirce, on the other hand, produced his ideas from the peripheries of the American academic system in the late nineteenth century, and some of his early disciples were too eminent in their own right to feel they had to be faithful to his thought. Some accounts of semiotics suggest that there are two traditions stemming from these two founding fathers: continental semiotics (or semiology), a rationalist, structuralist form deriving from Saussure, and American semiotics, more behaviourist and positivistic and deriving from Peirce. But though American semiotics does have its characteristic forms, the seeming deference to Peirce is not a decisive factor in it. Peirce's observations on semiotics, scattered through his collected works (1940–65), are potentially far more subtle and fluid than the mechanistic theories of those (like Morris 1971) who claim to follow him. There is not a Peircean counter-tradition, with solid achievements planted in American soil, ready to confront the European semiology of Saussure. But there *is* Peirce's own work, unsystematic but full of sharp and illuminating observations on semiosis and thought, still waiting to be properly assimilated into a general semiotic theory.

Peirce was a philosopher, in so far as he was an academic at all. Philosophy, at that stage in the institutionalization of knowledge, had a wide scope, addressing itself to general problems of language and thinking. Peirce actually used the term 'semiotic'; other philosophers reflected productively on problems of language and meaning without invoking the term. Thinkers like Husserl, in the phenomenological tradition, and Wittgenstein were developing semiotic notions which have largely remained outside the semiotic tradition. These of course have not been without their influence and their followers, but that influence was labelled 'philosophy'. Linguistics subsequently did without either semiotics or a philosophy of language, while linguistic philosophy, cut off from a broader range of semiotic phenomena, was reduced to endless analysis of the language of philosophy as its proper subject matter.

Two other thinkers must be included even in so limited an inventory of 'founding fathers'. One is Freud. Although he produced his ideas from as marginal a position as Peirce, there is no question of the magnitude of his general influence today. Since Lacan's advocacy (1977) his status as a proto-semiotician has been recognized, although Lacan's versions of both Freud and semiotics are not definitive or exhaustive, and the place of Freud's thought in a general semiotics is far from settled. Even more important, in the reconstitution of semiotics that we envisage, is the work of Voloshinov and the school of Bakhtin. Voloshinov's major work (1973), produced in Russia in the 1920s, offered a contemporary critique of Saussure that has only recently begun to have its effect in the West and to be recognized as a potentially decisive theoretical intervention. Voloshinov drew heavily on Marxism, a tradition which was effectively excluded in West European and American theories of language in the 1930s. But he and others in that group were also silenced for decades by Stalinism. The rediscovery of Voloshinov in effect makes a contemporary of Saussure as well, giving new life to the issues he set in motion, providing a powerful impetus and orientation to a new form of semiotics.

Saussure's rubbish bin

Saussure's *Course in General Linguistics* is at first glance a surprising text to have precipitated semiotics. Saussure's explicit references to 'semiology' amount to three pages. Most of his book draws on a very narrow range of semiotic phenomena. The examples come mainly from his field of special competence, the history of changes in sounds in the Indo-European group of languages. This contradiction is at the centre of the problematic legacy of Saussure. On the one hand he projected a discipline with the widest possible scope, while on the other he laid down a set of strictures which split his heritage in two, deforming linguistics, and preventing the coming of semiotics for decades.

We can see this contradiction in many aspects of Saussure's work. He was trained in the precise and scholarly tradition of comparative philology, whose primary goal was the historical reconstruction of the Indo-European group of languages, but that tradition had virtually run out of feasible tasks. Bally and Sechehaye, editors of the *Course*, described his motives as follows: 'We have often heard Ferdinand de Saussure lament the dearth of principles and methods that marked linguistics during his developmental period. Throughout his lifetime, he stubbornly continued to search out the laws that would give direction to his thought amid the chaos' (1974: xxix). In the *Course* Saussure set himself the task of constituting a new and broader field of study, and so he devised a simple, clear and comprehensive map, in terms of which the close, narrow work he found congenial could proceed again with the certainty he so desired. His basic strategy was to project a large, undifferentiated field, then divide it up by successive sharp dichotomies; and then proceed to eliminate one half of each dichotomy. The result was a set of boundaries, each regarded as absolute, and a successive narrowing of linguistics and semiotics. What needs to be challenged are the exclusions enforced by those boundaries; the original scope of these claims must be re-examined, in the coming to terms with Saussure which semiotics needs even today. The Saussurean scalpel cut deep, and his need for limits has found echoes in many others who have set up sterile barriers, in linguistics and in many other fields of cultural studies.

His famous pairs of categories are often discussed in isolation, but they must be understood both as part of a rigorous scheme, and as successive stages in a progression through that scheme. We will summarize that progression in our summary of his thought. In the search for a pure object of study, he first made a distinction between that which was internal to language, and that which was external to it although essential to an interest in language phenomena: ethnology, political and social history, history of institutions, geography. Having posited this first division, he proposed to exclude 'external linguistics' – even though he also insisted elsewhere that language is irreducibly a 'social fact'. The class of objects that was left he put together, and he proposed it as a larger object of study, that of sign systems generally. That study he named 'semiology', and prophesied its existence in advance, while not in fact studying it himself.

Verbal language as such (*Langage*) he designated as one such sign system. This object he then categorized into two: *langue* (the abstract system of rules underlying speech) and *parole* (human speech: literally 'words'), conceived of as an intrinsically unordered morass, an infinite and arbitrary combination of the elements of *langue* by individual speakers. He discarded *parole* as an impossible object for systematic study. *Langue* was then divided into two: the *synchronic*, the study of stages of language (the system as it exists at any one time, for a particular language community) and the *diachronic*, the study of changes in the system over time. Most of Saussure's lifetime had been spent on diachronic studies, but he categorized these as defeating systematization. Diachronic change, for him, was essentially piecemeal and irrational. He then described synchronic language phenomena on two axes: the plane of combination and the plane of selection, which he called the associative plane (Hjelmslev 1953 later renamed these the syntagmatic and the paradigmatic planes respectively.) Synchronic linguistics deals with signs which have a value, that is, a place in a system or structure, syntagmatic or paradigmatic, and a signification, that is, a relation of reference, existing outside language. For reasons that are consistent with the rest of the scheme, he opted for considerations of value (relations in a system) rather than signification. Signs themselves have a double form, consisting of signifiers (carriers of meaning) and signifieds, the concept or meaning. Saussure did not entirely neglect consideration of signifieds, but his main interest was with signifiers. The signifier, too, has a double form, made up of a material entity (e.g., a stroke of the pen, a physical sound) and an image of that entity, which is a mental event. Characteristically, Saussure relegated the study of the material sign to a discipline outside linguistics. The full scheme, then, looks like this:

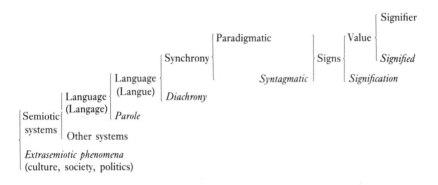

The underlining in this schema indicates the contents of Saussure's rubbish bin, what he chose to reject or seemed to minimize. So important are the things that he excluded that it is tempting to see him as that useful phenomenon, the person who is *always* wrong. On that reasoning, if Saussure rejects something it must be important. But that of course is too simple. His acts of exclusion, acts of repression, always see the return of the repressed. The repressed is the dynamic principle of his system. That repressed is invariably energy, movement, process: whatever changes, or causes or describes change. So he affirmed the social over the individual, but only as an abstract, immobilized version of the social order, potentially threatened by actions of innumerable individuals. At the level of language, however, he studied mainly words or phrases, not larger structures of discourse. This could be seen as a concern with the individual word, rather than with the structures in which words exist. But at a deeper level that concern betrays the same desire to stay with that which can be fixed and therefore known, even if the price is to see only chaos in the life and discourse that swirls outside the domain of linguistics or semiotics; in *parole*, in society, in history, in the intractable material world of objects and events. The strength of this attempt to escape the world of processes reveals his fascinated recognition of these forces, even if they appear in his theory only as negations.

Using Saussure as an antiguide, we can invert his prohibitions and rewrite them as basic premises for an alternative semiotics (an alternative which is implicit in his work). This alternative semiotics will incorporate the study of at least the following components:

1 Culture, society and politics as intrinsic to semiotics
2 Other semiotic systems alongside verbal language
3 *Parole*, the act of speaking, and concrete signifying practices in other codes
4 Diachrony, time, history, process and change
5 The processes of signification, the transactions between signifying systems and structures of reference
6 Structures of the signified
7 The material nature of signs.

Society and the sign

Voloshinov, writing in 1929, turned Saussure's doctrines on their head in essentially the same terms as we do above. His critique has an exemplary lucidity, and still repays close attention. He labelled the Saussurean tradition as 'abstract objectivism', and he diagnosed its central mistake, its *proton pseudos*, as follows: 'Abstract objectivism, by taking the system of language and regarding it as the entire crux of linguistic phenomena, rejected the speech act – the utterance – as something individual ... [But] *The utterance is a social phenomena* ...' This sees the separation of *langue* and *parole*, and the rejection of *parole* as too individual to be an object of theory, as the decisive error in Saussure's thought. Voloshinov also reconstituted the unity of semiotic phenomena, against Saussure's fatal dichotomies, in three propositions asserting the material and social dimensions as essential to semiotic analysis:

1 Ideology may not be divorced from the material reality of the sign
2 Signs may not be divorced from the concrete forms of social intercourse (seeing that the sign is part of organized social intercourse, and cannot exist, as such, outside it)
3 Communication and the forms of communication may not be divorced from the material basis.   (1973: 21)

Voloshinov's own position on the social determination of signs is not without problems of the relation of individual and collective structures: 'The form of signs is conditioned above all by the social organization of the participants involved and also by the immediate conditions of their interaction' (1973: 21). This 'also' links the general social organization and the immediate conditions of interaction, though it makes light of the problems a social semiotics must face in accounting for the constraints and determinations acting on participants in a semiotic act. Voloshinov's work foregrounds the speech act as an exchange between individuals whose consciousness is already socially constructed. It emphasizes the plane of production as decisive for semiotic analysis. His formulation, however, leaves unexplored the nexus of relationships between speech roles and social relationships in a class society, the complex structures of the logonomic systems at various levels. Moreover, a general semiotic theory must try to theorize the full range of semiotic acts, including writing, art, film and the mass media, where the relationships between participants are more complex and abstract than is the case with a face-to-face conversational exchange. But this is only to say that Voloshinov has left important tasks for social semiotics to explore. In that exploration, the two formulations 'social organization of participants' and 'immediate conditions of interaction' seem to us as good as any currently available.

Voloshinov makes a close link between semiotics and the study of ideology. 'Without signs there is no ideology . . . Everything ideological possesses semiotic value' (1973: 9). He uses the word 'ideology' here in a specific sense which we will examine later. The point to stress here is that for him, neither ideology nor language are monolithic phenomena, imposing their irresistible unity on a helpless society. On the contrary, society for him is characterized by struggle and conflict and constantly renegotiated relations, and semiosis reflects this process in its typical forms. Here his concept of the 'accent' is useful. An accent is a particular inflection which gives a different social meaning to an apparently common set of signs, just as happens with various accents of speech which mark class and regional identity. As well as this, for Voloshinov they affect the force and meaning of signs, by connecting them with different life experiences and values. He sees language systems as typically 'multiaccentual', with a seemingly common code refracted by different class or group positions. From this perspective it becomes impossible to see an ideology as a unitary set of meanings or texts, imposed from above in an absolute take-it-or-leave-it kind of way. For Saussure, language had to be a totally collective phenomenon, or it would be asocial and incomprehensible. For Voloshinov the processes of struggle, negotiation and creation and resolution of differences are both social and comprehensible, and indeed are at the centre of semiotic enquiry.

We believe that as an outline, Voloshinov's sketch of the basis for a social semiotics is essentially sound. The task that remains is to build on this basis, and confront the difficulties of implementing the programme. But it is worth pointing out moments in the Western

European tradition which could have led in this kind of direction. C. S. Peirce, for instance, had a dialogic conception of language and signs. 'Every thought is a sign', he declared (5. 470); 'All thinking is dialogic in form. Your self of one instant appeals to your deeper self for his assent' (6. 338). Unlike Voloshinov, he has internalized the transaction that constitutes thought, presenting it as a fact of personal psychology without explicit roots in the social process, and this is an important weakness in Peirce's theory. But otherwise, this is essentially the same kind of account of thinking processes as was developed later by the Russian psychologist Vygotsky (1962), himself influenced by Voloshinov and the Bakhtin group.

Peirce also stressed process in the study of signs. 'Semiotic' for him was 'the doctrine of the essential nature and fundamental varieties of semiosis' (5. 488). And semiosis here is a process, 'the action of a sign', not a language structure or a code. 'By semiosis I mean an action, an influence, which is, or involves, a co-operation of *three* subjects, such as a sign, its object and its interpretant, this tri-relative influence not being in any way resolvable into actions between pairs' (5. 484). Exactly what Peirce meant by 'interpretant' is not clear, and his theory has been disputed. But it is clear that semiosis involves a transaction, a process linking object, sign, and 'interpretants'. Interpretants are further ideas linked to a sign. 'The interpretant of a proposition is its predicate' (5. 473). The process of generation of interpretants is seemingly limitless, an infinite semiosis, rather like the process of free association. But Peirce insists on two limits to this freedom and infinitude. The relation between 'sign' and 'interpretant' is still controlled by the relations with the object, with material existence. And the endless flux of interpretants is also controlled by what he called 'habits' (4. 536), culturally specific rules of thought and inference that correspond to what we have called logonomic systems. So, unlike Saussure, Peirce sees meaning as intrinsically a process, not a quality of signs or texts, and he sees a place for both the material determinations of meaning, and general social cultural constraints on individual thought.

Even Saussure should not be seen as unequivocally opposed to a social basis for semiotics. In fact his work shows a deep division on precisely this topic, a contradiction that runs throughout his work. For instance he lists three aims that determine the scope of linguistics:

1   To describe and trace the history of all observable languages . . .
2   To determine the forces that are universally at work in all language, and to deduce the general laws to which all specific historical phenomena can be reduced, and
3   To delimit and define itself.

(1974: 11)

Aims (1) and (2) foreground the study of historical and social forces on language; aim (3) then attempts to cut linguistics off from semiotics, and from social and historical explanation. This set of aims does not show a hostility to this wider scope for the subject so much as a profound ambivalence towards that project. Saussure did not in fact dismiss what he called 'external linguistics': 'I believe that the study of external linguistic phenomena is most fruitful; but to say that we cannot understand the internal linguistic organism without studying external phenomena is wrong' (p. 22). This statement explicitly recognizes the value and importance of external linguistics, while making a plea for internal linguistics as well. Saussure has been invoked by later semioticians to justify a clear rejection of 'external linguistics' in the name of an abstract, autonomous internal linguistics. This is not entirely fair to him, although he was certainly not unambivalent about the issue.

How signs work

Saussure's confusion about the relations between semiosis and society affected some of his most influential pronouncements, even where that problem does not seem at issue. One example is his doctrine that the linguistic sign is *arbitrary*: by which he meant that (in verbal languages at least) there is no necessary or 'natural' connection between a signified and its signifier (e.g., the words 'horse', *equus* (Latin) and *hippos* (Greek) all refer to the same species of animal). There could therefore be no natural connection between the concept of 'horseness' and any of these words (and many others in other languages). Clearly this observation makes good sense, so far as it goes. However, Saussure's treatment of this topic attaches a surprising degree of importance to it. He declared it to be 'the first principle of language signs', no less.

This has proved a very influential and damaging overstatement. In practice, as some influential semioticians have argued, it is not absolutely and invariably true even of the sound of words (cf. Levi-Strauss 1963, Jakobson and Waugh 1979, and see below pp. 88–91). It certainly is not true of all signs in verbal language: Saussure himself recognized that syntactic patterns, for instance, are often what he called 'motivated', that is, connected in some rational, 'natural' way to their meaning. For example, the subject of a sentence in English comes first, which is a 'motivated' signifier of its importance. Outside verbal language, so many important classes of signs so obviously have some rationale (as Saussure himself recognized) that it becomes difficult to justify this doctrine as a universal doctrine in semiotics. Peirce had a more helpful classification of signs. He had three major types: *icon* (based on identity or likeness: e.g., road signs), *index* (based on contiguity or causality: e.g., smoke as a sign of fire), and *symbol* (a merely conventional link, as in Saussure's 'arbitrary' sign). The first two of these types are 'motivated' in Saussure's terms. Looking at the full range of sign types it seems incontrovertible that there is a continuum in signs, from more to less 'arbitrary' or 'motivated'. A dogmatic assertion that signs are all and equally 'arbitrary' is unjustifiable and unhelpful for general semiotics. Even Saussure's terms 'arbitrary' and 'motivated' have misleading implications. We will use instead the term 'transparent' to indicate a signifier whose connection with a signified can be seen easily by a user, whether producer or receiver, with the orientation always important. So the same sign could be transparent to a producer and not to a receiver, or vice versa. We will call the opposite quality 'opaque', again relative to specific agents.

But this alternative proposal does not explain why Saussure felt it necessary to insist on arbitrariness in the first place. Paradoxically, his motive was his sense of the overwhelming power of society in determining verbal semiotic systems. The logic of that position is as follows. Applying his habitually dichotomous ways of thinking to the relation between signifiers and signifieds, he saw two possibilities. Either there is a natural connection between signifiers and signifieds, based on their physical nature, or there is not. His interests, as we mentioned earlier, were largely confined to the study of sounds and of words. Scanning languages of the past and the present he saw such a variety of words corresponding to what he thought of as the same concept, and such continuous changes over time, that he felt forced to conclude that there was no natural bond to resist these social and historical forces. So the doctrine of the arbitrariness of the linguistic sign expresses, in a masked form and by negation, the principle of the social determination of the sign, in as strong a form as Voloshinov.

But the form of Saussure's version of this principle is not as helpful as Voloshinov's, and unsurprisingly has prevented the development of social semiotics in practice. This is because Saussure saw the social determination of language as not simply unlimited but also inherently incomprehensible. That is why he used the term 'arbitrary', as though the bonds between signifier and signified were subject to the whims of an inscrutably powerful collective being, Society. To call these signs 'conventional', as many including Saussure have done, is not much better, since it still attributes the source of determination to society without encouraging a study of how that determination works in practice. Voloshinov's work offers a clear framework for exploring the nature of the process of signification, by setting this process in a wider setting in which the action of social forces is powerful but by no means incomprehensible.

We will use the Marlboro BUGAUP advertisement (reproduced in chapter 1) again to illustrate the relevance for practical analysis of the

sue of the arbitrariness of the sign. On the one hand the change of mild' to 'vile' seems small but produces a sharply contrasting meaning, and this suggests the arbitrariness of the sounds of the two words, as Saussure would have argued. The word 'cough' is a less 'arbitrary', more transparent sign – it partly repeats the action of coughing – though the identity is not complete, and is supported by convention ('hack', 'cuck', 'cack', and other sounds would have served equally well). But the style of the lettering itself is a kind of sign with a clearer relation to its meaning. The crude scrawl of the campaigners contrasts strongly with the symmetrical machine-produced lettering of the original advertisement. In Peirce's terms, the style of the original is an index, a signifier of the cigarette industry's control over massive technological resources, while the scrawl signifies a repudiation of that hegemonic structure. This meaning, coded in the writing style, is an important component of the overall effect. (This sign is highly 'motivated' or transparent, yet it is also specific to a particular form of society, since it draws its meaning precisely from some assumptions about the structures and material practices of an advanced technological society. The fact that it is both transparent yet also socially specific helps it to play a powerful role, along with other more opaque sign systems, in creating the overall meanings of the text concerned.

Semiotics and reality

Equally important, a practical semiotics should have some account of the relationship of semiosis and 'reality', that is, the material world that provides the objects of semiosis and semiotic activity. Unless semiotics confronts this relationship, it can have no relevance to the world of practical affairs with its confident assumptions about 'reality', and it cannot account for the role of semiotic systems in that world. This relation between semiosis and reality bears on some problems that have bedevilled Western thought for millennia, the relationships between language and thought, thought and reality, and the problems of defining 'truth' and 'reality'. In practice, of course, people call each other liars with rather rough and ready criteria of truth. These criteria have their own problems and difficulties even at the level of practice. But the stance of trying to do without any criteria while waiting for absolute definitions of truth and reality has practical consequences too; not least because it leaves the field to the roughest and readiest definitions of truth to meet in head-on collision.

Saussure's contribution here as in so many other ways has been ambiguous. He drew attention to the problematic nature of this relationship, but he also devised a strategy that seemed to legitimize a

practice that ignored it. Part of his persuasiveness about the
(or non-relation) between language and reality is because he s.
little about it. Early in the *Course* he takes one popular notioı.
language as 'a naming process only' (p. 65). He labels this idea as
rather naïve approach', and so it is, in the form he summarizes. But
instead of offering a less naïve account of this process, he followed his
usual strategy of split and snip. First he saw an analogous split, within
the sign itself, between its material substance and the mental image of
that substance, and a further split, between signifiers and signifieds,
and between concepts and reality. The result was a four-tiered relation
instead of the naïve two-tiered form:

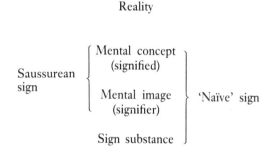

Saussure saw no necessary relationship between these levels, so each
could be studied entirely independently. But he also claimed that in
practice the union of mental concept and mental image was so total
that the two could not be distinguished. They are like the two sides of
a single sheet of paper: 'Thought is the front and the sound the back;
one cannot cut the front without cutting the back at the same time'
(p. 113). But he did not see a similarly close bond between signs (on
his account of them) and reality. On the contrary, he felt able to claim
that that relation was irrelevant to linguistics, which could focus
exclusively on the sign, as so defined: 'Linguistics then works in the
borderland where the elements of sound and thought combine; *their
combination produces a form, not a substance*' (p. 113, italics in the original).
What he has done, then, is to establish the sign, and hence semiotics,
in a realm between two material planes, the world that signs refer to
and the material that composes the sign itself (which in fact comes
from the same material world). The 'naïve' sign is superior in that it
avoids this double split imposed on material reality.

The Western philosophical tradition going back to Plato and beyond
has been concerned to the point of obsession with this set of problems.
In the twentieth century, the philosophy of the early Wittgenstein offers
a way out of the dilemma of the referentiality problem, that could

provide a basis for a semiotics of reference. In his *Tractatus Logico-Philosophicus* of 1921 (published only four years after Saussure's *Course*) he set out the following premises:

4.01 A proposition is a picture of reality.
A proposition is a model of reality as we imagine it.

4.011 At first sight a proposition – one set out on the printed page, for example – does not seem to be a picture of the reality with which it is concerned. But neither do written notes at first sight seem to be a picture of a piece of music, nor our phonetic notation (the alphabet) to be a picture of our speech.
And yet these sign-languages prove to be pictures, even in the ordinary sense, of what they represent . . .

4.021 A proposition is a picture of reality: for if I understand a proposition, I know the situation that it represents. And I understand the proposition without having had its sense explained to me.

What Wittgenstein is doing here is, in other terms, to make the smallest unit of signification not an *element* but a *combination of elements* (a 'syntagm' as this is commonly called in semiotics). Peirce also saw the sign as a proposition, and the proposition as a sign. Saussure at one stage debates what is the unit for semiotics. He specifically considers, not the proposition but the 'sentence', but rejects this because the infinite number of sentences takes them outside *langue* and outside linguistics. He also discounts the word, partly because some words break down into even smaller meaning-bearing units, which linguists call morphemes (e.g., *cats* which consist of the morphemes *cat* and *s*, the latter signifying plurality). However, with some provisos he does in effect take the word, considered as a free-standing entity that can enter into relationship with other such entities, as the most transparent example of a sign.

However, if words, or morphemes, are taken as the primary example of the verbal sign, there are well-known problems of referentiality. With a word like 'cat' for instance, we can point to furry four-legged animals running around, but what about a word like 'the'? How many legs does a 'the' have? But if the proposition is the chief site of the relation between language and reality, it becomes quite sensible to ask what is the effect on the proposition 'the cat sat on the mat' of changing 'the' to 'a'. The 'picture of the world' implied is quite different. The difference concerns not cats or mats, but claims about knowledge of specific cats and mats. It affects the semiosic plane rather than the mimetic plane. With 'the' the speaker claims to know the cat and the mat referred to, and specifically implies that the hearer knows too. With 'a' the claims are much weaker: any cat on any mat will do. With a physical picture, such as the horse-rider in the Marlboro advertisement, the pattern is reversed: the picture is easy to see, but not the proposition(s). But again, meaning resides in the version of the world projected – a world in this case where work is romantic and in close contact with nature, and is completed by leisure and a Marlboro cigarette as leisure's natural signifier.

One important consequence of Wittgenstein's proposal to see meaning in the relation of propositions to 'pictures' or 'models' of reality is that the analysis of meanings even in the verbal code inevitably goes outside the code of language and draws on general semiotics. This, of course, makes an autonomous linguistic analysis no longer viable, but it makes good sense of actual processes of interpretation as they are understood today. For instance, famous acts of code cracking known to Saussure, such as Champollion's decipherment of Egyptian hieroglyphs or Rawlinson's decipherment of Assyrian cuneiform, were dependent on knowing precisely what a specific text was talking about (Ptolemy and Cleopatra for Champollion, Darius, Xerxes, Hystaspes and others, in the Behistun inscription that provided Rawlinson with his breakthrough). Modern theories of reading (and misreading) show the power of 'top–down' strategies which go from prior expectations of the sense to meanings of the specific text. Information theory measures the 'information' of a text in terms of the uncertainty it resolves in a decoder, an uncertainty which is a function of the existing state of knowledge, and its interaction with the text. Students of cross-cultural communication know how often misunderstanding arises because of different assumptions in different cultural groups. Undoubtedly, it creates heavy demands to extend semiotics in this way, to include the description and analysis of the stock of cultural knowledge in a given society. However, if members of a society do in fact normally acquire the ability to accomplish this feat by the time they are adolescent, then it should not be beyond semiotics to develop its own strategies.

As long as the general relationship of semiosis and reality is avoided as too problematic, the study of strategies for relating specific acts of semiosis to reality also tends to be deferred or ignored. But for practical purposes, it is important to have ways of detecting different kinds of error, and different kinds of lie – or conversely, to develop ever more devious ways of lying or concealing ignorance of the truth. Saussure did not consider this class of problem. Peirce did give it some consideration. From logic he took the category of 'modality', that is, the kind of truth value attached to a proposition. There are three types of modality for Peirce: actuality, necessity, and possibility (i.e. actually true, logically necessary, and hypothetical). He considered tense as part of modality, something that linguists did not realize for over fifty years. His classification of signs into icons, indices, and symbols also had a modality-value built in. Icons, as picture-like signs which either are or resemble what they signify, have the modality of direct perception, and hence are the most persuasive of signs (as modern advertisers and news editors are aware). Indexical signs are formed from cause–effect chains (e.g., smoke–fire) or contiguity linkages (e.g., an arm for the person). These have a high modality (i.e., a close fit between sign and meaning), but since they are still based on an act of judgement or inference they have a lower modality than icons. Symbols, which relate sign to object by bonds of convention (like Saussure's linguistic sign) have the lowest modality, though Peirce also saw semiosis using symbols as the highest mode of thought, in an evolutionary schema.

Peirce's treatment of modality is fairly rudimentary. Three forms of modality, and three kinds of sign, are not adequate to account for the full range of strategies that are deployed in this area, and semioticians tend to overuse Peirce's terms for want of anything better. But at least Peirce has put this topic on the agenda for semiotic theory. And in so far as Eco is right to call semiotics a 'theory of the lie' (1976: 7), it cannot afford to neglect this whole class of strategies for lying more effectively by positioning readers and messages in different ways to normative accounts of reality. At the same time semiotics must also consider the means for controlling lies and their effects.

Structuralism and the materiality of signs

Thus far we have made Saussure's influence on semiotics seem largely negative. It is time to correct the balance somewhat. Saussure made important contributions to semiotics, and we believe that post-Saussurean semiotics still has something to learn from Saussure. Unsurprisingly, Saussure has most to offer in the two areas of semiotics to which he devoted most of his life's work, which modern semioticians suppose they have assimilated and gone beyond, or can safely neglect. In this section we will consider the Saussurean notion of value, especially as applied to structures of signifiers. In the next we take diachrony, history and the role of change.

Saussure's concept of value is at the basis of structuralism. Value to Saussure refers to the place of an element in a system or structure. Value consists of a complex of identities and oppositions. He illustrated the concept of value, as opposed to reference, by comparing the French word *mouton* to the two English words 'mutton' and 'sheep'. The French word can refer to the same segment of reality as the two English words, but it has a different value, since the two English words are opposed to each other, whereas *mouton* in French is undivided.

Saussure's illustration of 'value' by reference to semantic oppositions is suggestive, but it has problems when applied to systems of vocabulary in natural languages, and in fact no system of the signifieds of a natural verbal language has been adequately explained in these terms. The vindication of structuralist method came from its success in analysing the phonological code, the sound code of human languages. It was this success of structuralism, associated with the work of Troubetzkoy and Jakobson, that for Lévi-Strauss, writing in 1948, transformed linguistics into a science and the model for all the social sciences. An achievement of this kind, even on seemingly so narrow a front as this one, concerned only with the signifying system of one semiotic code, turns out to be a more substantial basis for theoretical development than any concept, however suggestive. And Saussure not only provided the concept of value to this enterprise, he foreshadowed clearly in his own work the kind of analysis that Troubetzkoy and Jakobson brought to completion.

It is important to observe that Saussure's achievement required him to go against what has seemed to many commentators to be one of his basic principles, his exclusion of material considerations, especially in relation to the analysis of signs, as we saw in the previous section. He titles his exploration of the sound code 'Phonology'. Culler, an influential modern interpreter, takes him to task for this title. For Culler, Saussure has confused the modern categories of 'phonology', the study of sound as a system of signifiers, and 'phonetics', the study of the physical medium of the phonological system, and Culler claims that much of what Saussure calls 'phonology' should be called 'phonetics'. He adds the judgement: 'It is as though in the study of sound he had . . . not realized the full import of his exclusion of physical sounds from the linguistic system' (1976: xxii). Culler is perfectly correct that Saussure here is inconsistent with his normal anti-materialist stance. But it is precisely because Saussure clearly recognized that the material basis of sound systems is indispensable to a study of their structure that he was able to achieve his theoretical breakthrough.

His analysis of the sounds of language takes as its basis the articulatory mechanism, the parts of the speech apparatus which are responsible for different sounds. Since 'the articulatory mechanism never changes' (p. 33) the material basis of sound production provides a universal basis for description of sounds in all languages, even though actual sound systems are various and unstable. In conventional phonology, sounds are labelled in terms of features that derive from that part of the vocal mechanism that is most characteristically involved in their production. For instance dentals like d or t are produced with the tongue touching the teeth: labials such as b, p are produced using lips. What is happening here is that the space of articulation is subdivided and assigned meanings, and these become the basis for the subdivisions of the stream of sound. Saussure pushes this kind of analysis to a more abstract level. He suggests a number of alternative schemes. In one, he projects four basic categories of sound, arising from the operation of four basic phonational acts: expiration, oral articulation, voice, and nasal resonance. He then goes one stage further, proposing to derive all sounds from a single principle, ± closed (or ± open). The various parts of the articulatory mechanism contribute to different degrees of openness or closure. Different languages may involve different ways of achieving this, producing unique sounds in their phonological system, but the very great variety of sounds is the realization of a single principle, constrained by a material reality that provides innumerable different realizations of it. Saussure's analysis finishes with seven categories of sound, in a continuum from open to closed. At one extreme are the most vowel-like vowels (maximum aperture), at the other are the most consonant-like consonants (maximum closure). His invention of seven categories obscures the radical simplicity of his proposal, which is essentially the structuralist analysis of the universal form of phonological systems, in terms similar to Jakobson's better-known but later formulation.

Saussure also analysed phonemes in the spoken chain: that is, syntagmatic structures of the phonological plane. Again he offered a radically reductive analysis, in terms of a single principle. He observed that sounds as they combine in speech involve either implosure (a process of closure) or explosure (a process of opening). The syntagmatic rules for the combination of syllables can then be specified in terms of movements of implosion or explosion, which build up syllable contours and boundaries. So the same abstract principle is responsible for both paradigmatic structures and syntagmatic structures in the phonological code. Saussure's proposal is impressive for its comprehensiveness, its elegance and its simplicity. He allows himself a certain pride in this achievement: 'For the first time we have broken away from abstraction. Now for the first time we have found the concrete, irreducible units that occupy a place and correspond to a beat in the spoken chain' (p. 53). It is interesting that far from being ashamed of his descent into 'concrete, irreducible units' of the actual spoken chain, as Culler's criticism would imply, he sees his success as inseparable from this materialist strategy.

Surprisingly, Saussure's analytic achievement has largely been ignored by later structuralists. His analysis of the syntagmatic chain has hardly been mentioned. Even the structural analysis of the phonological paradigm, as developed by Jakobson and Troubetzkoy, has been admired but not used by many semioticians as the basis of general semiotic method. Two major exceptions are Jakobson himself, and the anthropologist Lévi-Strauss. But Jakobson's extensions were over a narrow range, and Lévi-Strauss tended to be speculative and unsystematic in the uses he made of the phonological model. It remains a paradox of the structuralist tradition in semiotics that it has barely begun to assimilate the lessons from the achievement on which its prestige is based.

As a start to this overdue development, we will set out some principles of structuralism in a general semiotic form. In cracking the phonological code, Saussure accounted for its fundamental coherence and economy by reference to an abstract elemental binary principle, with infinite particular forms produced by this principle applied repeatedly to the material basis of the code. A dialectic of this kind can generate innumerable different forms which still make sense. The sense they make, however, is a function of both the binary principle and the material basis as they interact. The multiplicity of forms cannot be reduced to the underlying binary principle, and the binary principle itself does not remain a pure form. The same binary principle, again in an abstract or analogous form, will organize both syntagmatic and paradigmatic structures of a code, so that there will be a relation of homology between syntagm and paradigm. The paradigmatic structures of the phonological code are not only built up from a common principle to that of the syntagmatic plane, they are also derived from a human activity that takes place in space and time. The features that make up the code are derived from a single syntagm: the narrative of the journey of air from the lungs to the outside, past various obstructions, making use of various opportunities on the way. In structural analysis, paradigm and syntagm, structure and process, meaning and matter, unity and multiplicity are inseparable, and must be complementary aspects of a single description. We can sum up these principles of a materialistic structuralism, which have their surprising source in Saussure:

1   The structures of a semiotic code are built up by the interaction of a small number of binary principles interacting with the material nature of the coding medium. Its unity comes from its general principles and their relationships, its variety from the material base on which the principles act.
2   The source of the features of a paradigmatic structure, which seems to exist outside space and time, is the material world of human actions and purposes in space and time.
3   Syntagmatic and paradigmatic structures in a code are constituted by the same set of principles, and are bound together by a relationship of homology.

History, change, transformation

Saussure has usually been represented as opposed to historical explanation in language, and in fact his importance is often seen as lying in the break he supposedly made with the historical orientation of the comparative philological tradition he was reared in. This is essentially Culler's view: 'In short, Saussure, Freud, and Durkheim renovated the social sciences by rejecting historical and causal explanations in favour of the study of interpersonal systems of norms' (1976: xiii). This judgement represents the modern orthodoxy on structuralism, but it would be surprising if it represented the whole truth about Saussure, the distinguished exponent of the discipline of comparative philology with its essentially historical strategies and tasks. Certainly he insisted on a sharp distinction between two kinds of approach to language, the synchronic and the diachronic, and created a larger space for synchronic linguistics than his tradition had recognized, but he also saw history, process, flux as the normal condition of language. In the section on synchronic linguistics in the *Course* he established the notion of 'language state', but only as an approximation. In practice, he noted, 'There is really no such thing as absolute immobility' (III, i, p. 140). He rejected the notion of linguistic laws on the grounds that a law must be both general and obligatory. 'Synchronic laws', he says, 'have regularity but are not imperative, whereas diachronic laws are imperative but not regular' (I, iii, p. 6). That is, the synchronic is rational but without force. It is the diachronic, then, that Saussure sees as the site of causal explanations. This is hardly a rejection of historical explanations as Culler claims.

Speech unfolds in time, and Saussure was aware of this, too. In fact he insisted on this feature of spoken signs, elevating that to his second principle of signs. (In fact he probably overstated the role of the diachronic in verbal language. Words are articulated together with pitch or intonation at the one time, and there are synchronic syntagms in many other codes, as we shall see.) But with larger stretches of text, it is usually the case that there is only meaning in a text if elements across time are brought into a significant relationship. We can extend this generalization to include relations between texts or elements of text, produced at different times. If we use the general term diachrony here, to include the dimension of time whether long or short (a step Saussure did not take) we have the paradoxical conclusion that diachrony is indispensable to meaning even within the 'language state' of a synchrony. It is clear that Saussure is by no means to be identified with a rejection of temporality or history, though it is also clear that he finds it deeply problematic.

It is not our intention to attribute ideas to Saussure that it has only become possible to see with hindsight. What we want to argue is that a lifetime of working with diachronic linguistics could not have left Saussure without any strategies for dealing with such problems. It is deeply ironic that Saussure's arguments for synchronic linguistics have been used to legitimate an *a priori* dismissal of the diachronic dimension, which has meant that most of what Saussure had to offer as a practising semiotician is simply ignored. It is reasonable to suppose that the professor of general linguistics at Geneva University would have assumed his audience recognized the importance of diachronic linguistics, leaving him free to explore its problems. Modern semioticians assume that diachrony is so obviously uninteresting that they do not bother to take Saussure's concern with it seriously, or attempt to learn about it from him.

If we turn to the *Course*, there are innumerable acute observations on diachronic phenomena, as we would expect, lacking only an overall framework that could make sense of them. The diachronic phenomena Saussure studied so extensively were all examples of language change, mostly of the sounds of words. In more modern terms we can call the theory he is developing a theory of transformations. As with his theory of phonological structures, it is narrow in scope, and needs to be broadened to cover other semiotic systems. Because he characteristically ignores the social context of language, the source of the 'imperative' of diachronic laws, he is unable to explain the transformational operations he so meticulously describes. But given that there is this work to be done, Saussure's theory of transformations still repays study, because modern semiotics lacks an adequate transformational theory. Within linguistics, with the collapse of the Chomskyan paradigm serious interest in transformations has withered. The theory advanced in our *Language as Ideology* is an isolated exception to this trend. In structuralist semiotics, there has been only a limited and partial account of transformations. Freud does have a powerful and comprehensive theory of transformations, but it is insufficiently systematized and has not been incorporated into the semiotic mainstream.

In spite of his sharp distinction between synchrony and diachrony, Saussure insisted that any transformational sequence must first exist as alternatives in a synchronic state. 'An evolutionary fact is always preceded by a fact, or rather by a multitude of similar facts, in the sphere of speaking (*parole*)' (p. 98). Saussure's refusal to theorize *parole* or to accept it as an object of theory has obscured the importance of what he is saying here, which is in effect that transformations arise in a synchronic state, in the social conditions of language use. In this synchronic state, he says, at least two forms must coexist, however subtly distinguished, as the starting point for change. He does not offer any explanation for this divergence, although Voloshinov's theory of the fissive force on the sign coming from social conflict and class struggle would certainly provide one. Saussure specifically rules out a transformational relation between the two coexisting forms, a decision which makes it even harder for him to account successfully for change. What he does do is, however, a useful clarification. He insists that all the changes be listed in rigorously strict sequence, only one change at a time. For instance the modern French *chaud*, 'warm' (pronounced ṣo) is derived from the Latin *calidum*. The relationship is not visible on the surface, but follows this sequence: calidum – calidu – caldu – cald – calt – tsalt – tsaut – ṣaut – ṣot – ṣo. He notes the rationality of it, in this form, as against its incomprehensibility if we look only at the beginning and the end: 'Each step, when viewed separately, is absolutely certain and regular and limited in its effect; viewed as a whole, however, the word gives the impression of an unlimited number of modifications' (p. 152).

In such sequences, he noted two kinds of change. One he called, unhelpfully, 'spontaneous', the other 'combinatory'. Spontaneous changes are changes in the value of the sound in the paradigmatic system (e.g., c – ts), so we can call them paradigmatic transformations. Combinatory changes concern the syntagmatic arrangement of existing elements (e.g., calidu – caldu). We can call these syntagmatic transformations. He also had a further category he called 'conditioned spontaneous' changes, which were paradigmatic transformations dependent on specific syntagmatic conditions in their context (e.g., the place of the element in the word). So a precise transformational history of a form is the key to its understanding, and that history consists of both syntagmatic and paradigmatic transformations, acting separately and in unison.

It is salutary to compare Saussure's theory of transformations with Chomsky's later and better-known formulations (1957, 1965, 1976). Chomsky restricted his theory to syntagmatic transformations in a synchronic state, which he assumed were reversible, part of *langue* and the consciousness of the typical speaker. Saussure includes paradigmatic transformations as well as syntagmatic, and he follows changes back to the point where they are no longer reversible. So Chomsky's transformations are a specific subset of Saussurean transformations. If the state of mind of a normal member of a synchronic language state defines rationality, then Saussure is right to see the diachronic as reaching into the realm of the irrational, with history the determining irrational in a given society. Transformations that are difficult to reverse were also studied by Freud, as characteristic products of the processes of the unconscious. Saussure's inclinations did not take him in this direction, but he went further than Chomsky, who definitionally removes all kinds of irrational from the domain of linguistics.

Paradoxically, however, Chomsky's work suggests the opposite tendency in his notion of 'deep structure' and his siting of these processes in the unknowable depths of the human mind, out of reach of consciousness, whereas all the forms Saussure arranged in sequence had had a prior social and material existence. If Saussure was forced to reconstruct a hypothetical form it was only because that form had been lost, but was marked by the space or gap it had left. *Language as Ideology* offered a misleading account of the role and place of 'deep structure' in a transformational theory, overinfluenced by Chomsky's formulations. We would now posit a sequence of material texts or forms of texts as the explanatory core of the concept of transformation, with prior texts or structures not 'deeper' but simply 'earlier'. But in many semiosic instances this sequence is frequently not present, and has to be implied by producers and reconstructed by receivers. These implied or reconstructed sequences are partly an effect of textual qualities but are also strongly affected by the purposes and knowledge of semiotic participants. These are the content of what, in *Language as Ideology*, we used to call 'deep' structure. The analytic practice still seems defensible to us, but we are now uneasy about the illusion of three-dimensional solidity that the metaphor 'deep' suggests of texts or meanings whose most obvious characteristic is their insubstantiality. The term 'semiosic projection' is less misleading; although what matters more than the name is the importance and pervasiveness of this level of meanings in semiotic analysis.

Diachronic changes of the kind Saussure mainly dealt with raise other problems which he addressed. The full chain of diachronic changes often does go outside the scope of knowledge of the member of a specific community. How do we root them in human social processes, if the agent for the chain as a whole must exist outside any specific time and place? They are only visible at the metalinguistic level, accessible only to the pedant. The same problem would exist for another class of diachronic phenomenon that Saussure does not try to investigate, diachronic syntagmatic structures whose beginning or end are obscure or invisible. In both cases we seem to have to invoke a transhistorical subject or set of subjects occupying a single position, yet these are simply projections of innumerable structures of meaning in search of an author. On this issue, Saussure's observation is still valid: 'All these things exist in language, but as *abstract entities*; their study is difficult because we never know exactly whether or not the awareness of speakers goes as far as the analysis of the grammarian. But the important thing is that *abstract entities are always based, in the last analysis, on concrete entities*' (p. 138, italics in original). Here again we have a Saussure capable of subtle yet assured judgements about diachronic phenomena because of his sense of material and concrete facts as the basis of explanation, where the idealist Saussure abandons diachrony as an incomprehensible flux.

Our own work in *Language as Ideology* developed a reasonably powerful concept of transformations as applied to specific texts, but it did not integrate this explicitly with a theory or strategy of historical analysis. We now see the development of a comprehensive theory of the diachronic as an urgent need for the kind of semiotic project we are engaged in if it is to account for such crucial phenomena as change, process, crisis and revolution in the smaller and larger scale. One decisive superiority of Marxist social theory over other structuralist forms has long been its recognition and theorization of history; and we believe that no adequate social semiotics can afford to neglect the diachronic dimension.

From Saussure's work on diachrony and transformations and our reflections on this area we can draw the following principles:

1   All semiotic activity takes place in time: all semiotic phenomena are diachronic, whether on a small scale (the time to produce or interpret a single syntagm, the flow of syntagms in discourse) or a larger scale, including the history of human semiosis.
2   Every syntagm is a moment in a process of transformations, leading backwards in time (to earlier syntagms in the same exchange, to earlier discourses or semiotic acts) and forward (to later uses of the syntagm, by decoders or encoders); and this process, in its strict chronological order, is a key to the interpretation of that syntagm.
3   Every structure and relation in the field of semiotics is subject to transformational activity: so there are syntagmatic and paradigmatic transformations as well as other transformational processes, which act together to constitute every semiotic object.
4   Every transformation is a concrete event, with agents, and reasons, deriving from material and social life: and the base line for the interpretation of any diachronic chain is its intersection with the material world.
5   Transformations can have force and effectivity even if their full scope is not available to consciousness. So transformational analysis can reveal structures of meaning whose action is unconscious yet decisive in a given context of interpretation.

We can apply these principles to the account of the semiotic tradition in this chapter. We have interpreted the semiotic tradition as dynamic and open-ended, and not as a solid body of doctrine to be accepted or rejected, wholly or even bit by bit. We did not start with Saussure, nor did we try to determine where Saussure's thought ends. We have seen possibilities in his thought which connect with other possible lines of development offered by other thinkers, but we are not attributing a full recognition of these possibilities to Saussure, nor claiming their discovery to ourselves. So we have not gone back to what Saussure (or Peirce, or Voloshinov) 'really' thought, as though that was something fixed, which other commentators have seen or unaccountably missed. Our reading of Saussure in particular is a critical reading, a transformation of his work in many respects, so we do not suppose that if he were alive he would agree with everything we say. But that has not been an excuse for an inattentive reading of Saussure and these other founding fathers. On the contrary, precise recognition of the structures and the fissures, in Saussure as in the provisional starting point of any diachronic chain, is indispensible for this kind of critical-transformational work to proceed.

In the process, we have outlined the main terms and premises of our own theory of social semiotics. We could have done this as a set of axioms, complete with illustrations and supporting argument. But that form of presentation always has the effect of freezing thought, cutting it off from its roots, preventing its further growth, making it to some degree incomprehensible. A diachronic account of a tradition frees the reader from the oppressive sense that it is monolithic, unchanging, without inconsistencies. We hope our own theory is more comprehensible for being offered as provisional, a stage in a continuing debate, a continuing struggle for clarification.

3

Context as Meaning: the Semiosic Dimension

Voloshinov, as we have seen, focused his critique of Saussurean structuralism on a single error, its *proton pseudos*, as he called it; its rejection of the speech act as something individual. Against this he asserted the counter-proposition: *the utterance is a social phenomenon.* He then placed the utterance – that is, the unitary semiotic act – at the centre of social semiotics. He went on to the following formulation, which we have already quoted but which bears repeating: 'The form of signs is conditioned above all by the social organization of the participants and also by the immediate conditions of their interaction'.

This shift of focus marks a radical break from structuralist semiotics. In the last twenty years or so a number of theorists have begun to push in the same direction, often concentrating on different aspects of the context of semiotic acts, but sharing a sense of its importance. (See especially Benveniste 1971, Hymes 1972, Halliday 1978.)

To illustrate some of the implications of this new orientation, we will take the instance of traffic lights. Structuralists are fond of this example, because it seems a code of classic simplicity (see, for example, Leach 1970). There are three signifiers (red, green and amber/yellow) linked to three signifieds (stop, go and stop/go) by a conventional code. In practice there is usually a double code, since red is conventionally at the top, green at the bottom, and amber in the middle, but this seems a minor matter, since it merely repeats the other code. What more is there to say about such an elementary system?

The answer is: not much, if we persist in ignoring context. If we consider how these systems function in their context, however, we can immediately see that context is a crucial part of their meaning. We can also see that the meaning constituted by the interplay between text (a sequence of traffic signals) and its function is complex, far reaching and ultimately social and ideological. The traffic signals are, of course (it seems too obvious to mention), positioned beside roads, at intersections. This is not only their context of use: it contains the information essential to their meaning. They address their message primarily to motorists, and motorists and the cars they drive are included in their meaning. Red, for instance, doesn't simply mean 'stop'. It means 'motorists, stop'. In context, it carries other meanings, as part of its mimetic content. It promises that the behaviour of other motorists at other parts of the intersection will be predictable. These others will either stop or go themselves as the case may be. It has a mimetic content, then, implying a state of affairs in the physical world even though it's only a claim, which 'some lunatic shooting a red light' could disrupt, making a lie of its claim to power.

Indeed, in order to be able to drive safely in a particular place, we need to understand that such texts are constructed with different class, gender, or other cultural dialects. In Sydney the meaning of amber for a particular group of motorists is 'speed up if you are approaching the traffic lights'. Red itself has at least two signifiers in that dialect: 'just turned red' and 'red for a few seconds'. In the dialect just mentioned, 'just turned red' means 'proceed through the intersection'. 'Green' therefore has a different reading in that dialect. But what also becomes apparent is that motorists need to be 'multilingual', aware of the existence of different dialects, and of their meaning. 'Green' therefore becomes the signifier of a meaning 'proceed after checking for the possible presence of users of the other dialect' for *all* users of the code. Nor is it difficult to understand the complex of social factors that has given rise to the emergence of the second dialect: factors such as prevailing traffic conditions, commuting times, attitudes to authority, gender attitudes, ethnic differences, and so on.

The traffic signals as text, then, construct a specific context, which is both a physical context and an organization of participants. So important is it that its messages be seen and acted on that there is normally redundancy built in – several traffic lights saying the same thing, plus many other ancillary signs. Even the duplicated message of top-plus-red, bottom-plus-green is functionally redundant, so that the text can still be read even when one of the colours in the sequence is not lighting up, as happens with malfunctionings. But this is not the limit of the messages it conveys. Part of the social meaning of these signs is the absence of any human agent operating them. The 'agent' who issues these instructions is impersonal in two senses: an electrically operated device linking the complete set of lights so that their messages are synchronized, and a state which functions as invisibly and efficiently as the electrical device. This is a signifier of an absolute authority whose instructions are even-handed, rational and benign. But behind its commands, there is also a police force and a set of rules, specifying fines, etc., for non-compliance with the message of the lights. Just as there is a multiplicity of signs, so there is a possible double punishment for disobedience: injury, and legal penalties.

So this elementary code could not operate without the underpinning of a logonomic system which classifies people and actions, and whose action can only be guessed at by observing behaviours as well as signals. The system is directly connected to the legal system of the state, and enforced by its officers. Thus its meaning has the same scope. The traffic signals transmit an ideological message as well as particular instructions. They present a version of society, an image of impersonal rationality operating impartially on behalf of all. This ideological meaning is not a gratuitous addition but part of its effectivity, since it is a faith in this benign impartiality, transmitted with massive redundancy by countless traffic lights day after day, that conditions motorists to abide by their message almost unthinkingly.

The basic constituents of this as of every other such social message system concern two dimensions: power and solidarity. In the case of the traffic lights, power is the most obvious dimension, power understood as control by one social agent of the behaviour of others. But solidarity is an effect of power just as power is an effect of solidarity. The traffic lights separate out the streams of cars into two groups, each of which acts as a single entity, all either going, close to each other but not touching, or stationary. And if there was not this solidarity relationship, making a single entity, the 'stream of traffic', then the effortless assertion of power would not work.

What we have observed in this specialized case applies to many other cases of communication as well. In the case of speech, communication of any mimetic content is normally accompanied by innumerable clusters of messages about the conditions of semiosis transmitted with massive redundancy in a range of semiotic systems (tone of voice, expression, behaviours, etc.). Within the spoken text itself, there are many signifiers of relationship. Producers of messages construct a social identity for themselves and for their hearers. They also attend to reception messages from receivers which act as a kind of feedback that in turn is built into their own message. Just as the behaviour of drivers going through a green light is based on their (more or less qualified) confidence in the other drivers respecting a red light, so every exchange in a verbal text is in a sense co-authored by the main participants. The context, both the physical referents and the social conditions of semiosis, is decisive for communication to occur. This context can only enter into communication in so far as it is assigned meanings and made meaningful, though these meanings may not be common. The traditional illustration of traffic lights should be stripped of its implicit ideology of the communication process. Semiosis is never simple, clear and rational, even when it is operated by electricity. We assume that it always involves conflict, disagreement, a lack of clarity and consensus, even in the seemingly simple instance of the traffic lights.

We can summarize some of these observations about the functions of context as follows:

1 The context of semiosis is itself organized as a series of texts, with meanings assigned to categories of participants and relationships.
2 The behaviour of the participants is constrained by logonomic systems which operate through messages about their identity and relationships, signifying status, power and solidarity.
3 Participants in semiosis typically transmit a great profusion of messages in a number of codes about the status of the exchange and their own and others' roles.
4 Where a semiotic exchange does not involve direct contact by all participants, producers are likely to include instructions specifying producers, receivers and contexts into the form of their text.
5 The set of messages which organizes a particular semiotic exchange will imply a generalized version of social relations. That is, every semiotic act has an ideological content.

Messages of power and solidarity

In examining the logonomic systems that organize relationships of power and solidarity, we begin by looking at a classic linguistic study by Brown and Gilman, 'Pronouns of Power and Solidarity', first published in 1960. At first glance the scope of this article seems extremely limited. It looks only at pronouns of address ('you' and its forms) as used in a number of different European languages over a period of about four hundred years. In spite or because of this narrow scope, however, it has proved an exemplary analysis, with implications for many other semiotic codes. Other linguists, of course, had studied systems of pronouns, but they had treated the conditions of use as secondary, and they had not established the social meaning of these terms at the centre of their study. Brown and Gilman's achievement was to reverse these priorities. Their starting point was the social meaning of this set of pronouns which they analysed as falling into two dimensions, power and solidarity. Behind their own specific analysis lies the social theory of Durkheim, who had posited two fundamental dimensions of any form of social organization, solidarity (cohesion and discohesion, alliances and antagonisms, bonds and barriers) and power (order, control, hierarchy). These abstract categories have the virtues of scope and flexibility. They can apply to both macro and micro levels of society, to the relations between and within social classes in a class society or to the constitution of smaller groupings such as family, kin-group and so on.

Brown and Gilman's study started from the well-known fact that many European languages have two different forms of pronoun for the second person singular, with complex rules for their use. They label the two forms the T form (French and Italian 'tu', German 'du', English 'thou') and the V form (French 'vous', Italian 'lei' or 'voi', German 'Sie'). There is a double problem with their use. One concerns their meaning. Each pronoun carries meanings about both power and solidarity, so that each is potentially ambiguous. The T form, for instance, can signify intimacy if used to an equal, and superiority or contempt if used to a non-equal. The V form indicates respect to a potential superior, but coolness to a friend. The second problem is that the meaning of each depends on the response that is expected. Thus, their meaning is directly dependent on a shared knowledge of the social organization of the participants and acceptance of these terms. Correct usage requires a person to understand both directionality (who is speaking to whom) and system (where the person or persons are 'located' socially and how they can be expected to respond). This makes such forms fraught with difficulty for the unwary language learner, because of the precise social knowledge they require. It also makes them dangerous when social relationships are insufficiently clear, either for lack of clear supporting signifiers, or where negotiation or dispute render them unstable.

In its most basic terms, the code consists of not just one pair of elements (T or V form) but of two: reciprocity, $+R$ (mutual T or V) or non-reciprocity, $-R$ (T–V or V–T). We can set out the basic possibilities and their meanings as follows, where the bracketed form is that expected in return:

	Signifiers		*Signifieds*
T {	$+R$ (i.e. T)	—	Intimacy
	$-R$ (i.e. V)	—	Power/hostility
V {	$+R$ (i.e. V)	—	Formality, respect
	$-R$ (i.e. T)	—	Deference

One of the striking things about this system is the way it seems to conflate meanings of power and solidarity. In abstract terms, this code is constituted by two transparent oppositions, one between T and V, the other between reciprocity and non-reciprocity, which is a transparent signifier of inequality, and hence of power or its absence. The logic of the system signifies an antithetical relationship between power and solidarity at some points. For instance, the distinction between weak solidarity or politeness, and strong solidarity or intimacy, is signified by the difference between mutual T and mutual V, as though the greater distance signified by the mutual V indicates greater power, or the greater power of the two demands a greater distance. But the T form, used by the powerful to the non-powerful, uses intimacy as a sign of power, not of its opposite. When this usage is challenged, a failed claim to intimacy is treated as its opposite, as a declaration of intense hostility, as though the possibility of a meaning of power serves to invert the meaning of solidarity.

The complexities and instabilities of this system led to its being abandoned in English between the sixteenth and eighteenth centuries, so it is no longer a current form in English. Fortunately, however, Shakespeare was around to see the system in crisis, and he dramatized the process and its social implications in some of his greatest plays. One work we will look at for this purpose is the tragedy *King Lear*, written at the beginning of the seventeenth century.

In the first scene of the play King Lear 'tests' the love of his three daughters, requiring them to tell him how much they love him, in return for which he offers them power, one third of his kingdom. (For a fuller discussion see Aers and Kress 1981, Hodge and Kress, 1982). To his two elder daughters he uses the plural 'we' of himself, and addresses them as 'you' till after they have passed the test by insincere hyperboles of love. Assured of their love, having raised them to what he thinks is an equality of power, he addresses them as 'thou'. Cordelia, his favourite daughter, refuses to compromise her genuine feelings in this way, so his love turns to an equally intense fury. But this is again expressed through the 'thou' form, meant to be unreciprocal this time, therefore conveying contempt and superiority. But none of his daughters addresses him with the T form, so his intimacy with his elder daughters is an illusion, and the close but power-laden relationship he has with Cordelia is the only intimate relationship a man, a father and a king, can have with even a beloved and dutiful daughter. In the society of Lear, power and love are incompatible, but they are expressed through a common semiotic system, so that it is quite possible for him to fail to understand the meaning of his own sign. Similarly, when his action is opposed by the Earl of Kent, a faithful courtier, Lear fails to appreciate that love can express itself as opposition to power or authority. Kent uses the T form to challenge his king: 'What wouldst thou do, old man?' Again the T form is ambiguous. It asserts an intimacy which is real but which of its nature challenges Lear's power. Despite his professed concern with love not power, Lear fails to distinguish between the two, and with Kent he acts to safeguard his power not his love (he banishes him), after he has sacrificed power because he trusts in love. Or, more exactly, he has trusted in the signs of love that in his society are inseparable from systems expressing power.

One problem with this analysis of the thou/you system is that it's apt to seem too idiosyncratic, a system that has now disappeared from English. The set of meanings at issue, of course, is hardly likely to disappear. On the contrary, these are so fundamental to social life that they are bound to be conveyed through countless other sets of signs which will operate in similar ways to thou/you. Brown and Ford (1961) studied one of these, namely terms of address, which they found had similar functions in twentieth-century American English to the sixteenth-century thou/you. The sixteenth century had a system of terms of address too, to supplement thou/you. But in order to generalize more powerfully from the thou/you system, over the whole range of signifiers of power and solidarity, we need to understand how these signifiers are themselves constituted, and how they function within a larger system of signs to express semiosic meanings.

The key point to make is that when this was a functioning system, it was based on transparent signifiers of power and solidarity, and it is these basic signifiers which give us a sound base for generalizations. One component signifier, as we have seen, is reciprocity/non-reciprocity, or symmetry/asymmetry. This is a transparent signifier of power which is very widespread indeed. The difference between 'thou' and 'you' is also based on transparent signifiers. 'Thou' is the singular form, 'you' the plural. So when both are used of a single person, 'thou' is being used in its most direct sense, whereas 'you' is a transform, a displacement. So the difference is constituted by two signifiers, plurality and displacement/transformation. Plurality, like size, is a common signifier of power (plurality = magnitude = power). Transformation requires work, and introduces difference. The presence of transformational activity, then, is a transparent signifier of distance or non-solidarity and the recognition of power and constraint.

If we see it in these terms, the sixteenth-century system of terms of address is not a separate system parallel to thou/you, but another realization, one of many, of a common signifying system. To show how this works as a system, with the massive redundancy that is characteristic of such systems, we will look at two lines of dialogue from an early seventeenth-century play, *A Chaste Maid in Cheapside* by Thomas Middleton:

SIR WALTER WHOREHOUND   How dost, Jack?
MR ALLWIT   Proud of your worship's health, sir.

The power difference between these two is marked. The conversation occurs outside Allwit's house, which gives him some status, but Sir Walter is a wealthy aristocrat, while Mr Allwit is a struggling tradesman

who is financially supported by Sir Walter so that the aristocrat can
continue an affair with Allwit's wife. The solidarity relationship,
therefore, is inseparable from the power dimension, and Sir Walter
exploits the ambiguity to the maximum.

With this brief sketch of the context, we can turn to the systems
which not only reflect it but also sustain it. Both men are engaged in
phatic communication, in Malinowski's (1923) terms (communication
designed to sustain communication). Sir Walter, lusting after Mrs Allwit,
isn't really interested in how Allwit does, or what he does. Nor is Allwit
proud of Sir Walter's excessive health. The exchange serves instead to
rapidly recall and reinforce the relationship itself, with all its inequalities
of power and mystifications of solidarity. Sir Walter's contribution is
asymmetrical in two ways. He initiates the conversation, and he uses
the non-reciprocal form 'dost (thou)' in a compressed form which partly
conceals it. He also uses not simply first name, but intimate first name
'Jack', whereas Allwit responds with 'Sir'. So Sir Walter projects
effortless intimacy, relying on Mr Allwit to produce for himself the
markers of his own subservience. The whole exchange is a beautifully
economic instance of how many messages can pass so quickly, when
what is at issue is simply the replication of an ideological formula.

From Allwit's point of view, however, things are not so easy. What
he says, as an answer to Sir Walter's question, doesn't make good
sense. However, if we reconstruct a transformational sequence it does
work (with deleted elements in brackets):

> ↑ Proud of your worship's health, sir
> ↑ (I am) proud of your worship's health, sir
> ↑ (I am) proud/(I) worship (you)/(you are) healthy, sir
> ↑ (I am) proud/(I) worship (you)/(I am) healthy, sir
> ↑ (I am) proud/(I) worship (thee)/(I am) healthy, sir

Although the exact sequence might be open to some dispute, it seems
plausible that Allwit initially formed the simple and safe answer 'I am
healthy' in response to Sir Walter's phatic inquiry. But by the time the
platitude has reached the surface, it has been transformed almost out
of existence, changed to an irrelevant comment about Sir Walter's
health. This twist is part of a consistent pattern, whereby the
inferior deletes self-references and self-meanings (his own meanings).
Corresponding to this is a magnification of Sir Walter. Not only is the
direct singular 'thee' expanded to the honorific plural, he adds another
marker, 'sir'. Sir Walter does mention Allwit's name, but deletes the
pronoun ('thou'). From this we can see a more general rule of which
the 'you' form is an illustration. Inferiority is signalled by a suppression
of meanings of the self, and expansion of the meanings of the other.
Superiority is signalled by the opposite.

This explains why Allwit can speak at greater length while still not signifying power. He says six words to Sir Walter's three, and behind his six are three truncated sentences to Sir Walter's one. But this simply demonstrates how much more difficult it is for him to produce his meanings. His elaborate form of words, easily recognized as 'polite speech', clearly functions as the equivalent of the 'you' form. Like forms of address, this realization of non-power is still alive and well in the twentieth century. English, like most other contemporary languages, has prestige forms which are seen as markers of status (cf. Labov 1978). These forms are characterized by extensive transformations which make such speech difficult to produce and to understand. But 'polite' speech, like the 'polite' pronoun form, is created by self-negation, self-suppression. Mutual polite speech, in the sixteenth as in the twentieth century, signifies a kind of equality constructed out of mutual self-constraint. It signifies weak solidarity and acknowledgement of the power of the other. But the status that is believed to be associated with this code comes not from use of it, but from being offered it by another, in return for offering it to the other. Real power, now as then, is signified by the non-reciprocal use of direct speech which expresses meanings of the self.

It isn't the case, of course, that excessive speech is always a marker of weakness. Clearly, silence is a transparent signifier of exclusion from a relationship and lack of power. In this exchange of Allwit's, servants were standing round in deferential silence, which means what it seems to mean in social terms. Allwit is in fact caught in a contradiction, trying to express both power and lack of power. (One of his transformed utterances is 'I am proud' – which in some ways he is, in spite of being a servile cuckold). The servants, if they followed the logonomic rules for servants in the seventeenth century, would delete themselves as communicators, not only in the verbal mode, but also in non-verbal systems. As good servants their faces should be impassive (even eagerness to see and serve Sir Walter would be inappropriate, if they felt it). Their bodies should stand at attention, not communicating nothing, because that would be impossible, but communicating as little as possible, and those only the preconstructed meanings that they as servants are required to produce: signs indicating their lack of any possible status as participants.

In interactions like this, many other codes play a part, including clothing codes, gestures, and so on, and others, such as architectural codes, which establish not simply the status of a context but also what pattern of relationships will prevail in it. The specific signals change from society to society and from time to time, so that a system like the thou/you one in English is incomprehensible in the twentieth century. Most modern readers of seventeenth-century plays probably do not even notice that there is a system of this kind there, much less understand how it works. But these systems are too vital to social functions to be intrinsically difficult to learn. Logonomic systems cover this problem by a double strategy: massive redundancy (so that if one sign-system doesn't work, others will translate for them) and by use of transparent signifiers at their base.

We can summarize a number of points about this type of sign system:

1 Interrelated systems of signs of power and solidarity are used to organize and make sense of the relationships of participants in all semiotic acts.
2 Systems of signifiers of power and solidarity are based on the assumption of both opposition and identity between these dimensions, leading to systematic ambiguity and multiple redundancy.
3 Transparent signifiers of solidarity are based on a number of principles, including analogies with equality, reciprocity, self-reference, and simplicity or lack of transformational modification. These can also signify absence of power; and, conversely, absence of signifiers of power can signify solidarity.
4 Transparent signifiers of power are based on a number of principles, including analogies with asymmetry, self-suppression, magnitude and elaboration. These can also signify absence of solidarity; and signifiers of the absence of power can signify solidarity.
5 Logonomic systems specify and assume specific relations of power and solidarity between categories of participant, projecting an ideological vision of reality.

Media constructions of power and solidarity

In contemporary Western societies, power and solidarity cannot be exercised solely through countless individual exchanges. The mass media act like communication technologies of the past, including writing, art and architecture, in having to construct communication exchanges that bind distant participants into an effective community, so that they can be subject to effects of power. But this does not mean that they have no need for existing systems of signifiers of power and solidarity. On the contrary, their need for these is just as strong, although they have had to develop alternative systems and strategies to reinforce or replace those that mediate face-to-face communication. To begin to examine some of these specialized systems, we will take the following text: a television interview between Mike Willesee, of the Australian current affairs programme *Willesee*, and Sir Joh Bjelke-Peterson, the former right-wing populist premier of the State of Queensland, in Australia. (Our transcription is an attempt to represent the grammatical organization of relatively spontaneous speech – other than in the scripted introduction – for which the sentence-based forms of punctuation are inappropriate. Dots signal pauses and hesitations.)

WILLESEE Hello. Thank you for joining us. The Queensland Premier, Mr Joh Bjelke-Peterson suffered what appears to be his worst political defeat last night. His controversial Abortion Bill was voted down in Parliament. Eleven Liberal Party members, four of them Ministers, broke from the Coalition ranks to vote with the Opposition and from the Premier's normally cohesive National Party there were four defections and three abstentions, er, one indeed by a Minister. The defeat had begun seeming apparent on Tuesday night after a headcount of Liberals and National Party members, but it was not until ten minutes before yesterday's defeat that Mr Bjelke-Peterson agreed to cut his losses and have the Bill sponsored not by the Government but by a private member. But that barely lessened the size or impact of the defeat for the Government. Political commentators are now starting to guess about Mr Bjelke-Peterson's own political future, with elections due before the end of the year. Mr Bjelke-Peterson is in our Brisbane studios now. Mr Premier, thanks for coming to talk with us.

BJELKE-P Er . thanks . . that's a pleasure . a . a great pleasure . hm . hm.

WILLESEE You've had a tough couple of days.

BJELKE-P Well . that's just politics . . that's nothing unusual . . they come and they go . those sort of days . and there's been many of them in the . . hm . . years that I've been in politics . particularly the twelve years that I've been Premier . that's nothing unusual.

WILLESEE Many as tough as this?

BJELKE-P Oh yes . I think they . they . . er . . there are many . yes . sure . . there's . . that comes and goes all the time . all sorts of things.

WILLESEE It doesn't bother you more than all the other problems.

BJELKE-P No . it doesn't . . we . . we . . yesterday . . that's er . . well . as I said once you are in politics . . when you've been there 33 years like I have . Mike . as you know . I've . . I've had to deal with all sorts of problems . . all sorts of people . . people like yourself . . and others . so . no . . that's . . that's nothing unusual.

WILLESEE So it doesn't bother you . . you don't lose sleep on occasions like this.

BJELKE-P No . No . I don't . I . . I . . matter of fact I have no problems that way.

There are two exchanges here, both involving Willesee, the interviewer: the first with the audience, the second with the politician. We will take the interview itself first. Both participants have a source of power: Willesee as the interviewer, Bjelke-Peterson as a political leader. The two men live in different cities, and the interview is by link-up between two television studios. Their political affiliations are opposed – Willesee's background being left of centre, Bjelke-Peterson's to the right – and there is an age difference of 30 years between them. Real solidarity and intimacy is not to be expected.

A convenient starting point for the analysis is with terms of address, as they signal and construct relationships within the interview itself. Willesee addresses Bjelke-Peterson as 'Mr Premier', which is one step more formal than 'Mr Bjelke-Peterson', and he is referred to as 'Mike' – one step more familiar than 'Michael'. That is, there is extreme non-reciprocity between the two. There is even a discontinuity between the two classification systems, since 'Premier' implies an orientation to the public domain, and 'Mike' to the private domain, to individual private existence. Willesee's term indicates that he sees the situation as power-laden, Bjelke-Peterson indicates that he does not. The asymmetry forms a syntagm of power, Bjelke-Peterson's power and Willesee's weakness. Willesee initiates each exchange, as interviewer, and this power to initiate signifies power generally, but it is interesting to see that the question form – one common surface signal of that power – is hardly ever used by him, or at least never untransformed. His first 'question' seems a statement: it has the syntactic form of 'declarative'. We have added a question mark to his second question, which is syntactically an interrogative, though he has deleted the syntactic marker of the question at the beginning (i.e., 'Have you had . . .?') Intonationally this is a question. His other two interventions are both statements: syntactically they are declaratives, and there is only a slightly raised intonation contour to suggest a question. The inequality of power between Willesee and this senior politician has virtually deleted Willesee's power as an interviewer to use the question form.

There are a large number of asymmetries in the exchange, which all carry the same message. Willesee says much less than Bjelke-Peterson – the contrast is marked in contrast with his opening statement – and this is because what he might have said has been so drastically deleted. This severely reduced form still contains a content which is antagonistic to Bjelke-Peterson's, and his repetition of his point of view 'It doesn't bother you . . .' 'So it doesn't bother you . . .' is an assertion of his power, though that assertion is transformed into surface agreement with the meanings of the other. His antagonism, such as it is, leaves no traces of affectual content on the verbal surface, perhaps only in the intonation; and that only slightly.

Bjelke-Peterson's language is very speech-like. That is, it is characteristic of the grammatical structure of relatively spontaneous speech, with a structure of clauses which are loosely 'chained' ('Well . that's just politics . . that's nothing unusual . . they come and they go . those sort of days . and there's been many . . .') rather than strongly integrated as in the more characteristic structure of sentences in the written form, as for instance, in the interviewer's introduction. To take an example sentence: 'The *defeat had begun seeming* apparent on Tuesday night after a *headcount* of Liberals and National Party members, but it *was* not until ten minutes before yesterday's *defeat* that Mr Bjelke-Peterson *agreed to cut* his *losses* and *have* the Bill *sponsored* not by . . .' This sentence consists of at least eight clauses (marked by the italicized verbs) and possibly twelve, if we treat the words *headcount, defeat,* and *losses* as derived from clauses. Bjelke-Peterson's speech is also marked by the hesitation characteristic of spoken language in relatively spontaneous, informal situations. This leads to an equivocal signal: an indication of power on the one hand, for instance through the naming practice, and an indication of solidarity on the other, through the use of the more intimate forms of casual speech. (More detailed accounts of the characteristics of the speech-writing distinction can be found in Kress 1982 and Halliday 1985). Since the interviewer seemingly cannot respond using similar forms, we have to assume that the premier is signalling power towards the interviewer. Yet he does this by using forms which signal solidarity.

This ambiguity is not merely hypothetical. In fact Bjelke-Peterson like Willesee functions simultaneously in two semiosic contexts, one the interview, the other the communication involving the viewers of this programme. This second semiosic context is crucial to the effect of the programme for both politician and interviewer. Like pronoun-systems, this relationship must be left open, so that receivers can dutifully construct the appropriate model, and will their part in it. Viewers are in fact totally excluded from the exchange, with even less power than Willesee, but one possibility for them is to imagine responding in familiar tones, as intimates of this powerful figure. Hence the intimacy of the forms of speech is directed to them. Bjelke-Peterson's double image, projecting both power and solidarity with the same words and style, is very effective as a carrier of the contradiction which is at the basis of a populist autocratic leader. To the 'populace' he speaks in their idiom – or what is constructed as their idiom. To his addressee he asserts power. Willesee's semiotic repertoire in this situation would not allow him to project such an image even if he spoke at much greater length.

The audience options are different in the first part of the transcript. In the interview itself, the audience overhears an exchange, and has more freedom to relate to any participant. In the first part, Willesee looks straight out of the screen, and says 'Hello'. The language has the specific forms of the written code, signifying power and formality. The only person on the end of the gaze is the viewer, a listener not a reader, replicated in thousands of homes. The primary semiosic structure that gives meaning to the semiotic codes here is the dyad formed by television speaker and television viewer. For the analyst, there is the seductive illusion that the meaning of the exchange is fixed, on the screen and in our transcript. The significance of the exchange, though, is dependent on the other part of the dyad also, and that is not fixed. The audience might switch off the set, reducing Willesee to silence and a spot of light on the screen, a total deletion. If they listen, they might be sitting relaxed in their lounge, talking casually and directly about what they think of Willesee and Bjelke-Peterson. Or they might be sitting with their eyes fixed on the screen, silently watching and listening, all their own messages transformed to zero. This last relationship is what is taken as the norm for the TV relationship: the passive narcoticized viewer. But appearances can be deceptive. Two equally impassive viewers (the same applies to readers of books, or someone looking at paintings, audiences at plays, sermons, debates) might have significantly different relationships to a common text. One crucial difference is transformational capacity. Anyone who can go from a transformed text to project a fuller set of prior structures is engaged in a process which mirrors the original act of production, so such an interpreter can feel on an equality with the producer. He or she may be silent, but that is a temporary and surface self-repression. Internally, the message is reproduced, recreated as by an equal, who therefore feels solidarity with the speaker. But for the receiver who would never produce those transformations, and at best can only partly reverse them, the relationship is one of exclusion, the feeling one of powerlessness and alienation.

We set out in figure 3.1 the possible responses as a network of choices, each of which defines the relationship with Willesee differently. With each successive option, the viewer is weaker in relation to Willesee, though this subjective variation coexists with the objective relationship which is the same each time, with Willesee a high status communicator, and the audience contained within a privatized sphere. Options 1–3 all attribute some power to the viewer, but this coexists with its opposite, the power that Willesee has to communicate on the mass media without anyone having immediate right of reply. Only option 4 does not contain any contradiction, except in so far as the viewer who does not physically switch off will inevitably switch off mentally, because interpretation which is unable to interpret is itself a contradiction.

Some of these responses we can recognize as 'preferred' in some sense. Willesee and Channel 9 wouldn't have broadcast the show, we deduce, simply so that viewers would switch off. We can also recognize regularities in the exchange between Willesee and Bjelke-Peterson, again making some seemingly common-sense assumptions. Willesee is a professional interviewer, whose forms of language are similar enough to those of most other TV interviewers in Australia, Britain and America, and Bjelke-Peterson likewise is a seasoned interviewee, as he points out. Like old campaigners, neither can surprise the other or the seasoned viewer. We can capture this sense of shared assumptions

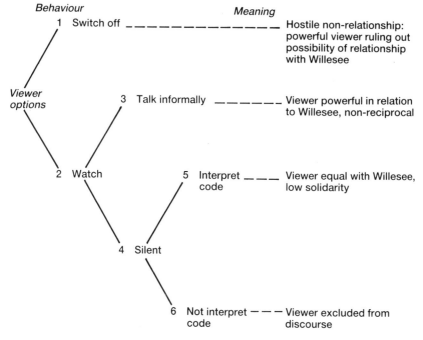

Figure 3.1 Willesee viewers' options

through the concept of genre, seeing the genre of TV interviews as implying a set of reception and production regimes, carrying a pre-existing set of undertandings about roles, meanings and styles that are shared by all participants, including viewers.

Yet although a knowledge of this genre does exist and has explanatory power, it is important to recognize its limitations also. Willesee and Bjelke-Peterson draw on a set of signifiers of power and solidarity which governs everyday interaction in twentieth-century Australia, similar to systems operating in Britain and America. A genre isn't a charmed area where all other systems cease to apply. It is one specific instance of their operation, a syntagm of options prescribing behaviours in a specific class of situations. Through these prescriptions, genres encode and enforce a version of society, an ideological form, which, because it is enshrined in interlocking production and reception regimes, seems like a prerequisite for meaning to occur. But in practice the set of meanings and relationships projected by genres are by no means inevitable. In fact the logonomic system readily assigns a meaning to the acts of 'rebellion' we indicated. Switching off or talking through a programme of this kind are very common responses, even if Willesee might wish otherwise, and neither act is in any way meaningless. At the same time, to the extent that such responses have become 'usual' and encode possible relations among the participants, they indicate a change to and extension of the genre at issue here. In every case, ultimately what is at issue is a complex set of relations of power and solidarity, in which power and solidarity are equivocally related, both opposed and conflated through signifiers of power and solidarity that are themselves ambiguous.

Ideology and bodies in space

Of all the dimensions of the semiotic situation, the most fundamental is the physical relationships of the (bodies of) participants in space. In English as in other languages, there are many forms of speech which express social meanings in spatial terms: 'keeping one's distance', 'being stand-offish', 'high status', 'grovelling', 'knowing your place', 'upper management', and so on. These turns of speech are sometimes called metaphors, but what they express is a basic equation between the ordering of bodies in physical space and the relationships between persons in social space. This forms the basis for a system of transparent signs that is fundamental to the organization of social life among humans as well as among countless other species. Territorial behaviour among canines, for instance, is organized by a complex set of signals which declare what distances are too close, for particular sets of relations among specific individuals. From the hierarchical ordering mechanisms of chickens has come the term 'pecking order'.

There is no doubt that there is a biological basis for these codes in 'lower' species. This basis may have survived to some extent in humans. However, it is equally important to stress that although the basic form may have biological predispositions, the elaborations which it undergoes in different social groups are too various to be attributed purely to an innate predisposition. And the meanings carried by the codes unmistakeably come from social life, not from biology. These meanings concern the primary categories of social relationships: the relations of power and solidarity which constitute every social formation.

The anthropologist Edward Hall (1966) has coined the term 'proxemic' to refer to the set of meanings carried by physical relationships in space, specifically by closeness ('proximity', hence his name for the codes) and distance. This is undoubtedly an important transparent signifier of social meanings, especially those concerned with solidarity relations. Yet in spite of its seemingly elemental form and 'naturalness', it turns out to be surprisingly complex, ambiguous and open to a variety of other determinations. Non-closeness normally signifies weakness, indifference, or alienation in a relationship, either positive or negative.

Closeness, however, signifies a strong relationship which can be either positive (love, intimacy) or negative (aggression, hostility). Closeness, on its own, thus carries a contradiction. It is a strongly ambiguous sign which is only disambiguated if there are other reasons or signs which control interpretation. Remoteness is similarly ambiguous, though less acutely so. Any particular culture provides a basic interpretative grid for this code. So for instance, a distance which signals solidarity in one culture (say, English) may signal non-solidarity/power in another (say, Italian); and of course there are 'dialects' within each culture. Further possibilities for ambiguity come from the fact that these terms are not absolute, but mark points on a continuum. So a distance of 2 metres is closer than 4 (= intimacy/aggression) but more distant than 1 (= non-intimacy). And proxemic codes, with their meanings about presence or absence of solidarity, cannot be taken in isolation, since relations of solidarity are intermixed with relations of power in any social formation, and these latter are commonly signalled through the dimension up–down (or higher–lower). The two axes of space act together to create ideological meanings. So intermixed are these two dimensions of the signifying system and their social meanings that it is preferable to talk of spatial codes rather than proxemic codes.

Plate 3.1   The Annunciation: a study in relationships

To illustrate some of the forms and functions of this set of codes, we will look at a black-and-white reproduction of *The Annunciation*, an alter-piece painted by the Siennese painter Simone Martini in 1333, originally placed in Sienna Cathedral, now in the Uffizi Gallery, Florence. We need to acknowledge immediately that we are dealing with a form of these codes coming out of a distinct culture, early Renaissance Italy, with aesthetic, social and economic organizations specific to that culture. The modes of cultural production and reception – the logonomic rules – are systematically different to those operating in 'our' culture, twentieth-century 'Western international' culture. Our reading is thus an attempt at a reconstruction of the relevant elements of the semiosic plane, and of the place of Simone Martini as the socially located producer of that painting, responsive not only to the broad elements of semiosis of his time but no doubt also to quite local factors, such as local ecclesiastical politics. We have some confidence in the plausibility of our reading for although it focuses on one painting, it is embedded in the analysis by many readers of a large number of similar texts. That is, the Martini painting is not an isolated text, but one of very many, with similar signals, read over a long time. The painting represents the angel Gabriel, kneeling on the left, announcing to Mary that she will give birth to the Son of God. The words are stamped in a background of gold, shooting like an arrow from the angel to Mary. We will begin analysing the subject of the picture as though it was a realistic depiction of reality, and then we will consider its status as a work of art.

Taking it literally, then, the angel Gabriel is about 2 metres, or one body length, from Mary, and though she is seated, he is kneeling, which leaves her about 10 cm higher. The first point to make about this fact is that on its own its meaning has considerable uncertainty. Hall has shown cultural differences in the meaning of distance, specifically in what counts as too close, for given categories of people and relationships. So we can ask: is Gabriel too close, by fourteenth-century Siennese standards? And is Mary high enough – for herself, or for Gabriel? One crucial problem of spatial codes comes from the fact that the distance-syntagm relates at least two people, and hence carries meanings about both of them, yet either one or both may not be in control of that spatial relationship, and thus might not mean its meaning. The behaviour of people jammed in a lift is a case in point. Such close proximity on its own might signify extreme intimacy, but the passengers may be total strangers to each other. There is a reception regime invoked, which all members of that culture can rely on, which cancels the message of intimacy; or else one person may control the syntagm by moving close to another person, who does not accept that meaning but who cannot, for some reason, move out of the way.

For this reason, distance is normally supplemented by a whole set of other signifiers which are understood as transformations of physical distance, and which act as comments on the implied meaning of the physical space, expressing a specific reception regime. Mary twists her body and face away, and draws her robe across her throat, signalling that Gabriel is too close, thereby counteracting the overt meaning of the distance. However, she still looks at him, out of the corners of her eyes, and she is, seemingly inadvertently, offering her ear to his rod of speech. Gabriel is kneeling, which both lowers his height and immobilizes him, guaranteeing that he will not immediately leap on the cowering maiden. His body is upright, inclined slightly forward into her space. His head is thrust sharply forward, his upper arms hanging down more or less vertically, the lower arms positioned in her direction, the hands however going upwards or downwards. His left hand holds a branch, which is almost exactly vertical.

From the contradictions signalled by both participants, we gain a general impression of ambivalence, especially marked for Mary. We can be more precise than this, about how this meaning has been coded and conveyed, and how we can decode it. The starting point is the basic spatial syntagm, consisting not simply of a distance, but also of categories of people. One of these is clearly female. The other, the angel, is more ambiguous in terms of gender-markers. Also, he has wings on his back. Just how familiar should a well brought-up girl be with a strange angel who has just dropped in? Mary is sitting in a chair. Clearly it is the angel who has determined the precise space between them. It is in the first place his meaning. At 2 metres it is relatively close, but ambiguously so; and also potentially aggressive in the intimacy it is claiming. Mary's responses can thus be read as a comment on Gabriel's proxemic statement, just as Gabriel's gestures can be read as anticipatory answers to her anxieties, markers of his own reception-regime.

The signals Mary uses, in our analysis, consist of body movement (turning upper body away) head movement (downwards, and away) adjustment of the clothing code (holding robe to cover her bosom) facial expression (mouth held down, unsmiling) and gaze (looking at Gabriel). In addition, before this exchange, she had clothed herself so that very little flesh showed, and she was sitting down reading a book. All the signal systems she uses in response to Gabriel's intrusions clearly function to signify meanings about space. They are transformations of the spatial code, carrying with apparent redundancy many statements about perceived distance, which clearly code statements about social distance. The twist of the body away from Gabriel is signalling non-close. The hand covering the bosom reinforces this meaning, and reveals the basic meaning of the clothing code as a signifier of barriers, or non-close. The pout and the head facing away and downwards reinforce this meaning of non-close. But the gaze contradicts all these meanings, establishing eye contact, and thus accepting a relationship. The meaning is not simply the sum total of these signs (5 minus close, 2 plus close). The meaning resides in the process, including the order of the signs. The order of the semiotic operations can often be guessed at, and hypothetically recovered, as here, and it is that order which in effect records a dialectic process which gives, as it were, the formula of the relationship. The formula for her attitude is $(+ - - - - - +)$ close. Translating this into speech, this says: 'You're very close; too close; still too close; still too close; still too close; still too close; that's OK'. The eye movement, the gaze, is a particularly significant sign system, since it is the most flexible, the most easily under control, and it is, so to speak, the last word, the most surface signal. Decoding typically starts from both ends of the chain, the initial statement (physical distance) and the final statement (cognitive distance, communicated through gaze). Sometimes an interpreter will guess at a different order, or miss a number of steps, but will draw on the same general procedure, to give a different meaning, where meaning refers not to a different ideational content, but to a different interpersonal content.

We can decode Gabriel's complex attitude in the same way to recover a pattern of advances and retreats whose overall meaning is a restrained insertion of his self into Mary's intimate space. But distance is not the only dimension of space which signifies here. As we noted, Gabriel is kneeling. Kneeling reduces the height of a person and so it is a transparent signifier of minus power. It also interacts with signifiers of solidarity. If Gabriel had been standing, his distance would have been perceived as more aggressive and threatening. This reflects the general tendency for power and solidarity to be inversely related, so that minus power signifies plus solidarity, and vice versa.

Mary, however, is seated. If 'high' automatically signified plus power, then to sit down should signify minus power (though not as strongly minus power as lying down). However, there are too many apparent counter-examples for this to be a convincing reading. Seats of various kinds have signified power at many times in many cultures, from the thrones of old-style kings to the chairs of modern chairpersons and professors. What seems to be at issue is not high or low, but stasis or movement, with high status signified by no need to move. The signifier of power in this case has some motivation, some rationale, but it also allows scope for ambiguity. An obvious way of resolving the ambiguity is to attach other signifiers of power to the powerful seated one, for instance by raising the chair, by requiring everyone else to kneel, crawl or grovel, or by raising a canopy or other construction above the sitter.

Gabriel has signalled Mary's power by kneeling so that he is lower than she, but this signal of her power is not under her control. So she does not have power, except in so far as he gives it to her. The relation of power between the two is therefore fundamentally ambiguous, with an ambiguity that is intrinsically related to the complex relationship of intimacy/formality between them.

The spatial code and its transformations carry complex social meanings, and the decoding of the text reveals both general social categories and processes of negotiation in terms of them. But to understand the exchange (and the picture) properly we need to know what it is about, that is, its mimetic relation to a world of referents. The angel's speech provides the way in to this dimension of the transaction. The biblical narrative of the incident, better known in medieval Sienna than now, runs: 'And the angel came in unto her, and said, Hail, thou that art highly favoured, the Lord is with thee: blessed art thou among women. And when she saw him, she was troubled at his saying, and cast in her mind what manner of salutation this should be' (Luke 1: 28–9). The angel then announced to Mary that she would give birth to Jesus, with God as father, and the means of conception left obscure. We have no intention of becoming entangled with the vast body of doctrine and exegesis that surrounds this episode in the Bible. What can be said, however, is that a description of the Annunciation is as close as the Bible gets to a description of the divine act of conception, so paintings of the Annunciation, a common theme in medieval painting, are representations of the sex act displaced at several removes. The transformation was partly enabled by a systematic analogy that was made between communication and sexuality. Jesus was referred to as 'the word', and the act of conception is referred to, in St John's Gospel, by the phrase 'And the Word was made flesh, and dwelt among us' (1: 14).

In medieval and Renaissance paintings of the theme, Mary is usually shown, as here, as having been occupied by reading, putting a book (the Bible) aside to receive a more fertile verbal message. The anxiety or unease she communicates, in this painting, is a response to an act of verbal rape. The phallus of Gabriel's speech passes across the empty space to penetrate her ear and her mind. Phallic images proliferate: the upraised finger of his right hand, the branch, the traditional lilies, the cloak rising inexplicably upwards behind him. Meanwhile from the top centre of the picture a bird, surrounded by a cluster of infant faces, represents the Holy Ghost (who in turn represents God the Father) directing a beam that intersects Gabriel's rod of speech at Mary's ear. This is another convention of this type of picture, to have either God the Father or the Holy Ghost represented as simultaneously sending down, from His position of power, a divine beam of conception, so that Gabriel's verbal act is paralleled by a conventional signifier of sexual action.

With this sense of what the transaction is about, its reference to a world of events as explanatory context, we can understand better the complex shifts and contradictions carried by the spatial code. It is not enough to know the gender and social status of the participants in a communication act, as though those categories are fixed and permanent and determine all possibilities of social behaviour. The kind of activity is also crucial, since specific tasks require specific forms of social organization if they are to be carried out effectively. This picture presents in almost a parody form the problem of love and sexuality within a patriarchal family framework. Mary has a relationship with two males: Gabriel kneeling in front of her, and God the Father, who is so powerful that he cannot be in the same frame as the Virgin, but must relate to her through intermediaries. Such power, semiotically expressed through extremes of height and distance, is thus rendered incapable of the intimacy which is essential to sexuality. Power is incompatible with solidarity, and hence with power itself, because without solidarity, power becomes impotence. So the absent God becomes the signifier of patriarchy, and the present Gabriel becomes the signifier of what the patriarch must in practice do if he is to fulfil his marital functions with satisfaction to all concerned. Hence his self-subordination, signified by kneeling, and his youthful feminine appearance, establishing the basis of relative equality without which solidarity is impossible. God signifies the male as a figure of patriarchal power, while Gabriel is more equivocal in meaning (hence the contradictory signals) but includes the signification of male as lover, attempting to achieve intimacy under the shadow of the power of the Father.

So the picture represents two semiotic acts superimposed on each other, each a version of social relations of men and women. The superimposition declares a contradiction, which splits the male figure in two, as ancient remote male and youthful feminine present figure. It also specifies contradictory roles and behaviours for the woman, as submissive passive inferior and as potentially powerful active equal. One of these versions of gender relations can be recognized as the ideology of patriarchy. The other seems its opposite, yet the artist has presented it as a necessary companion, a *doppelgänger* of patriarchy. Martini allows us to see the functional relationship of the two ideological schemes. This 'Martini effect' is in fact a widespread phenomenon. Ideology often has a double face in exactly this way, for reasons that this example makes clear. A dominant group within a larger formation typically is concerned to maintain its own power and right to rule, and will generate an ideology which expresses these relations of power in a heightened form. However, an obsession with the expression of power leads to a paralysis within the larger group, an ineffectuality which ultimately erodes the real basis of power of the dominant group. The illusion that the dominant group is the sole site of effectivity becomes an embarrassment if that means the dominant group needs to do everything. Bonds of solidarity must exist, and the subordinate must be allowed a measure of freedom and initiative and even control. So within the world of education, the authority of teachers is buttressed by an ideology that gives them a monopoly of knowledge, yet if they retain that monopoly intact at the end of a student's school career, then they will have failed in their task as teachers. Bosses and management justify their profits because of their expertise and authority and role in imposing work discipline, yet none of that produces commodities without a responsive and co-operative work-force, who must be to some extent trusted and integrated with management. Within the family the patriarch who is feared and obeyed suffers from deprivation of love, and without bonds of solidarity the family like any other social group will fall apart. The two apparently opposite ideological forms are both essential in sustaining the rule of the rulers in all these instances, and many more. The potential ruler must be assimilated into both, and be able to manage the contradictions, for the system as a whole to survive.

The meaning of frames

It is time to acknowledge that this is a painting, a text produced by an artist, not a fragment of reality that has conveniently been preserved. As such it must be situated in terms of the plane of semiosis, with Simone Martini now involved in the production of the message. The text can be read by persons remote in time and culture from Martini – by us, for instance – but we will begin by considering it in its initial moment of production, as far as we can. This is not to imply that this is the 'real' or only legitimate meaning of the text, and all others are distortions. It is simply to respect the unity constituted by the social organization of participants and textual forms at a specific point of time, and to recognize their importance in the economy of the logonomic regimes which operated at the time.

The painting was originally designed as an altar-piece for Sienna Cathedral, though it is no longer there. Simone Martini signed and dated the work – not an invariable procedure at the time. Otherwise he is as absent from the painting as God the Father, detected only through his effects. The absence of the author in medieval paintings is so common that it usually goes without comment, yet this absence is still a relationship, part of the dynamic of the text. And the text doesn't exist, semiotically, unless it has an audience, which must set the text in some kind of social relationship, as well as attributing a relationship of text to world. The social relationship is crucial to the effectivity of the painting. Without it, its ideological content will be inert. We can put the case more strongly: the ideological effect of this text is constituted by the interaction of the structures on the two planes, the ideological forms represented through the text, and the ideological forms constituted by the semiotic act itself. This concept of ideology owes something to Althusser's (1971) definition of it as 'an imaginary relation to real conditions of existence', which envisages ideological forms at right angles to each other. Althusser also stressed the relation between ideology and individual subjects through the concept of 'interpellation', a metaphor that suggests an actual summoning by ideology, personified and hailing passers-by to establish a semiotic relation with them. With painstaking literalmindedness we insist that ideologies are without a voice. Only human agency can have social effects. Yet something like the interpellation effect does occur, and it is our task to explain it in terms of concrete social fact.

We will start with the physical positioning of bodies in space. The painting was originally in a fixed position, behind an altar table, set on a raised platform, with a barrier round it that only a priest could pass, except on specific occasions. The cathedral surrounding it was a large building in the Gothic style, opulently decorated with green and white marble, and an elaborate mosaic floor. All these facts have a coercive effect on potential viewers, 'hailing' them silently through marble and stone and gold. They know where they may stand, and where they are excluded from. The ideological effect is stronger for the absence or invisibility of its agent – who can therefore be more easily named as 'God' or 'the Church' by the person so summoned.

The structure of the setting contains signals that offer two major viewing positions: one for priests, close up, the other for lay people, from a discreet distance. We will take the lay viewers first. They are positioned below the painting, and at least 10 metres from it. From this position, the painting makes one kind of sense. Physically the viewer may not be centrally placed, but the symmetries of the picture indicate clearly enough that that is the appropriate viewing position. From here, the overwhelming impression is one of gold. More than half the painting is covered with gold, which makes it a very expensive painting indeed. The painting style itself is not highly realistic, thus asserting distance, formality and power. From this distance and angle, the viewer can be impressed, but not strongly involved in the scene itself. Here the direction of the gaze is a decisive signifier. Gabriel and Mary form a dyad, engaging with each other through their eye contact.

This leaves onlookers free to choose their distance. The fact that these two eternally do not notice the viewers allows viewers either to enter close into this primal scene and become pivotal in it, or else to keep remote from it and uninvolved. But the first option is discouraged by the surrounding context and its constraints. The spectator is thus positioned as the humble and remote receiver of a message of power, issuing from an entity so grand it must be named the Church, not Simone Martini. Though dimly glimpsed, there is the other more · intimate subversive message contained within the larger one.

Surprisingly it is the priest, celibate functionary of the church, who is positioned close to the painting, in a position of intimacy where the intimate meanings become more accessible. The members of the Church hierarchy who commissioned and paid Simone Martini for his painting would have had even more close access. And what they have access to is a demystified account of how gender relations must be managed under patriarchy, in spite of the official ideology of male power. The difference between the two viewing positions, of course, is not absolute: it is a matter of emphasis and foregrounding through signals that encourage viewers to read one set of meanings and not to read another. From both positions, the ambiguity and contradiction can be decoded, for those who can and wish to do so. The coercion of the physical signals is typically reinforced by reception regimes. The low railing around the altar area, for instance, could be leapt at a bound if there were not also rules, adequately taught and policed, reinforcing the rail's meaning of 'barrier'. Similarly a reading of patriarchal forms of sexuality as intrinsically sterile would be specifically forbidden, chastised and discouraged in lay people, while having to be recognized by the spiritual guides of the emotional victims, male and female, of unrestrained patriarchy.

The ideology of ways of sitting

Spatial codes are frequently the primary medium for ideological statements, as mediated through other codes in a wide range of situations. Take the photograph, reproduced as plate 3.2, of a committee meeting chaired by Mary Quant, famous as a textile designer, published in an article in the *Sunday Telegraph* magazine on Mary Quant as successful business woman (29 March 1981).

The table's rigid form and the chairs act to impose a structuring of space on everyone concerned, which carries clear ideological messages about power and solidarity in the company. People across the table are separated by about 2 metres – the same distance as between Gabriel and Mary. People sitting alongside each other are separated by about

Plate 3.2   Mary Quant as signifier of power

20 cm, physically a smaller distance but equivalent in psychological distance, since they are facing parallel, and do not have the eye contact which completes a proxemic syntagm. The men both wear jackets and ties, the women have no part of their throat showing. In this covering up they are like Gabriel and Mary, even though Mary Quant was famous as a designer of daring clothes. All these signals are strictly prescribed by logonomic rules which reinforce a conception of the

prevailing relationships within the group. With this underpinning, the conception does not need to be stated in words, but is endlessly restated in every committee meeting: that the individuals are equal in power, equally respectful of the power of all others, enclosed in a grid-like structure, able to modify relationships (for instance by turning to one side, or leaning across the table) but only within the prescribed limits. This arrangement vividly expresses the logonomic rules that typically govern speech in this kind of situation. Comments must be directed to the chair, or with her permission, 'through the chair' to anyone else.

The major exception, of course, is Mary Quant, presiding at the head of the table, the position of power. Other spatial locations can have the same meaning as high–low, or can be seen as transformations of high–low. The 'head' of a table is regarded as higher, even though it is actually on the same level. Another transparent signifier of power is centre versus periphery. Mary Quant is placed so that she looks down the axis between the rows of people; so in a sense she is in the centre, and people would refer to her equally. This photo carries messages about the Mary Quant organization simply by reproducing the messages carried, through proxemic and spatial codes, in committee meetings, which themselves reproduce that set of messages (which may be counter-factual) about the dominant relationships within the organization: a harmonious structure of independent equals, linked to the relaxed, smiling boss.

But this boss is female. That is the point of the article, the reason for reproducing the photograph. The same spatial relationships carry a different ideological content if one of the persons is categorized differently. Precisely because it reproduces the dominant form it challenges it, and the less it signals its aberrant status, the more strongly it challenges it. This is where an asocial, purely textual form of analysis is most liable to go wrong. The syntagmatic relationships are observable in the text: the paradigmatic categories and reception regimes which complete their meaning are not. This photograph, like Simone Martini's painting, is itself an act of communication, existing on the semiosic plane. The photograph situates the viewer in a specific position, as photography and film typically do, thus establishing a significant spatial–social syntagm. In this case the disturbing phenomenon of a successful female boss is viewed by the spectator from a distance. She is at the centre of the picture and of her domain, but remote and inaccessible, far removed from the viewer, who is therefore situated in a position of minus power. In this situation she is difficult to relate to or identify with, by male or female readers of the basically conservative *Telegraph*. In so far as the threat of her example can be neutralized, the photographer has helped to do so.

Ideology and the construction of gender

Since ideology is only effective in so far as it conditions actual behaviours, its most potent form of expression is when it is inscribed in and and organized though spatial codes and their transforms. Gender messages can be instilled by rules of etiquette – such as the requirement that 'gentlemen' must stand up when 'ladies' enter a room. Here the role of verbal language is important but ancillary to the physical spatial codes. Styles of dress, appearance and behaviour are overt enough to be strictly policed, so that the ideological meanings they carry can be obligatory and ubiquitous. Verbal language thus plays a secondary role, acting as a commentary whose real meaning is given by the underlying behavioural text it invokes. To illustrate the process, we will take the following extract from an article in the Australian women's magazine *Cleo* for June 1984 (see also Kress 1985). The article was entitled 'Body Talk'. It described different types of women found in an office, and instructed each type how to modify their behaviour in order to improve their situation at work. The 'types' addressed were 'Miss Mouse', 'Miss Seductress', 'Ms Winner', 'Miss Nonchalant' and 'Ms Power-broker'. Here are the descriptions of Miss Seductress and Ms Winner:

Miss Seductress

There's always one of this type in every gathering: at parties she laughs alluringly and touches everyone (even your man); when meeting men she pouts, flutters eyelashes and makes her body do the talking. Even in the supermarket she totters in high sling backs and wears clingy angora. Yes, she's the one who always believes that everything will come to her as long as she looks gorgeous. She attracts men like bees to the honey pot and keeps their attention by direct eye contact while always flashing a dazzling smile. She's all teeth, luscious lips, glossy hair, painted fingernails and seductive curves. Men love her, even if women don't, and that's just the way she likes it. She's managed to get good jobs in the past (always male bosses) and never has to 'go dutch' on dinner dates. The trouble with Miss Seductress is that half the world is made up of women, and the men who enjoy her type go down on record as having short attention spans. Which leaves her high and dry much of the time.

You, Miss Seductress, need a lot of help. Turn down the sirens for a start – you won't miss out on the men. You may miss out on the bounders, but you could score with Mr Nice-Guy, the one who's likely to stay for more than the first act. Office harmony hasn't been your strong point because you alienate your female co-workers. Rising in the hierarchy takes enthusiasm and ability, not low cut dresses and knowing looks. Restraint is the key word, in all aspects of your life.

Ms Winner

Ms Winner isn't always easy to categorize at once, because her self-confidence is so unassuming. She's the type who doesn't need to impress others with her abilities – she knows they will shine through anyway. Her self-assurance comes through in every mannerism, every item of clothing, her relaxed posture, her confident speech. She dresses with flair, knowing how to combine basically conservative clothes with innovative extras to form a completely co-ordinated outfit which exudes her personal style. Basically, Ms Winner has panache. She dresses well for the occasion whether it's a job interview or dinner party. Her hair is cut in a modern, but not outrageous style, her make-up is subtle. But Ms Winner's strongest point is her well-modulated conversation which is always lively and intelligent. She has many friends of both sexes who never feel threatened by her. She doesn't talk behind people's back, but is no sycophant either. She has a mind of her own, but doesn't impose it on others. Ms Winner, you're on the right track, so don't change a thing.

The general ideological point of the two descriptions is clear. As the 'Miss Seductress' passage concludes, 'Restraint is the key word.' The recipe for success for women in both cases is self-limitation. The description of Ms Winner makes it clear that she isn't meant to win too much – not as much as Mary Quant, for instance. The character assassination of Miss Seductress works in the first place by describing a stereotyped set of semiotic transactions that define her in social-ideological terms. The focus is on her signals in a range of codes, but these imply the rest of the communication model as an image of the social relationships that define her meaning. Basic proxemic signals of extreme intimacy are listed, from 'touching' (everyone) to 'direct eye contact' (from very close range, we assume). Her facial expressions ('pouts, flutters eyelashes . . . dazzling smile') and clothing ('high sling backs', 'clingy angora', 'low cut dresses') send similarly unmodified messages of intimacy which are at the opposite extreme to those of the Virgin Mary (and Mary Quant).

This list, however, doesn't explain the ideological effect of this description. Certainly all the signals are exaggerated stereotypes of the 'office siren', but such signal-systems are always conventionalized and predictable. Wearing a coat and tie to work is equally conventional and hence could be called stereotyped but isn't. There are occasional hints of a negative attitude (for instance, in words like 'totters', 'bounder', 'Mr Nice-Guy') but these are counterbalanced by what might in other contexts be positive ('alluringly', 'gorgeous', 'luscious'). The key to the strategy of the article is not here, but in the social relations of the semiotic process itself, in the semiosic plane, in the positions constructed for the reader and the social organization that implicates her.

Cleo is a women's magazine, targeted on 'liberated' women, middle-class women who work and have a disposable income of their own. Its readership already has an assumed gender, and although many men may also read it we can legitimately emphasize the position and role of women readers, in contrast to the Mary Quant article and photo, which had a bi-gendered audience, and a double ideological effect. The gender of the reader is decisive here, because it is crucial to the meaning of the semiotic transaction. In the first paragraph, this reader is explicitly addressed (through 'your man' – sufficiently implying her gender). Miss Seductress is referred to in the 'third person' as 'she', therefore as outside the transaction that constitutes the text, equally distant from author and reader. The transactions she engages in all consist, as we have seen, of signals of strong intimacy, with clear gender-marking. Words like 'alluringly' are a massive shorthand, indicating a range of sexual signals specifically from a woman to a man (men don't laugh or do anything 'alluringly'). So the intimacy and solidarity offered by 'Miss Seductress' is specifically unavailable to the female reader. Similarly with the 'everyone' (male gender assumed again) whom she touches. Since this 'everyone' includes 'your' man, Miss Seductress's intimacy signals cannot but be interpreted as aggression, towards the reader and also towards the man. The description of her as 'all teeth, luscious lips, glossy hair' in effect inserts the helpless reader 3 cm from Miss Seductress and recategorizes the gender of this reader, if the relation is to be one of solidarity, as a male about to be swallowed by those enormous teeth, or about to devour those 'luscious' lips. But the reader has already been explicitly constructed as female. The result is to release the powerful hostile meanings of closeness. The lack of discrimination increases the sense of potential danger from Miss Seductress, to both stray males and stray female readers. The implication is that the complex social organization of everyday life has been collapsed into innumerable uncontrolled sexual encounters.

Because the female reader is positioned in the text as an uncomfortable victim of unrestrained aggressive intimacy at the hands of Miss Seductress, there is no real need for the author to condemn it. What the author does do is to offer two alternative semiotic models and reception positions. In the first paragraph the author addresses the reader with very little direct contact, though she has the power of the person in control of the discourse. This implies a distant, formal relationship, with the imbalance in power held in check. It contrasts with the aggressive contact of a Miss Seductress. It also contrasts with the receiver-position offered in the second paragraph. Here there is direct contact with Miss Seductress, but it is the closeness of outright aggression. She is on the receiving end of commands, advice and observations which are highly insulting. But the ideological effect of this harangue is not to improve Miss Seductress, who isn't likely to be reading it by this stage (can she read, anyway?). What it offers is an untenable reader position, the experience of being Miss Seductress getting her come-uppance. So much better to be the uninvolved audience of the writer's character assassination.

The second stereotype, Ms Winner, is not only described differently, but set in a different semiotic transaction. Ms Winner's signals are so characterized by multiple contradictions – like Gabriel's and Mary's – that she is hard to categorize. The author lists some of the codes – mannerisms, clothing, posture, manner of speech – but hardly bothers to indicate how the clusters of contradictory messages are put together or how the contradictions will be resolved. The problems of different audiences for her signals are resolved by suppressing their receivers, half suppressing even the fact that she is producing the signals ('she knows [her abilities] will shine through anyway'). By these means the transactions she is represented as being engaged in are left vague but comfortably distant. No one feels 'threatened' by her, by signals of power or solidarity that are too strong, and because of the coolness of the relationship it is easy for the reader to insert herself into either of the two major semiotic positions, as like her, or as her female 'friend'. The address from the author to Ms Winner which closes the piece is very different from what Miss Seductress receives. Not only is it positive, it is short and unspecific, a compliment rather than a command. Even the approval of this author is an unpleasant experience, because of the power difference, but at least it doesn't last long, and the brevity is itself a kind of withholding of power and an assertion of Ms Winner's near equality.

As with the Simone Martini painting, the ideological potency of the text is established by the semiotic transaction on the semiosic plane interacting with the semiosic relations of the represented world. In both cases there is a double reception-position, offering different possibilities of solidarity and power or submission to the author/authority. In both cases, the represented world contains conventional signals for different versions of social relations, two contradictory ideologies of gender relationships, one characterized by power, the other by intimacy. In spite of the fictional nature of both texts (Ms Winner is hardly more realistic than Martini's Virgin Mary), the social relations invoked both by the semiotic transaction which is its framework and by the transactions represented within the text are coded fairly transparently, drawing directly on major spatial codes and their transformations. Some theorists have emphasized the specific demands on readers/receivers made by different genres or by texts from different cultures or periods. It is true that it should not be assumed that gender relations are identical in fourteenth-century Sienna and in twentieth-century Britain, Australia or the United States. Nor, of course, can we assume that everyone in Western societies today understands them in the same way. Some of the enabling knowledge which logonomic systems rely on is culturally specific. But nor should it be assumed that there are always insuperable difficulties preventing entry into specific receiver-positions. If that were so, incorporation into ideological forms would be a privilege reserved for an elite few, which is manifestly not the case. On occasions where there is a kind of exclusion being exercised, as there is in different ways in both the Martini painting and *Cleo*, it is likely to be motivated and safeguarded by social forces and interests, and achieved through specific social agencies. Otherwise, ideologues like to be understood, and when their target is the common man (or woman) their techniques and systems of signifiers are likely to be rather common too. That commonness or commonality resides in the relatively greater transparency of the signifiers employed in such texts.

Domain and antiworld

The site in which a text occurs typically contains instructions as to how it should be read and what meanings should be found in it. The same text – Simone Martini's *Annunciation* for instance – will tend to be read in different ways if it is in a museum, or in the pages of a book on social semiotics, compared to the readings given it by a Siennese priest or by his congregation, when it was an altar-piece in Sienna Cathedral. Settings exert a coercive force on the meanings that can be produced or received within them. In practice, what happens is that specific categories of settings are socially classified as domains, sites where the specific meanings of specific groups can be expected to prevail.

What is at issue is not simply difference. Conflict and hostility between competing groups is typically expressed by actual inversion. Marx described ideology as 'the world turned upside-down': a version of reality literally turned on its head. Within linguistics, Halliday (1978) has developed a theory of what he calls antilanguages. These are languages generated not by agents of the state but the opposite: criminals, prisoners, groups that have been marginalized by the state, who express their opposition by creating a language which excludes outsiders. A primary function of antilanguages, according to Halliday, is to create an antiworld, a set of meanings and values that inverts those of the dominant society. These antilanguages characteristically are built up by a series of transformations whose meaning is negation, opposition, inversion (see Kress and Hodge 1979). Members of an antisociety do not use their language all the time. On the contrary, they protect it, using it only when and where they feel secure. It is confined to their own domain, to a social space which is beyond the reach of the power which dominates public life, even though the rules of this antilanguage are formed out of those of the dominant language, created out of resistance to it.

A major role of architecture in Western societies is to mark out separate domains. A house for instance marks out a distinct area, where different rules of power prevail (for instance, police may not enter without a warrant; acts that would elsewhere be banned may be permitted). These differences may seem to be simply relaxations of dominant rules. However, 'relaxation' is strictly a form of negation. In a classic study of housing arrangements in Berber society, the French sociologist Bourdieu (1971) has shown that houses in this culture present what he terms 'a world turned upside-down'. His analysis is worth close attention, because it provides an exemplary instance of the function of domains as creators of inverse forms.

As Bourdieu describes it, the typical Berber house has a two-part division, as in figure 3.2. The primary social division he isolates is between men and women. The meaning of the spatial organization is a transformation of this social division. The lower part, to the south, is the place of reproductive functions, the place of darkness, wetness, fecundity, animality. The upper part is the place where guests are entertained, where social activities occur, though it is also where women do their work, weaving and cooking, during the day when the men are out. The front door facing the east is the men's door, through which they go out to work each morning. The back door, out to the garden, is the women's door, facing the west. From Bourdieu's analysis two things emerge. One is that North–South and East–West both express the primary social opposition male–female, with North–South a

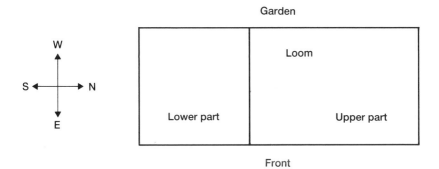

Figure 3.2 Bourdieu's analysis of the typical Berber house

transformation of the primary East–West opposition. The other is that the world inside the house, across the threshold, is an inverted world, with all the spatial values of the outside world (the public domain) recreated as their opposite (in the private domain). As the man faces East as he commences his work, so the woman faces West to commence hers (the loom is on the Western wall). Not only are the spatial orientations reversed, so are the valuations of men and women. Bourdieu notes that it is no more true to say that the women are shut in the house all day than that the men are shut out. The house by day is the site of female power and male powerlessness, even though the men's work, by day, is regarded as more prestigious and important. He reports the significance attached to the main pillar of the house, and the beam which rests on it. The main pillar is seen as the woman and the beam is her husband. That is, the woman supports the husband, an ideological inversion of the economic dependence of the women on her husband in Berber society.

Bourdieu's analysis is schematic, removing differences of social class from the account. It is, in essence, an extreme example of patriarchal gender relations, but its simplicity allows us to see the main outlines of the process in clear relief. He takes a primary social division (men versus women), and the division of labour that gives content to that division. This is the minimal syntagmatic form in which classifications of people have existence: a kind of agent with a kind of verb (function). He then sees a classification of places (primarily inside–outside, private–public, transformationally replicated to structure the whole environment) and of times (day–night, plus other transformations of the opposition of light and darkness). We have not included in this account the classification of objects on which the respective functions are performed, which would provide the grammatical category of object.

Given this most simple of classifications, the syntagmatic possibilities are as in figure 3.3. Social rules prescribe syntagms. As we follow the scheme, using Bourdieu's findings for Berbers, we see that for males to perform female tasks in female places would challenge their status as males. It would involve a double contradiction. To perform male tasks in female places would seem to be less of a contradiction; or female tasks in male places. Gender rules take different forms in different societies, but what is common is the presence and difficulties of mediating transformations. The movement of women into certain levels of the work-force in modern Western societies, for instance, has forced a reclassification of kinds of work and systems/signs in the work-place which both retain and modify traditional gender systems (cf. Game and Pringle 1983). The category of time, however, functions differently in the syntactic chain. Time is different from space in that some places can be avoided but time is unavoidable. Men cannot cease

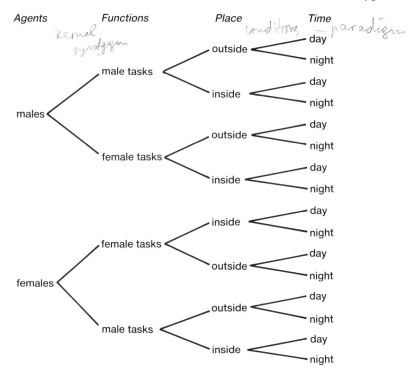

Figure 3.3 Syntagmatic possibilities of Bourdieu's analysis

to exist in whatever part of time is classified as female time. They do not want to avoid the inside of the house all the time, either. In the Berber syntagm, although night and darkness (and winter) are associated with woman, the effect of time is apparently simply to reverse the valency of the rest of the syntagm. 'Day' is like a positive marker, to indicate that all values remain valid: a male performing male acts in a male place is a male. 'Night' cancels all or some of these. By night the man returns home, he sleeps and engages in reproductive activities, in the lower, female part of the house, all this fulfilling his status as male. The converse is not true. By night woman does not leave the house and earn a living. For her, it is day that acts as a negation. By day she works productively (at the loom, or in other economic activities) and she does go outside, in a limited way, into the garden.

In this case we divide the syntagm into two parts: kernel (agents and functions) and conditions (place and time). In the Berber scheme, problems created by an extreme opposition of the two classes (males:females, corresponding to production:reproduction) are resolved by the same opposition applying to conditions, so that under some conditions, of time and/or place, males can be involved in reproduction and females in production. Because the contradiction is resolved by applying the constitutive categories, it does not challenge the primacy of those categories, even though its effect is to produce counter-syntagms whose force is opposed to the kernel-syntagms which are the basis of the rules. But as a general rule we can say that counter-syntagms exist as a recognition of the strength of opposition to the kernel-syntagms, or their practical inconvenience, and the conditions are rule-governed attempts to contain that opposition or remove the inconvenience. The neatness that characterizes Bourdieu's analysis of the Berber household will be exceptional. The conditions will usually be related by quite complex paradigmatic transformations acting on the underlying rule-system.

The set of rules (kernels plus conditions) which characterizes a social form will be specific in its details to specific social groups, just as verbal languages formed by common processes lead to innumerable different dialects and languages. Bourdieu's analysis focuses on one major division in most if not all societies. To take the scheme to its most abstract and general form we would need to take syntagms in terms of power, socially ascribed power, assigned by different paradigmatic schemes in different societies, but following common forms in all societies, starting from universal principles of classification in all societies. The essential syntagm of power, also transformed into an adjective, 'powerful' in English, is in fact a sentence of the form 'X controls Y', a social relationship, from which follow further syntagms 'X does/has A: Y does not'. But social life demonstrates in innumerable ways, in innumerable cases, that Freud's 'return of the repressed' is as fundamental a rule in the social as in the psychic economy. The 'return of the repressed' may be systematically achieved through regular transformations, whose function is to contain disruptive energies. It may appear as 'leakage', with a similar effect. Or it may return cataclysmically, as a radical challenge to the social order. And the site of the return is likely to coincide with a domain of inversion, whose presence indicates a point of fissure, a fault-line in the dominant structure.

This tendency is inherent in the nature of such systems. Syntagms of power require the relevant world to be classified in terms of power: people, places, things, times. Potential agents are powerful in terms of specific criteria: age, gender, and social status being three ubiquitous criteria which divide up the world of social agents. But in a society with any degree of cohesion, as all societies generally are, these classifications obscure the continuous nature of the phenomenon, and relationships of dependence and interdependence. Male–female in most cases can seem an unequivocal categorization, although there are problems of bisexuality, sex changes, transvestism and homosexuality. But the dependence-relations between men and women constantly challenge the separation needed to sustain power. Age is more obviously a continuum, and it has the further difficulty that every old individual was once young, and that as people get old they decline to a similar state of dependence as when they were young. Nevertheless, the natural category of age, like the biological category of sex, is given specific cultural significance: school age, military age, voting age, marriage age, middle age, retirement age, are all cultural classifications superimposed on the continuum. Differences in class or status typically have to describe a continuum of degrees of power, as well as separating off separate groups. There may also be some degree of social mobility to challenge the neatness of the classification scheme derived from this principle. Every classification scheme is tidier than the reality it classifies. Social conflict puts pressure on the paradigmatic system, which employs its very defects to accommodate the pressure. So conflict emerges as contradiction, which since it is systemic can be contained in systemic ways, as the special domains, or conditions of space or time, where the dominant syntagms do not fully apply.

Ritual space and time

In the case analysed by Bourdieu, it is categorizations of the diachronic plane which allow conditions of reversal. Night is a special time, in which rules of the day are reversed. Time is used in this way in many cultures. In holidays, feast-days, tea-breaks, divisions of the year and divisions of the day, periods are allowed when the normal rules do not apply. The principle is general, though the paradigmatic structures and transformations will be specific. Faris (1968), for instance, studied the structure of 'occasions', among the inhabitants of Cat Harbour, a small fishing community off the coast of Newfoundland. He found the paradigmatic structure depicted in figure 3.4. 'Scoffs', shown therein, are a traditional form of party,unique to Cat Harbour, where a small group of people eat food which has been stolen from someone not invited, and the normally puritanical community indulges in drink and *risqué* conversation. Faris interprets these as examples of sanctioned deviation. That is, they are times when social syntagms lose their force, are in fact reversed. Bakhtin (1968) uses the term 'carnival' to refer to a similar phenomenon. Sansom (1980) has analysed drinking bouts among a fringe-dwelling Aboriginal community in Darwin, and finds rules governing this behaviour which require everyone drinking to get equally drunk, and equally to repudiate the canons of everyday rationality. But all of the times labelled 'occasions' by the Cat Harbour

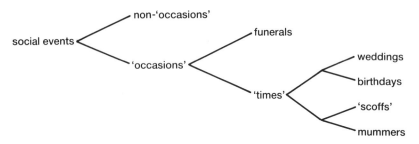

Figure 3.4 'Occasions': the structure at Cat Harbour

people contain an element of sanctioned deviation, in Faris's analysis. In all of them, behaviour is permitted or prescribed that would be disapproved of at normal times.

Weddings and funerals are very common focuses of special behaviour in many cultures. Van Gennep (1960) coined the term *rites de passage* for these and other ritual forms. Birthdays are minor rites of passage. Rites of passage typically are concerned to mediate the progression of individuals or groups from one status to another, a progression that is inevitable because of the flow of time (people being born and growing older, sexually mature and independent, and finally dying, or being left by the dead). The interface between the socially defined stages are moments of inconsistency in the scheme. Rituals account for this, or find a way of managing the inconsistencies. They are also a convenient site for the expression of other inconsistencies. As at Cat Harbour, rites of passage are often 'occasions' where some social rules are waived or reversed, or transformed in some way.

Weddings are one such occasion. In Britain and Australia there are a number of forms of wedding, but in both countries the so-called 'traditional wedding' is an important form as codified in the Book of Common Prayer of the Anglican Church. We will look at one crucial moment, the putting on of the ring. The groom is required to place a gold ring on the bride's second finger of the left hand. The bride may do the same for the groom, in a less common form, but this is an optional extra, not intrinsic as is the man's act in the English form, though in the German-speaking world an exchange of rings is the norm. The man then says the following words: 'With this ring I thee wed, with my body I thee worship, and with all my worldly goods I thee endow'. Two things about this are interesting. The placing of ring on finger is a fairly transparent enactment of the sexual act, the vaginal ring enclosing the phallic finger. But it is the man who is placing the ring on the woman's finger. During the space of the ceremony, at this crucial point, the classification male–female is reversed, even though the wedding is ostensibly about the proper organization of the sexes.

The same reversal occurs in the speech. It is the man speaking, but he says 'with all my worldly goods I thee endow' of a relationship where in the past at least, when the formula was devised, this form of marriage made the woman economically totally dependent on the husband. It was the woman who endowed the husband with all her worldly goods, while he retained control over his. The promise 'with my body I thee worship' could apply equally to a man or a woman, though for a husband to 'worship' his wife is carrying the traditional marriage relationship a little far. Respect, perhaps, but 'worship', in a church, sounds blasphemously excessive. But the phrase is glossed by the ring, which is the 'body' which is to worship the 'thee': the vagina-body of the woman that will worship the phallus-body of the man. The content, here, is an authoritarian relationship with the man as economic controller, but it is said by the man on behalf of the woman, that is, by the man transformed into woman, to the woman transformed to or reclassified briefly as man.

At many points in this ceremony whose function is to assert the proper forms governing relations between the sexes, the surface content is the primacy of the woman, the relative insignificance of the man. It is known as 'the Bride's Day'. Attention focuses on the bride, who is semiotically central, surrounded by signals of her importance. It is her entrance into the church that starts the ceremony. Visual reproductions of the happy couple frequently indicate her importance. In *Wedding Day*, for instance, which proclaims itself 'Britain's own bridal magazine' (there is no equivalent 'Britain's own groomal magazine') the target is prospective brides. The majority of the advertisements feature only a bride – the groom is so unimportant that he can be dispensed with – and representations of the two together signify the importance of the bride. In greetings cards the convention has the bride taller than the groom (with the lower half obscured, so that it is not clear how the extra height is achieved) and/or slightly in front of the groom and/or closer to the centre of the card. The same conventions apply to British royal weddings. In the case of the marriage of Lady Diana Spencer and Prince Charles, the bride was physically tall by nature but socially of far lower status. However, an official engagement photograph showed Lady Diana in the centre of a group of three, with her future mother-in-law, though the reigning queen, on one side, and the prospective groom, heir to the throne, on the other. The ubiquitous picture of the couple that was sold on souvenirs throughout the land showed Lady Diana in front, as though the more significant of the two. The apparent meaning of the picture was the greater importance of women than of men, and even of a commoner compared to a member of the Royal Family. The picture, however, has never been suspected of being subversive because the conditions are sufficiently displayed: the specific time when women, briefly, are allowed or even required to seem pre-eminent.

In some parts of Australia and Britain there is a small anti-ceremony concerned with a ring, which has some of the qualities of an 'occasion'. The bride wears a garter, and after the ceremony, outside the church, a male, usually unmarried, is selected by lot, and is allowed the privilege of taking the garter off, to the accompaniment of ribald comments. The anti-ceremony reverses many details of the ceremony itself: a ring is taken off instead of put on, and it is made of cheap perishable material, not valuable durable metal. The surface meaning of the anti-ceremony is that the bride's vagina is possessed by some strange male, who feels the real fleshly leg as he does so. It is a ritualized act of promiscuity, apparently contradicting the main force of the ceremony that has just been conducted, which entails a strict monogamous union. The two ceremonies can be put alongside each other:

Ceremony: bride acquires a man's vagina

⇓ ⇑

Anti-ceremony: man acquires the bride's vagina

The sexual transformation performed by the anti-ceremony simply reverses the values of the ceremony, but the ceremony had performed the same transformation itself on the real nature of the sexuality involved. One effect of the original transformation was to deny the groom's sexuality (except as the provider of a vagina for his wife's phallus). The anti-ceremony restores male sexuality, but assigns it to another male since the groom has renounced it. The anti-ceremony, however, must be seen as a transformation of a transformation (which is why it is not read as subversive), not as the direct presentation of the relevant reality. The repressed returns, but under given conditions, controlled.

As well as classifying time, society classifies space or location, the context of a social syntagm. Certain contexts allow or enforce certain transformations, just as the inside of a house, by day, reversed male superiority in Berber society as studied by Bourdieu. Conditions of deviations will normally specify both place and time: the wedding day, plus place, inside or outside the church, together specify conditions for different transformations. But domains of deviance are only one kind of domain, only to be understood in terms of the general structure of domains which they transform. The general form of the structures of domains in British and other forms of Western society is given by a rudimentary division in terms of power, predicating a society where agents, functions and conditions are homogenous, the powerful performing acts of power continuously, the non-powerful excluded from power – see figure 3.5.

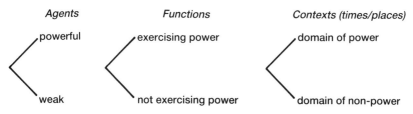

Figure 3.5 Domains: the general structure in Western society

But a minimal modification of this scheme is required to allow the powerful to perform other functions, and the functions of living performed by the non-powerful. So we have a classification of domains into public and private – see figure 3.6. A whole set of signifiers normally exists in most semiotic systems to indicate public versus private. Sometimes the verbal language used is actually distinct from the language used for other functions, by other agents (as in Arabic, Greek and Chinese, to name but three). Linguists call this situation diglossia, or a double-language situation (cf. Fergusson 1959). The clothing code normally has the recognizably different forms, 'formal', and 'informal' clothing, and so on with the other codes.

But the full structures of domains in contemporary Western societies is more complex than would be predicated by public–private even with a continuum between these extremes. Religion, for instance, has constituted a separate domain for millennia. Marx's definition of it is famous: 'Religion is the sigh of the oppressed creature, the heart of a heartless world, and the soul of soulless circumstances. It is the opium

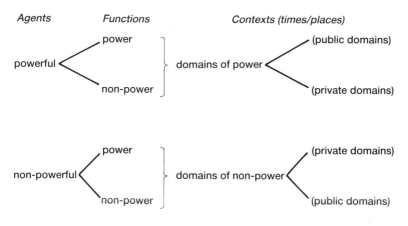

Figure 3.6 Domains in Western society: public and private

of the people'. Christianity legitimates the celebration of the weak. Its central symbol, the crucified Christ, shows a 'saviour' defeated, helpless, near dead, and alone on a cross, this negation of power, a symbol of power itself, negated again by its context. The realm of the aesthetic is also recognized to be a domain where separate rules apply, where syntagmatic forms may be reversed. Less obviously to many, the realm of the scientific is a privileged domain, where within limits (there are always limits) dominant syntagms, the syntagms of dominance, are allowed to be replaced by the order of things as prescribed by the science concerned. Outside of the fields of knowledge institutionalized in educational institutions, the same phenomenon appears. Sport, for instance, typically transforms syntagms of conflict into syntagms of harmony by establishing the conditions and outcomes of the conflict. 'Jokes' of all kind – from verbal humour to savage practical jokes – are similarly a kind of legitimate reversal of normal syntagms. Typically there are rules about where and when and to whom jokes are allowable – even if these rules are sometimes broken. The 'scoffs' described by Faris are probably an instance of this kind of reversal: *ad hoc*, strongly subversive, tolerated by society, exacted from the overall system of control rather than a regular systemic element.

In all these examples, and many more, we have the same phenomenon: oppositional discourse which constructs various kinds of inversion, and a process by which the availability of these oppositional practices is mapped on to social time and space, organized into a system of domains. If we use Halliday's term antilanguage in an extended sense, to cover all semiotic codes, including codes of action and behaviour as well as expressive codes like speech and writing, we can summarize how the domains and antilanguages typically function.

1. Conflict and hostility between an antigroup and a dominant group is expressed through the transparent signifiers of inversion and displacement, to produce an antilanguage, that is, opposite or displaced meanings, values and ideologies.
2. Domains of inversion are specific sites in social space or time where antigroups produce antilanguage forms, under relatively controlled conditions.
3. The social meaning of domain of inversion is unstable and ambiguous, since it is established by an ongoing struggle between two groups. From the point of view of the dominant, a domain inverts or neutralizes the subversive meanings expressed in it, labelling them as permitted transgressions incorporated into an overall orjder. From the point of view of an antigroup, this label is always liajble to be contested.

4

Style as Ideology

Style, accent, grammar as metasign

Just as individual acts of semiosis are organized by systems of signifiers
of power and solidarity, so also are the relationships between groups
in a broader social formation. These broader signifying systems are
essential for the smooth operation of systems governing particular
semiotic acts. They link the social organization of semiotic participants
with social organization on a larger scale. Any group of any size needs
markers of group membership to give it identity and cohesion, and to
differentiate it from other groups. It is theoretically possible that these
markers might be empty of any meaning, with the single function of
marking the group. In practice, these sign systems normally carry
important social meanings as well. Typically, groups are marked not
with a single label but with a cluster of them. Some of these markers
will have a common meaning, and the duplication functions as
redundancy to underline the message. Others have different meanings,
modifying or contradicting other sets of signs within the complex.
Overall, these sets of signs not only act as markers, which their profusion
enables them to do satisfactorily enough, they also define what
constitutes group membership. That is, they declare a specific version
of social relations. The meanings they communicate are an important
instance of the ideology of the group concerned. We will call a set of
markers of this kind a metasign. Our usage is influenced by
Bateson's (1973) term 'metacommunication', or communication about
communication. Metasigns take a number of forms, but typically they
are pervasive in messages, and they continually refer to and monitor
the social relations of semiotic participants.
    One influential word that is traditionally used to describe this
phenomenon is 'style'. Style originally derived from the Latin word
stilus, referring to the pointed iron rod which Roman schoolboys used

to incise letters on wax tablets. In this context, 'good style' meant an approved use of the *stilus* to form correct letters and correct content conforming to the canons of literacy. Later, in an educational system which rewarded excellence and difference, *stilus*, like English 'style', expressed the notion of valued individuality, a unique way of using the stilus that was associated with particular persons. This has been crystallized in the common understanding of Buffon's famous phrase, 'Style, is the man himself'.

The core meaning of this word today is a 'manner of writing, speaking, or doing, esp. as contrasted with the matter to be expressed or thing done' (*Concise Oxford Dictionary*) – with style normally seen as indicative of a particular 'person or school or period or subject' in 'painting, architecture, furniture, dress, etc.' This, then, is one word in popular use that has made the semiotic leap, integrating phenomena in a range of media, typically studied by different disciplines. As a specialist academic term, however, it has some difficulties. Both literary criticism and art history have appropriated it as a primary object of study for the respective disciplines. Typically they treat it as an asocial category. A hybrid discipline, 'stylistics', developed from a mixture of literary criticism and linguistics, but it was never a vigorous or productive discipline, in spite of a small number of distinguished proponents (e.g., Spitzer, Auerbach, Halliday). But in a different and more recent tradition, the sociolinguistics of the American William Labov (1978) has a more emphatically social orientation. For Labov, 'style' refers to a kind of variation which is free in some respects, yet serves to mark specific social agents and occasions within a broader language community. His own focus is relatively narrow, concerned with verbal codes and their social meaning, but this work is compatible with the broader more semiotic sense of 'style' in popular use. His work has made the concept of 'style' available for social semiotics, by bringing out its essentially social meanings and functions, and stressing its role in sustaining difference and identity and in carrying ideological meaning.

But 'style' is not the only term that has been used to refer to this general phenomenon outside semiotics. From the study of verbal language came two other terms which we can also use in this area. One is 'accent' (Voloshinov 1973). In speech, 'accent' refers to a further marking attached to words or syllables which serves to create difference, much like 'style'. A Scottish accent is a metasign of Scottishness. It distinguishes Scots from other English-speakers, expressing Scottishness for Scots and non-Scots alike. 'Accent' is the distinctive use of the vocal apparatus that corresponds to the distinctive use of the metal *stilus*.

Another term we can use is 'grammar'. Its basic meaning nowadays seems opposed to that of 'style'. 'Grammar' typically refers to common rules, 'style' to individual variation. However, the word comes from the Greek *gramme*, meaning a stroke of the pen in writing, a similar origin to that of 'style'. Grammar was taught in the same classrooms as 'style'. It came to be the set of prescriptions that distinguished the alien codes of Greek and Latin from familiar vernaculars. Essential to it were notions of 'correctness' and 'rules' (also originally present in the concept of 'style'). These notions are both social and comparative categories, distinguishing the speech of one group (an elite, a class or a nation) from that of others. So 'grammar' referred and still refers to a similar phenomenon as style, but at a different level. Grammar, too, incorporates a kind of metasign.

The notion of 'grammar' has been theorized by later writers in a number of ways that have relevance for social semiotics. Linguists in the tradition of Boas, Sapir and Whorf early this century, working with a large number of different languages, came to argue a connection between a language and a 'world view', a 'cosmology' or 'metaphysic'. They saw the distinctive grammar of a language as a major repository of these sources of difference. Our own work in *Language as Ideology* built on this tradition to assert an intrinsic connection between language and ideology, between the system of a specific language as encoded in its grammar and rules of use, and social meanings and functions of dominant and dominated groups. Languages differ in their vocabulary and their semantic systems and the paradigmatic structures that constitute them. They also differ in their 'grammars'. An important part of a grammar concerns a subset of the vocabulary system, one that provided the main focus for 'grammar teaching' in Latin and Greek classrooms. In every language there is a small set of signifiers which seem to serve primarily a 'grammatical' function, not a content function. Usually these words are very common, and also short, sometimes a single syllable (like *the*) or a morpheme unable to stand on its own (like -*s* to mark a plural). The specific meaning of these signifiers is usually vague and ambiguous, sometimes seeming almost non-existent. Yet their usage is normally controlled by strict rules. Fluent and 'correct' use of these items in the language is usually difficult for foreigners to acquire, so that they are convenient markers of group membership. Like other markers of group membership such as accent and style, they function with massive redundancy. It is difficult to speak a single utterance without having to show knowledge of at least a few of these items and the rules for their use. Semiotic codes other than verbal language have a similar kind of sign: for instance, the taken-for-granted frame around a painting, the columns and headings of newspapers. This kind of sign is often seen as being too humble and common to be worthy of notice. But nothing so common could be without its effects.

One useful feature of the concept of 'grammar', as against 'style' or 'accent', is the way it foregrounds the notion of rule. It is true that many linguists try to erode the force of this term by distinguishing between 'prescriptive grammars' (whose rules are imposed by the will of rule-givers) and 'descriptive grammars' (whose 'rules' are 'simply' regularities of a particular language, observed and catalogued by a scientific, neutral linguist). Behind this distinction is a valid recognition of an important difference in two kinds of 'rule': constitutive rules (e.g., the statement that -s is among other things a signifier of present tense and singular, as affixed to verb stems) and prescriptive rules (e.g., the statement that a singular subject should agree with its verb, marking the agreement by, among other signifiers, the -s present attached to the verb stem, as in 'The boy runs'). The first category of rule is part of the set of conventions that makes meaning possible in that code. The second category leaves specific meanings largely unaffected ('The boy run' is easily comprehensible). Even if it is observed with very few exceptions among sentences of English, it remains a prescriptive rule. Part of its meaning is that the speaker has obeyed the prescription, and is self-labelled as a full and conforming member of the group whose language it is. Children or dialect speakers who do not observe this rule are classified as imperfect members of the dominant group, or as members of another group one of whose defining features is their imperfection. As with other markers, the rules expressed through required syntagms are themselves meaningful, with meanings that are part of the identity of the group. In this instance the singular–plural agreement signifies a precision of mind (see *Language as Ideology*, ch. 4). These rules are social in origin and essence, not quasi-scientific. Although the author of these rules on any given occasion will not be a single identifiable individual, the process of construction of these rules and their sanctions has been the responsibility of concrete social agents over time; and it can be studied and understood as a social fact.

We can summarize these observations about style, accent and grammar as follows:

1 'Style', 'accent' and 'grammar' all refer to the same broad semiotic phenomenon, the metasign, whose function is to sustain difference and cohesion, and to declare the ideology of a group.

2 Metasigns are sets of markers of social allegiance (solidarity, group identity and ideology) which permeate the majority of texts.

3 These markers primarily refer to relations in the plane of semiosis (the production of meaning) rather than the mimetic plane (what is referred to). They can therefore seem arbitrary or meaningless, whereas they carry consistent ideological meanings which become clearly evident by reference to the semiosic plane.

Accent, difference, community

The most convenient starting point for analysis of how metasign systems work is the sound system of spoken languages, including 'accent' in the most limited sense of the word. This is partly because its social function is so easily recognizable and well known. The word 'shibboleth' has come to refer to party labels or slogans, because of an incident recorded in the Bible as occurring over three thousand years ago. In a bloody incident involving two groups of Jews, the Gileadites and the Ephraimites, the victorious Gileadites imposed a linguistic test on their opponents. Those who could not pronounce the 'sh' of 'shibboleth' (meaning a river) but adopted the Ephraimite 's' were to be killed. 42,000 men of Ephraim perished for this reason (Judges 12: 6). It is a dramatic illustration of the effectivity of a seemingly trivial phenomenon, types of pronunciation. 'Accent' typically plays a similar role to this in communities which have a mutually intelligible common language. In class societies, accents perform the same function as the Jewish shibboleth, usually affecting the social and economic position of millions rather than causing the deaths of thousands. For these purposes speech accents do not usually have to work on their own – there are many other systems of metasigns to supplement them. Nor is the accent powerful in itself. The Ephraimite 's' wouldn't have been fatal if there had not been hostility and conflict of interests between the two tribes. The energies attached to accents are social, not intrinsic to the sounds themselves; but this misperception is what makes conflicts over accents or languages seem so trivial to outsiders.

For social semiotics, the most useful starting point is Voloshinov's concept of the 'multi-accentuality of the sign'. Unlike structuralists, Voloshinov sets this phenomenon at the centre of his semiotic theory. Instead of assuming the coherence of society, Voloshinov posits conflict and contradiction as the norm. He sees language as normally dialogic, as the site of competing voices and competing interests. Where it is monologic, that signals the active suppression of difference, and even the possibility of difference, by an overwhelming social force. Monologic texts, then, rest on strictly policed logonomic rules which do not allow opposition or even participation by the non-powerful. The meaning that they encode is an ideology of absolute power. Dialogic and pluralist codes signify the existence of various kinds of opposition, resistance, negotiation within a group. At the level of the individual sign, this opposition is expressed through the phenomenon of multi-accentuality. If we take individual words as linguistic signs, this principle is realized through the existence of different 'accents' applied to the 'same' word. The example of 'shibboleth' will illustrate the point. This word had the same meaning for both Ephraimites and Gileadites, referring to a river, the same kind of river. Only its phonological substance was slightly different. The difference between 's' and 'sh' did not label reality differently: its main function was in the plane of semiosis, to label the kinds of speaker differently. Social difference can be signified at many other levels of the system of verbal language. We can represent some of the possibilities schematically in a semiotic hierarchy, as in figure 4.1. Items from any level can be used to mark difference, and there is also 'leakage' between levels within one group's language code. We do not know why, of all the words containing 's' the Gileadites chose 'shibboleth', river, for their test, though a river was the boundary between the two areas, and there were no rivers in the Ephraimites' mountainous region. Shibboleths which draw on accents from several levels function more economically as group labels, though this is not necessary for them to serve their function. The lower down in the table, the less significant the difference seems to be, the less concerned with mimetic (referential) meaning, but this allows them a more exclusive concern with semiosic/ideological reference. This quality is precisely why markers with low mimetic value are so widely used for this social purpose.

Saussure bequeathed to structuralism a precise system for describing the phenomenon of accent in sound, but also acute problems in explaining or accounting for it. For Saussure, as we have seen, the problems focused on sound change. Change in sound systems was evidently ubiquitous, but for Saussure it was also inexplicable. Saussure could see that the forces producing language change came from outside language, from society itself, but he excluded these dimensions from semiotics and linguistics, and since he regarded the linguistic sign as

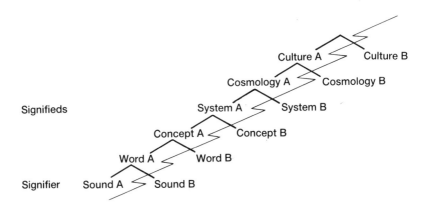

Figure 4.1 A semiotic hierarchy

definitionally non-rational, he had to see language change as both motiveless and meaningless. It has been the sociolinguist William Labov (1978) who has resolved many of the problems left by Saussure. As a sociologist, Labov did not leave out the social dimension of language. On the contrary, the relations between social and linguistic structures were his primary object of study. He integrated historical and sociolinguistic inquiry by a single powerful assumption: that the same forces and processes which create small differences over a short time in a single language community will produce over a longer time the large differences which ultimately constitute separate languages. The motor of linguistic change in the present, and therefore presumably in the past, is the desire to express social difference and its other face, solidarity.

Labov's basic method was to isolate an element subject to significant variation within a linguistic community, that is, an element subject to a social accent, to use Voloshinov's term. One such element he studied was post-vocalic *r* in New York speech (that is, *r* as in *port* or *party*). In order to isolate its effects, he manufactured texts which differed only in terms of this variable. He then established its function as a marker or label of socio-economic position, and for whom it functioned. He found that this variable acted as a prestige-marker, correlating significantly with judgements about the speaker's socio-economic status. He also found that it signified the status of an occasion, ranging from formal to casual. The same marker, therefore, could signify both a prestigious speaker and a formal occasion. That is, it indicated power in the semiosic plane, but ambiguously, referring either to the power of the producer or to power associated with the situation itself.

Labov elicited what he called 'subjective' meanings assigned to these markers, judgements made on speakers purely on the basis of the chosen markers. What he found was a consensus by all classes on some meanings, and divergences on others. In the dimension of power, all classes rated users of prestige forms as possessing high earning power, but in terms of physical power ('good in a fight') those of high socio-economic status tended to rate users of low-prestige forms higher than did those who used those forms. Predictably, in the solidarity dimension, high-status speakers reacted more positively to users of prestige forms, and low-status speakers the opposite. The differences and the agreements form a pattern which fits well with a process in which a common set of metasigns are given different values by different groups.

In broad outline, none of this is surprising. But as well as demonstrating quantitatively what had previously been understood impressionistically as linguistic prejudice, Labov was able to show that these same meanings were present in the atoms of linguistic prejudice (just as the Gileadites had suspected). He also opened up a precise new instrument for studying the mechanisms and processes of group formation, and the complex ideological meanings that sustain them. Since the sounds of language have a material existence, they can be analysed by precise instruments. Labov was able to show both the considerable material difference that is treated as the 'same sound', as non-significant variation, and differences that exist systematically but beneath the level of consciousness, indicating that an incipient change is under way. He was also able to show minute differences between the signals sent, and what was believed to have been sent, or what would be norms for the social group concerned – evidence of ideological shifts and contradictions in group allegiance. So for instance, women often 'hypercorrect', (using 'plummier' vowels than speakers from a higher social group, and/or hearing their own vowels as plummier than they are). Further, Labov was able to explain convincingly why users of non-prestige forms continued to use them when there seemed to be rewards for 'speaking correctly'. Labov pointed out the role of what he called 'covert prestige forms' in low-status groups. In his view, these strengthen solidarity bonds and act as potent carriers of a counter-ideological meaning. All groups have their metasign systems, which are so crucial to group identity and group survival that they won't lightly abandon them.

Labov distinguished between a number of kinds of difference, each with a different social function and meaning. Some differences have expressive value, so that they are meaningful to speakers, but do not mark off speech communities. Other differences have this second function, and Labov called these 'markers'. They are what together constitute an accent. Finally there is a sub-set of markers which have particularly high visibility within and outside the community. These are signs which have a special relationship to the metasign of the accent itself. Labov calls these 'stereotypes'. One important difference with stereotypes is that these are an accent of an accent. They are the selection, inflection and reading of a whole system of accents by a hostile community, a recuperation of the deviancy of the accent by reducing it to something simple, manageable and under the control of people outside the accent-community. So English speakers fancy their 'Irish' accent, Americans do their 'Negro' take-off, and Australians are delighted with their Aboriginal imitations. In each case, the real accent expresses the identity of the community, and excludes all other speakers. The stereotype constitutes the counter-claim that membership of that speech community is easy but worthless.

Labov's work can be complemented by Halliday's (1978) concept of antilanguage, which we have already mentioned. Where Labov worked mostly though not exclusively with sound signifiers, Halliday looked at other levels where meaning was more obviously important, at words and syntax. Halliday was clearer about the social functions of an antilanguage for its antigroup, and how these functions affected the typical forms of the language itself. In an antilanguage, language exists primarily to create group identity and to assert group difference from a dominant group. In Halliday's terms, the interpersonal function predominates over the ideational. In our terms, language is oriented towards the semiosic plane, not to the mimetic plane. One result is deliberate difficulty, often unintelligibility. Antilanguages simultaneously exclude outsiders, and express the ideology of the antigroup. Yet the antilanguage is derived from the dominant language, parasitic on it, typically achieving its incomprehensible forms by a series of simple but *ad hoc* transformations. For example 'look' becomes, by rhyming slang, 'butcher's hook'. Another transformation deletes 'hook', and the phrase 'take a butchers' (meaning 'take a look') becomes unintelligible to outsiders. In the process of creating the forms of an antilanguage, difference is first created by normal transformational processes. The terms of that difference are then assigned a social label. Finally the transformational processes are suppressed, so that the language becomes exclusive to its users. An antilanguage differs from an accent only in its assertion of stronger difference and more intense opposition; or, conversely, an accent is a partial antilanguage. The meaning at the core of the metasign of antilanguages is hostility and rejection of the dominant order. Where possible, antigroups usually draw on other semiotic systems – such as the use of black clothing, by many outlaw groups – to express the same basic set of meanings.

Antilanguages as studied by Halliday seem to be associated with subordinate oppositional groups – prisoners, thieves and so on. But a related phenomenon is very general in languages in stratified societies. Many language communities have two distinct languages, one of which is labelled 'high', and is identified with high-status speakers on public occasions, the other 'low', for the converse. Corresponding to 'high' languages, in such communities, there is normally 'high' culture, with the same social meaning and function as the high language, and usually mediated through the relevant 'high' language (cf. Bourdieu 1984). The nature, existence and role of 'high' culture and its opposing category, 'low' or 'popular' culture, have been extensively theorized. From a general semiotic point of view it is necessary to establish the unity of this set of phenomena, so that a 'high' language can be treated as one component of a 'high' culture, which operates ultimately as a single semiotic system that consists of overlapping sets of metasigns. We can also observe that whereas in Halliday's account an 'antilanguage' typically marks an oppositional and marginalized group, a 'high' culture and language normally signify the values of the dominant group. Yet 'high' languages have the typical qualities of an antilanguage. They are oriented towards the semiosic plane rather than the mimetic, they are full of complex transformations that obscure referential meanings while signifying kinds of power and solidarity, and they function to exclude those outside the high-status language community. Similarly, 'high' art, 'high' music, and 'high' culture itself characteristically are difficult, with mimetic meanings usually made inaccessible. They are full of complex transformations which are valorized to ensure that high culture forms are, for one reason or another, not available to the ordinary person. The metasigns of the elite who control high culture incorporate meanings of hostility towards the majority just as much as do metasigns of punks, bikies and mafiosi.

From the point of view of social semiotics it is not enough to note the existence and function of competing accents in a culture. This profusion of markers has a second major function, which is to declare ideological meanings; and social semiotics must be able to read them. Labov's study of the 'subjective' meaning of these signs goes some of the way towards this. But Labov was held back by his acceptance of the Saussurean doctrine of the intrinsic arbitrariness of the linguistic sign. His methods were salutary in showing the variety of meanings a single sign might have, for different groups. However, in order to explore their ideological meanings, we need a theory that can conceive of these signs as being themselves organized as texts. For this we draw on the concept of transparent signifiers.

Surprisingly, it was the structuralist tradition itself which provided the most useful starting point for this concept. Here the first important contribution to look at is Jakobson's arguments for 'phonetic symbolism' (1968). Jakobson's work on the phonological code has been extremely influential. Jakobson built on Saussure's and Troubetzkoy's theories of universal structural principles underlying the diversity of actual sounds in the various languages of the world. He also saw an inherent but vague meaning in the categories which constituted these codes. The opposition which Saussure termed 'open–closed', Jakobson saw as defined by an opposition 'energy–constraint', with vowels generally signifying energy (or absence of constraint) and consonants signifying constraint (or absence of energy). Relatively constrained vowels thus could signal 'constraint' (as opposed to open vowels), or 'energy' (as opposed to consonants). Their positioning within the continuum also carries another transparent signified: mediation or contradiction. All the sounds that make up a phonological code, then, will carry this set of meanings, but with considerable redundancy (so that one meaning will be carried by many different phonemes, even in a given language) and also variability (so that a given sound element might signify different meanings, depending on what it was opposed to). Allophones (the variant forms of phonemes that make up accents in speech) will build up the same kinds of meaning by the same principles. So will an individual's 'expressive' ways of producing the 'same' phonemes or sounds.

These two qualities, redundancy and variability, might seem to make the concept of phonetic symbolism implausible in theory and useless in practice. In fact, both these qualities are essential to the normal functioning of these semiotic systems. They also make it important to insist that transparent signs like these do not have a single inherent set of meanings, independent of context. Rather, they constitute a set of meaning-potentials, which are controlled by specific codes and regimes of interpretation, different logonomic systems, in response to the efforts of specific social groups at specific times. Jakobson extended these principles of natural symbolism to include colours systems, where the primary colours have long been recognized to encode symbolic values. This principle is compatible with seeming contradictions. For instance red in European cultures conventionally symbolizes energy (red for blood, as in the Red Cross organization, red as the sign of revolution as in the Red Flag) and also cessation of energy (red as in stop lights). But the underlying meaning of energy can be seen to be common to this full set of meanings, depending on its semiosic orientation. The red light of a traffic sign signals danger, but only from one point of view, the danger coming from the energy of the other. Similarly, the red flag, like the proverbial red rag to a bull, signals positive energy to Communists or bulls, but is a threat to capitalists or toreadors. Contradiction in the value of signs arises out of different positions and interests in the semiosic plane. Far from being a problem, it is precisely what social semiotics would expect. Lévi-Strauss has extended Jakobson's principles to other codes. His analysis – 1969(a) – of food and cooking codes for instance shows how they are constructed by the same principles out of a small set of transparent signifiers.

Sapir, the influential German-American linguist, made a contribution to the theory of phonetic symbolism which at first glance seems less consequential, and not related to Jakobson's theory. Sapir demonstrated that certain types of vowels and consonants seem to signify size. Wide aperture vowels like *a*, or vowels produced with a large oval cavity as in *or*, tend to signify largeness. Conversely vowels with narrow aperture and small cavity like *ee* or *i*, tend to signify smallness. Similarly, voiced consonants (like *b* or *g* or *d*) tend to signify largeness, as against unvoiced (*p*, *k*, *t*). This phenomenon has proved surprisingly widespread, present in a large number of languages. However, there are two problems with it as a theory. One is that it seems motiveless. Why have so many ways of signifying physical size? The other problem is the seemingly great number of inconsistencies in detail. To take just one example, the vowel of 'small' ought to signify big, and the vowel of 'big' ought to signify small (though their consonants would invert these meanings).

In terms of the theory we have been developing, the first problem is easy to resolve. Size is a transparent signifier of power, a crucial social category. The plane of semiosis is typically full of signifiers of power and solidarity, and massive redundancy in this class of meanings is the norm in social semiotics. And because signifiers on this plane can refer to any of the elements of the semiosic plane rather than just to the mimetic plane, we would expect considerable inconsistencies, if meanings are judged purely in terms of reference. For instance, the vowel in the Latin word *pater* (father) is consistent with largeness and power. But the vowels in the words *parvus* (small), *paucus* (few) and *paulus* (small, mean) also ought to signify largeness, yet all these words mean the opposite, and they are laden with negative social values. But in terms of relations in the plane of semiosis, the insignificance of the item labelled in this way attests to the power of those speakers who are not small/few/lowly, and are free to talk about these others. The power here defines the speaker not the object. With *pater* the power defines the subject and also the situation (*pater* was a formal term of address, like the English 'father'). As with accents, significant phonemes can label a number of aspects of the semiosic plane separately or simultaneously, with an ambiguity that is itself functional.

At this point it will be useful to draw together a number of observations about the role of metasigns in creating and sustaining difference and identity.

1   The motor of semiotic change is the desire to express difference. This desire proceeds from the need of specific groups to create internal solidarity and to exclude others, as antigroups constructing antilanguages, antimeanings, anticultures and antiworlds.

2   Differences can be expressed by marked choices and significant transformations at any level in a semiotic hierarchy, from the micro level ('accent', 'style' or 'grammar') through the meso level (item, phrase, ensemble) to the macro level (topic, theme, cosmology, metaphysics).

3   These differences exist to express group ideology and group identity. They normally form functional sets of metasigns (pervasive markers of group allegiance), whose meaning is social rather than referential, oriented to the semiosic rather than the mimetic plane.

4   Metasigns of group identity are normally constructed out of transparent signifiers. But since antilanguages and anticultures aim to exclude and mystify others, and since metasigns are normally pervasive in the production of texts, an accumulation of transparent metasigns of group identity will normally lead to forms of language and text whose mimetic meanings seem impenetrable, inexplicable and opaque to outsiders. Incomprehensibility, that is, is never an accident.

5 The 'culture' of a group performs the same functions for it as the metasigns in individual codes. A culture, then, is a complex that consists of metasigns from a range of codes (speech, clothing, food, etc.) with a common core of social meanings.

Class, culture and stereotype

In order to illustrate something of the complexity of these principles as they underlie specific texts and discursive processes, we will look at a cartoon (plate 4.1), published in the paper *The Australian* of 17–18 August 1985. The main point of this as a satire is straightforward enough without help from social semiotics. The trade union movement (the Australian Congress of Trade Unions, ACTU) is represented as obsessed with power but impotent and destructive. The Labour prime minister, Bob Hawke, is shown as an egoistic producer of bombastic claims and very little action. Mitchell's cartoons are a regular feature

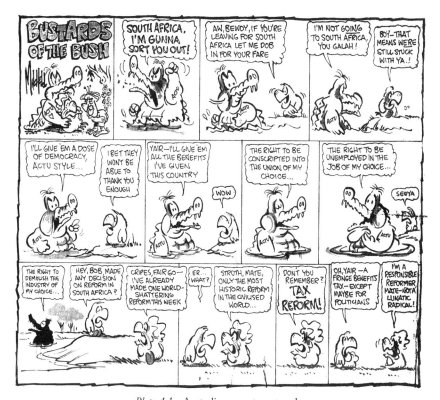

Plate 4.1 Australianness stereotyped

in *The Australian*, Australia's only national newspaper, the 'quality' paper of Rupert Murdoch's Australian stable, a kind of *Times* down under, with a similarly conservative political stance. A reading of the style and accent in this cartoon doesn't produce any great surprises, but it does reveal the processes by which the effects are achieved.

The text itself draws on and represents a number of codes that together construct specific accents and styles within Australia. The ACTU monster is represented as a crocodile, a large, dangerous and primitive reptile (one of the very few survivors from the age of dinosaurs). It has a number of differences from crocodiles including a hair-style that is parted in the middle, and which seems to be 'short-back-and-sides'. This style, in Australia in 1985, was a sign of both class and generation, referring to 1950s male working class, or middle-aged people who have not modified their style since then. We can read its meaning as a syntagm of transparent signifiers. Long hair is usually opposed to short as a signifier of nature, energy, lack of constraint, like an open vowel. Short hair seems to be the polar opposite, signifying curtailment of energy, but shaving is the most direct way of transforming hair, so it is a transparent signifier of negative energy, or energetic negativity. Puritans in sixteenth-century England and punks in the twentieth century used this signifier, with this meaning: so have monks, Buddhist and Christian, and so did Australian males of the 1950s and 1960s. The meaning of a parting in the hair is similar. A straight parting signifies culture in the midst of nature, if it is obvious and central, rejecting both the natural contours of the head and the complex possibilities of art. It signifies an opposition to nature that is so elemental and extreme as itself to be not yet fully part of culture.

The meaning of the hair-style is complemented by representations of the Australian accent. (For a discussion of the Australian cultural accent in more detail see Fiske, Hodge and Turner 1987.) Most of the speech of all characters is in normal spelling. 'Incorrect' spelling is then used to highlight a few items of vocabulary and pronunciation and we present them as stereotypes, to signify a whole accent and speech style and its ideological meanings and valuation. There are two main phonetic signifiers to which attention is drawn. One is a tendency to eliminate consonants (e.g., *gunna* for *going to*, *you're* for *you are*, *give 'em* for *give them*). This is not uniquely Australian. In many languages and cultures it is a signifier of informality, of low levels of constraint, and low status. As a quality of the Australian accent, it serves to mark it as a 'low' language. Vowel quality is the other carrier of accent. Here there are only a few examples: oo → a (*to* → *a* in *gunna*, *you* to *ya*), e → air (*yes* → *yair*), oh + i → a (*going* → *gun*). There is also a consonant shift, t → d (*beauty* → *bewdy*). This may seem a small selection, though it's several times more generous than 'shibboleth'.

Each of the items stands for a whole class of transformations that make up the full accent, so we will take them individually.

The three vowel shifts show a common quality; a shift from closed vowels (= constraint, control, culture) to open vowels, (= energy, lack of constraint). In the process, the Australian accent (like other informal forms of English) has created a new T form in pronouns of address, one hitherto unnoticed by grammarians. The formal or V form in Australian is 'you': the informal or T form is 'ya', with the open vowel 'a' acting as a transparent signifier of non-constraint. In the process, the Australian dialect has reversed the change in the dominant language, codified in its grammar, which banned this distinction sometime during the eighteenth century. In this as in many other such changes, shifts in sound and grammar systems are interrelated, and motivated by considerations of meaning whose basis is ideological.

All the words deformed by markers of the Australian accent in this text are also marker items of vocabulary. The example chosen to show voicing of a dental (t → d) is the distinctive Australian use of 'beauty', referring to something desirable but not either sexual or aesthetic. (So for instance 'bewdy' indicates generalized approval and can describe a fast horse, a good deal, a fine shot in cricket, or as here, a convenient departure). So the word, precisely because it conflates the categories of gender (male/female) and the aesthetic (art/non-art) signifies a language and culture whose paradigmatic structures lack even those basic distinctions – a 'culture' that in the eyes of an elite seems hardly worthy of the name since it lacks the categories to recognize what culture is. The spelling of the word is designed to emphasize its difference from the English word 'beauty', even though 'correct' English speakers do not pronounce the vowel like its written components (e–a–u). To unvoice the dental plosive, following the vowel, requires vocal precision, constraint. The voicing of the sound as 'd', then, signifies energy, or lack of constraint. This meaning is compatible with the notion of size or emphasis, as in Sapir's theories. 'Bewdy' is a convenient stereotype because the meanings implicit in its phonological characteristics and its status in the paradigmatic structures of the language converge. It thus becomes a potent sign of Australianness, drawing on and distorting the meanings of the accent-metasign to signify a dense and persuasive judgement on ordinary Australians.

'Yair' is another case in point. The vowel, with its diphthong, contrasts with the standard (dominant) form of 'yes', in being oriented towards open vowels, and the word also eliminates the final consonant. So of the two words for affirmation, 'yes' and 'yair', the second signals either a stronger affirmation or a closer solidarity bond with the listener. But there is a third form in common use in Australia, 'yup', with an open vowel cut short by an unvoiced consonant, p. This form is equally colloquial, but signifies strong constraint. Prime Minister Bob Hawke's frequent use of this form, especially when answering difficult questions, has been widely parodied. Where 'yair' signifies increased solidarity, 'yup' breaks it, signifying a hostile relationship closing off the debate, and hence reluctant agreement. The Australian accent as a whole then, projects contradictory ideological forms: markers of solidarity and markers of aggression and hostility. But contradiction within an ideological complex is the norm, not the exception, and the contradictions of the Australian accent are typical.

In addition to the markers of Australianness, there are two different kinds of language used in the strip, easily classified by English speakers (not only Australians) as colloquial and formal respectively. The ACTU crocodile's first speech is clearly colloquial. His last three speeches (before he fades into the distance) are recognizably examples of the formal code. Some of the markers of the formal code, apart from specialized vocabulary, are to be found in its syntax. It is heavily transformed, full of inversions and deletions. Such transformations are one of the most common transparent signifiers of non-solidarity, and hence power. This example is large in scope (a single sentence already 41 words long, and still not finished), and it has a rigid stylistic frame (the words 'the right to . . .' repeated with each new clause). This principle of organization involves some element of subordination, but mainly works through parallelism. Structures of this kind we term 'paratactic'. They are transparent signifiers of social structures that differ systematically from those of hypotactic organization.

In the text itself, these two speech forms are represented along with other semiotic signals of the semiosic plane. When he uses colloquial language, ACTU's expression signifies direct contact with his addressee (though this is illusory in the case of South Africa, in the first frame). As soon as he begins his long speech, his eyes first lose their focus and he looks away from the galah (an Australian parrot, or colloquial for 'fool') then he closes his eyes and turns his back, and seems not to notice the galah walking away as he continues. The signifiers of non-solidarity are strong, and they attach to the code he is using as well. He begins with the language of energy and solidarity, and finishes with the language of power and non-solidarity, but the non-solidarity is so extreme that the power (ACTU's illusions of his omnipotence, and the prestige accruing to his mastery of formal codes) turns into its opposite, the impotence of someone excluded from discourse. So ACTU's ability to use two forms of language is not represented as an asset, but the contrary. He is shown as ridiculous and ineffective both when using colloquial, working class Australian forms, and also when breaking with these forms; though he is seen as even more ineffective when using the language of power, because this form of language excludes him from his own potential allies.

In the case of Bob Hawke, the two forms of language are distinguishable, but they are not so polarized. 'Only the most historic reform in the civilized world . . .' is formal language, though it is more excessive in its claims than it should be to be felt to be fully 'correct'. And it is preceded by the colloquial 'struth, mate'. Bob Hawke may be equally bombastic and ineffective as ACTU, according to Mitchell, and involved in the same contradiction, but he retains contact and solidarity with his representative listener, as both his language and body posture show.

In the plane of semiosis which completes the ideological work of this text, similar oppositions apply. This cartoon is surrounded by print text, whose conventions follow those of 'quality' papers in Australia, Europe and America. The print face is small, with ruled lines separating articles or categories of article. The syntax and vocabulary are typical of the 'high' code variety, as appropriate for the small elite of 'top' people the paper is aimed at. This is especially true of the editorial, which sits immediately to the left of this cartoon. The style of the cartoon, then, is exactly opposed to the style of the paper, especially in its implications about power and solidarity. The cartoon is surrounded by a jagged, hand-drawn line. The draughtsmanship, similarly, is casual, deleting most of the visual information of the drawn characters, displaying, not concealing, the personal energy of Mitchell in his brush strokes. The writing is hand drawn also, not using type of any kind. Only the lines between the frames have been ruled, though the frames themselves have not been reduced to tidy regularity.

All these signifiers work primarily on the plane of semiosis, to create a high degree of solidarity between artist and audience. 'High' styles always involve a sense of strain between producers and receivers. The cartoon creates a space in which informality, humour and relaxation are possible for these otherwise important and serious journalists and readers. The methods of the cartoon style draw on essentially the same semiotic systems as underlie the verbal styles.

There are other codes Mitchell uses to position the reader, all of them developments of well-known codes. He uses four sizes of print, with underlinings and use of double lines giving a paradigmatic set of seven. The principle could be applied to produce more varieties, but they all express the same dimension as the vowel and consonant system, size as a signifier of emphasis or importance. The same principle underlies the conventions of headlines in newspapers. Very large typeface, like shouting (or lack of consonants), signifies unrestrained energy, which is incompatible with the ideology underlying the high code. So headlines of a 'quality' paper, like *The Australian*, are normally smaller than those of popular papers, like *The Sun* in Britain, or *Truth* in Australia. The size of the image, signifying proximity by reference to proxemic codes, also positions the viewer. These two codes converge in the first frame, where letter size and image size create maximum proximity. The verbal code used ought to reinforce this, as a colloquial form. In practice, however, these forms are class-marked, in Australian speech. The prestigious readers of *The Australian* would not use quite these forms, not even when relaxing. That makes them non-reciprocal and thus, non-solidary. The effect of the markers of closeness, coming from drawing style, combined with the markers of exclusion enshrined in the implied accent, inverts the high positive solidarity into equally high negative solidarity. This has a specific effect here, alienating this kind of reader from the sentiment ACTU is expressing (hostility to South Africa is not a policy *The Australian* endorses strongly, though its editorial on that day, printed immediately to the left of this cartoon, mildly rebuked President Botha for his tardiness on reform). It also has a more general effect, which is reinforced in every cartoon that uses the same codes, of confirming the antagonism between the readers of the paper and speakers like ACTU, a division along class lines made cruder and more overt than is the case in everyday Australian discourse. But even this effect is by no means inevitable. Commitment to an oppositional group can invert this bias, as a letter to the editor printed in this issue claimed: 'So many recent newspaper editorials seem to be advising the ACTU as to what policy is good for Australia. The ACTU appreciates the information. It then knows what to oppose,' wrote Tom Robinson, of Bayswater, WA.

It is important to stress that we are analysing a stereotype here, not an accent. The difference between the two is clarified in terms of relations in the plane of semiosis. As we have said, a stereotype is an accent of an accent, a version of it which expresses the interests of an opposing group. The normal producer of a stereotype is a category of person specifically excluded from that accent, an accent whose complex forms are designed to make its penetration difficult or impossible for outsiders. The set of stereotypes in effect declares this difficulty irrelevant. They enable anyone to enter the closed world of the antilanguage and anticulture. Sometimes they can economically invoke and dismiss a whole group and its ideological viewpoints in a few gestures. They can also appear more benign, declaring an essential oneness that incorporates the users of the accent into a higher consensus, appropriating the energy of its difference and the potency of its ideological forms. This cartoon in fact performs both strategies. It appears in a paper called *The Australian*. The Australian accent strongly signifies oppositional working-class affiliations and values, as we have seen, and hence is parodied and repudiated here. But the middle class, achieving readers of *The Australian*, are distinguished from similar readers in England and America only by being Australian. A form of the Australian accent is also their own marker of difference, the only statement of identity they have. So in practice they speak a modified or reduced form of Australian accent which has a double reference: a repudiation of standard English (in the direction of Australian) and a repudiation of 'broad' Australian (in the direction of middle-class norms and ideologies). The same will be true of metasigns in other semiotic media. The low-class style or accent is a major signifier of solidarity and identity for all Australians precisely because of its low-class associations, though these are an embarrassment when power is at issue. So the style of this cartoon, with its signifiers of a solidarity which is low class or 'popular' and Australian, is not simply anti-Australian and anti-popular. If *The Australian* commits itself to being anti-Australian and unpopular, where has it got to go, and who is it selling to?

Signs are the units of meaning in semiotics and reading signs is a primary skill for semioticians. But signs exist at many levels, in many forms. They are always part of another structure which itself functions as a complex sign, with a complex meaning. These meanings of signs are never neutral and objective. They are always part of a semiotic strategy which determines their social meaning and effect. So in reading signs, it is often convenient to look at relatively simple and self-contained signs, such as the crocodile used to signify the ACTU, or his hair-style as a defining feature. But it is also important to look at more diffuse signs, metasigns and signifiers of metasigns, because these, having become 'naturalized', are more likely to be missed or taken for granted and therefore ignored in any analysis of the effects of a text, dropping out of consciousness and therefore freer to work at an unconscious level.

Metasigns of gender

Gender is an important category in every human society. Every society recognizes the facts of biology and distinguishes between men and women. Built on to that biological base are innumerable cultural rules that specify and control behaviour along gender lines. These gender systems rest on and are part of semiotic systems and processes, without which they could not be known and sustained. Crucial here are gender components of logonomic systems, which prescribe semiotic meanings along gender lines: what meanings women and men can produce, to themselves and to the other, about themselves and about the other, in what codes and in which contexts. These logonomic systems in turn rely on systems of gender metasigns, which construct gender identities and transmit a continuous and pervasive set of messages about gender. The meaning of these metasigns undoubtedly reflects the dominant conception of gender relations. As with every other sign in social use, though, they will also incorporate oppositional meanings, responding to moments of resistance (to the dominant ideology) by both women and men. Studies of gender systems generally assume that a gender system will be a coherent set of meanings working in the interests of the dominant. This generally leads to one of two strategies: trimming the system down till it fits the model of coherence, or acknowledging the diversity and despairing of finding a system at all. Ours is a contrary expectation: we assume that gender systems are marked by contradiction and instability, that they are sites of struggle in the past as well as in the present.

The term 'gender' comes from Latin and Greek grammars, describing a pervasive feature of those languages, and it is useful to go back to this origin to begin to understand the term. Latin and Greek classified all nouns into three categories, masculine, feminine and neuter. In many instances this classification was based on biological sex, which made it seem unproblematic and 'natural', though why it should be marked so insistently was less evident. But both these gender systems went beyond biological sex in many other instances. A sexual identity was attributed by the systems to many nouns whose referents have no sexual characteristics. In the case of animals (which do have sex) they were often assigned to one or other gender irrespective of their actual sex, unless there was a reason to emphasize it (just as all dogs in English are assumed to be masculine unless their status as 'bitch' is foregrounded).

This gap between biological sex and gender as a social construct is what creates the need for gender as a separate category. One aspect of a gender system is a classification of reality which projects social meanings about men and women on to the non-human world, inscribing an ideology of sex roles and sex identities into the language itself. The other aspect is the set of markers that make up the system of metasigns. In order to know the language, you have to know the gender scheme in minute detail. So the gender scheme is absorbed from the earliest years and is effortlessly replicated in every act of speech; in this way it acts as a condition of entry into 'correct' language. This is clearly a powerful way of socializing individuals into the ideology of gender of a particular society.

This account, however, is too neat when faced with the complications of actual gender systems – complications which we have suggested are not accidents or excrescences but integral to their function. So we will take Latin as one example of such systems in verbal language. The choice of Latin has some disadvantages which we need to acknowledge at the outset. Latin is now a 'dead' language, so our reconstruction of its gender system is necessarily hypothetical, and cannot be tested against the responses of actual speakers of the language, who would have been aware of the many complications and anomalies that must have arisen in conditions of use by speakers of different gender, class and locality. But the example of Latin has been used persuasively to buttress claims that gender systems were meaningless in later European languages over the past two thousand years. A study of the signifiers of gender as transparent signifiers is only the beginning of an account of Latin gender, but it is a very good starting point.

Latin nouns were divided by Latin grammarians into three genders, masculine, feminine and neuter. The categories masculine and feminine include many entities without biological sex. The Latin system, then, is a typical example of gender used as a generalized ideological system. However, Latin has not just three sets of gender markers; it has five declensions. These declensions include different case-markings, though for this discussion we will restrict ourselves to masculine and feminine in the nominative case, which marks the subject of an action. The most common nominative form for feminine nouns ends in *a*, the so-called 'first declension', and *us* for masculine nouns in the second declension. There are three other declensions, however. The third declension ends in a variety of forms, with *is* as the most common, though *es* and *as*, and consonant plus *s* are also found, plus *io* and other forms. These nouns are predominantly feminine, although there are many exceptions. The fourth declension ends in *us*, a longer, more frontal vowel than the second declension *us*. These nouns similarly are mostly masculine, though with many exceptions. The fifth declension, mainly feminine, ends in *es*. But to confuse the picture even more, there are some further specialized gender markers; *er* in the second declension (*magister*, master) and *or* in the fourth (*creator*, creator, or *imperator*, ruler or emperor). Corresponding to *or* is a feminine marker *rix* (as in *creatrix*, female creator, or *imperatrix*, an empress or female ruler).

A system that has to operate so quickly and frequently would seem to need to be based on transparent signifiers. But if we try to interpret Latin gender markers in these terms, drawing on the use of vowels and consonants as transparent signifiers of power and solidarity, the results initially seem opposite to what would be predicted. The strong male marker, *or* or *er*, follows the basic pattern, with its large aperture vowel (plus power), but this is a minority form. The *us* of the second declension, the main marker of masculinity, has both *s*, which signifies smallness and hence non-power, and a relatively low aperture vowel, *u* (minus power). In contrast, the main marker for femininity, *a* in the first declension, is a transparent signifier of energy or lack of constraint (plus power). Neither Roman women nor their modern daughters were obviously liberated, powerful and free of constraint. Both markers, in fact, invert known valuations of gender roles in Roman society. The third and fifth declensions, however, mostly feminine, mainly use short, low aperture vowels or no vowel plus *s* (minus power). So the Latin system seems not to be consistent even in itself, much less with the set of transparent signifiers.

However, if we set out the system in two parts, a gender system plus a set of markers with transparent meanings, it does have a kind of consistency:

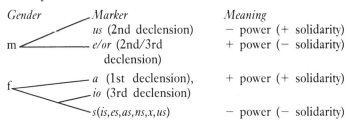

Gender	Marker	Meaning
m	*us* (2nd declension)	− power (+ solidarity)
	e/or (2nd/3rd declension)	+ power (− solidarity)
f	*a* (1st declension),	+ power (+ solidarity)
	io (3rd declension)	
	s(*is,es,as,ns,x,us*)	− power (− solidarity)

The system, in this form, makes sense if we assume that its marker system does not signify gender directly, but classifies gender in basic terms of power and solidarity. The contradictory classifications then make sense either in relation to the plane of semiosis or to the mimetic plane, and this explains many of the apparent gender-exceptions. For the common masculine form to be the more discreet *us* form, rather than the more overtly power-laden *or* or *er* forms, is in line with what is typical of high languages, languages of power. Many other apparent gender exceptions also make sense in these terms. For instance *mater*, mother, is feminine but powerful, especially within the normal contexts of its use. Conversely, *a* as marking the object of desire, unrestrained energy, can be used to mark females, seen from the male point of view in the plane of semiosis. The forms ending in *s*, in the third and fifth declensions, signify both constraint and powerlessness, a characterization which is not as strongly linked to a specific gender as the other two are, though it is more usually linked to female than to male entities.

The gender markers in Latin, then, define gender flexibly in terms of power and solidarity relations, referring to relations in the plane of semiosis as much as to characteristics in the mimetic plane. The overall effect is not a simple construction of homogeneous gender identities, but a repertoire of constructions of gender in terms of power and solidarity. The system itself has an overriding male orientation in that it normally implies a social world and semiosic plane seen from the point of view of a male producer of meanings, this being the point from which it makes best sense. Although it is not true that 'men made language' (cf. Spender 1980), men did control its grammatical forms to a large extent with Latin. The Latin language that has been transmitted to us is a male construction, described by male grammarians, describing the language of predominantly male writers. Of 207 authors whose language provided the basis for the authoritative Liddell and White dictionary, only two were women. Yet in spite of this male gendered point of view, the construction of femininity carried by the gender system does not imply a purely derogatory or dismissive view of women. The *a* declension was called the first declension by Latin grammarians themselves, thus giving it primacy (just as the first of the four declensions of verbs is the *a* class, whose paradigm example is *amare*, to love.) This deference to the feminine can be found in other male codes, in other cultures, such as codes of etiquette. It is found especially in domains devoted to pleasure rather than to power. Feminists will recognize this *a* as the signifier of desire, of women as the objects of men's energy and desire, not their own. Nonetheless, the object of desire can still have energies attributed to it and even a kind of effectivity. Ambiguity here as elsewhere in social semiotics is systemic and functional.

Linguists writing about gender in Latin normally treat it as virtually without meaning or function, a hangover from an earlier stage. In fact the system has survived with remarkable tenacity for over two thousand years, to be alive and well in modern French and Italian. Contemporary English is often said to have lost its gender system (without society becoming non-sexist). But as Whorf first pointed out (see Whorf 1956, Kress and Hodge 1979) English has developed a covert gender system which is nearly as comprehensive and contradictory as Latin, and is still capable of growth. Generally, it operates with fewer markers which are therefore easier to avoid. But some forms of English have developed a set of markers which have a close similarity to those of Latin. In Australian English, as in some other colloquial varieties of English, the suffixes *ie* and *o* are often added to first names to create nicknames (that is, high-solidarity names). Both indicate solidarity, but the *o* form implies respect, especially for the physical powers of the person, whereas *ie* is an affectionate diminutive. These also have gender implications which, like the Latin system, do not show a simple correspondence. So Jacko must be male, but Jacky/ie may be male or female. Orthography can be used to distinguish the two, where the general rule is that the more letters used to convey a given sound (hence the more constraints accepted) the more 'feminine' the name is. So 'Jackie' is more feminine than 'Jacky', but still not unequivocally so. But 'Jacqui' is unequivocally feminine, signifying both minus power and plus constraint.

The system, in Australian English, has produced an embryonic gender system. A tin of beer is known affectionately as a 'tinnie', and it is carried in an iced container called an 'esky'. The attitude to a 'wino' is quite different. He (the term has implied gender) is likely to be nearly always 'blotto', perhaps even a 'metho', (on 'meths') because he's so obviously a 'derro' (derelict). As the last example shows, the size or power signified by *o* may not apply to entities in the mimetic plane, only those in the plane of semiosis, here signalling intense hostility. 'Masculinity' and 'femininity' are not only signified by markers of power and solidarity, they also signify kinds of power and solidarity themselves, leading to some complexity even in this relatively simple system. So tins of beer, in spite of their phallic shape and association with male drinking and male solidarity, are classified with the 'ie' of implicitly feminine solidarity, as safe objects of male desire. Words with this suffix added that make up an 'Australian' language also build a gendered accent into it. They imply a gendered classification of drinks, in terms of which beer is a man's proper drink. They also create a semiosic orientation, backed up by logonomic rules, in terms of which Australian women should not use the word 'tinnie' except in so far as they are implicitly quoting males, because the marker system itself implies a male semiosic position. The same form also signifies social class (working class) and situation (informal). This kind of multiple meaning of metasigns is not unusual. It is in fact the typical consequence of metasigns being constructed out of a common set of signifiers.

Gender meanings are also constructed through specific styles of speech, dress, behaviour, and so on. One of the most important codes for constructing gender has been the clothing code. Clothes typically distinguish men and women, and help to declare what it is to be a woman or a man for that social group. To do this, they draw on transparent signifiers whose basic meaning concerns relations of power and solidarity. Out of these raw materials, particular styles construct complex meanings which go beyond gender to include meanings about status, class and other general social categories.

In order to examine how the meanings of clothing styles can be incorporated into constructions of gender and other ideological complexes, we will take as text the clothes of Princess Diana, using the photographs published in the *Australian Women's Weekly*, which covered her 1985 tour of Australia. The issue of the magazine had four pages of photos, plus a fold-out section including more photos, along with a cut-out of the 'prettiest' dress. There were 27 photographs in all, showing 17 different dresses, dresses with different colours, patterns, textures and shapes. This amount of difference declares itself as a signifier in its own right, carrying a meaning which is important in the world of fashion. Where an accent marks a consistent identity and a consistent difference, this aspect of fashion signifies the opposite, self-difference. A fashion-leader like Princess Diana offers 17 different versions of herself within four pages, a plenitude of selves. This plurality is a transparent signifier of power, similar to the royal 'we'. Following the same principle, fashions for top people are changed frequently, so that they can demonstrate their ability to 'keep up' with the multiplicity that signifies their status.

Yet there are also regularities and continuities, which give a consistent gender identity to Princess Diana. We will start by contrasting Princess Diana with her husband for comparison. She has essentially the same hair-style and the same make-up throughout, both serving to signify gender. The Princess Diana hair-style has become a well-known marker. Her hair is longer than Prince Charles's, but not long for a woman. That is, it has a double reference, defined against male norms (Prince Charles) and female norms (e.g., Princess Anne). The same is true of its styling: more carefully styled than a man's, but not tightly permed like the Queen's. Similarly her make-up is light by female standards, for this culture (unobtrusive lipstick, rouge and eye-shadow) though gender-marked compared to Prince Charles, who doesn't wear any make-up. Another difference lies in hats. In over half the photos she is shown wearing a hat. Only once is Prince Charles shown with one – a safety helmet, on a visit to an aluminium smelter, when she also wears one.

Except for that one instance, we might be tempted to see hats as marked for gender, even though Princess Diana doesn't always wear one. Of course, at different times and in different cultures this has not always been the case: even in these pictures, men other than Prince Charles are shown wearing hats – three out of five of these being military personnel. The meaning of hats, then, is not specifically indicative of gender, but of constraint (whether submission to discipline, as in the military, or for reasons of safety, as with safety helmets, or for both reasons, as with women like Princess Diana in public). The logonomic rules which in some cultures at some periods have rigidly prescribed headgear for women, especially in public (hats, shawls, veils) have usually done so with an explicit conception of women as dangerous objects of desire. Long hair is a common signifier of energy or lack of constraint, so that hat-plus-hair forms a self-contradictory syntagm (though Princess Diana's hair is not excessively long). It might seem simpler to have logonomic rules requiring women to shave their heads. But simplicity and consistency are not the only criteria motivating logonomic systems.

Although every difference is significant, here we will confine our attention to two dimensions of difference only. One is the general meaning of clothing as a transformation of the body. In every picture, Princess Diana wears a kind of dress. Prince Charles wears trousers. These are conventional signifiers of female versus male in contemporary Western culture, although there are exceptions (e.g., monks, priests, and monarchs seen from behind; and modern women's fashions including trouser suits and jeans. Richard Blackwell nominated Princess Stephanie of Monaco as the world's worst-dressed woman in 1986 for precisely this reason: 'Her royal unisex wardrobe entitles her to use either bathroom'). A decisive difference between trousers and dresses is that dresses conceal the anatomy more, especially in the genital area, and therefore signify constraint more strongly – though as we shall see, innumerable counter-messages can combine with this basic meaning to convey complex overall messages.

Princess Diana's dresses in this collection are relatively constrained, as dresses go. All but one reach below the knee. Only one shows the flesh of her upper arm and shoulders. One dress opens 15 cm down the front: the rest cover all but her throat. These styles all signify constraint. However, Prince Charles's clothing signifies constraint even more strongly. Except for one occasion, when he is shown playing polo, he wears collar and tie, suit coat or jacket, long trousers and shoes. No flesh is showing except below his wrists and above his Adam's apple. In spite of the meaning of trousers, constraint is not restricted to the one gender. But as the example of the Prince shows, these constraints partly signify the power of the persons and the formality of the occasion.

Another marker of difference is colour. Jakobson (1968) argued that primary colours universally have meanings analogous to the meaning of vowels, with red corresponding to high-energy vowels like *a*, and blue to low-energy vowels like *oo* or *i*. With all such universalistic claims it is important to recognize that what is at issue is a system of transparent signs, which is subject to the modifications of particular cultural and social groups. In the contemporary world of fashion however, the transparent meaning of colours as signifiers of energy provides the basis for the complex meanings constructed out of them. Mary Quant is authoritatively explicit about colour and gender: 'Masculine fabrics should be in masculine colours – grey, white, black, herringbone, etc., with one romantic lapse of *eau de nil* or *bois de rose*. This perversity delights me but panics the marketing experts who say that it will not sell. But it's wonderful to exaggerate femaleness' (1984: 8). She is here exploiting the inbuilt gender meaning of colours and textures precisely by creating new cross-gender meanings, relying on other signs (the green of *eau de nil* or the pink of *bois de rose* plus other signifiers of femininity) to invert the value of the initial colour sign so that the meaning is 'perverse' (a daring feminine appropriation of the masculine) and not a signifier of the anti-feminine (as her marketing experts feared). It is this kind of complex use of colour-meanings that can make colour seem arbitrary, when the 'arbitrariness' is in fact a deliberate negation or displacement of a basic meaning. At this level Quant sees red as expressing raw energy: '– hard, hot, alive, sure, pushy and crude, blood and guts, cruel, sex, tomato, Spain, rampant, and it always works', while navy blue is 'hard, cold and officious, but navy and white can be deliciously Gigi and Deauville'. On the other hand, pastels 'are difficult. They quickly look cheap and

boring. Especially when printed on thin white synthetics. On natural
fabrics – leather, silk, linen and wool – they look expensive, luxurious
and extravagant, because they are!' (1984: 8–9).

It is possible, then, to begin to read the social meaning of colours
in contemporary English fashion by using as a starting point the
transparent signifier system of plus/minus colour/luminosity = plus/
minus energy. In terms of this system, Prince Charles's clothes show
less variety, all of it within the range of the masculine in Quant's
description: one black dinner-jacket, the rest variations on blue-grey.
Of Princess Diana's dresses, 13 are in light shades and pastel colours,
half of them shades of blue. Five are in strong primary colours: two
bright red, one a bright green, one blue and one black. These colours
are organized as transparent signifiers. Light pastel colours signify
minus energy, that is, smallness, lack of importance. Most of Princess
Diana's dresses and Prince Charles's suits carry this message, a
cancellation of their royal status in the interests of possible solidarity
with their subjects. Of the dresses in primary colours, two are in bright
red, a colour that corresponds, in the visual dimension, to *a* in the
phonological.

The gender associations of red are interesting, in many ways
comparable with the role of *a* in verbal gender-systems. Traditionally,
pink is the colour for baby girls and blue for boys. Pink is a modified,
restrained red, suitable for young children, but it is a form of red none
the less, a marker of energy, labelling the female as an object of desire,
while blue (pale blue again) labels the boy with power purely by not
labelling him with energy or desire: the colour equivalent of the Latin
us form. Adult women signify their sexuality especially through the
colour red: lipstick, rouge, nail varnish. Princess Diana's light lipstick
and rouge signals this quality, though in a restrained way. In this
reading, she seems to signify mostly the suppression of desire.

However, some of these figures are misleading. The text of Princess
Diana's clothes is mediated by the *Women's Weekly*, a magazine largely
produced by women, for women. In its pages, Princess Diana is inflected
by a female accent, positioned by female producers and receivers in
the plane of semiosis. One effect of this can be seen in the selection
of dress-colours. Although only five dresses in primary colours are
shown, the two red dresses appear in five pictures, and the green one
appears in three pictures, one greatly enlarged, and readers are offered
a step-by-step model of this last so that they can make it and wear it
themselves. These women readers are positioned differently in the
plane of semiosis, oriented more strongly to signifiers of energy than
to signifiers of constraint. The dresses marked by colours are marked
for energy in other ways. The dress which plunges 15 cm downwards
is one of the red ones, and it has a slit at the front rising above the

knee. The green dress has a high bow on one shoulder but leaves the other shoulder bare, showing more flesh than any other dress depicted in the magazine.

In explaining the original semiosic plane, the magazine announced, 'It was a meet-the-people royal tour, with the Prince and Princess of Wales delighting crowds, especially children, wherever they went in both city and country'. This statement represents the major semiosic event, of which these clothes are part, as a relationship between the royal couple (with Prince Charles in the leading position) and 'the people'/'crowds', in which the Royals are objects of 'delight' especially to 'children'. Many children are in fact pictured, but not on the occasions when Princess Diana wore red or green. The magazine's ideological construction of the royal tour as a relationship primarily with children connects with one role specification for women, that of mother, but Princess Diana simply 'delights' this multitude of children and passes on, leaving others to feed, clothe and wash them. And the semiosic plane of the magazine links women to women in a bond of solidarity established by a common set of reference points. The women producers of the magazine signify the existence of female energy and desire through unobtrusive shifts in the dominant code. Princess Diana signifies both female restraint and potential female power. She also surreptitiously signifies female irresponsibility and gratification, through her signals which are magnified by the magazine. Princess Diana herself is silenced in the verbal channel – there are no quotations of what she says, only how she looks – but so is Prince Charles. The verbal text is created by Ann Pilmar and Pat von Wolff, so her silence is compensated for by the speech of other women.

Women's magazines like the *Women's Weekly* are part of women's culture in a country like Australia. This particular magazine projects a conservative ideology which offers small gratifications to women, along with considerable constraints. Like all ideological forms, constructions of gender are the site of struggles and renegotiations of meanings. They have their own inconsistencies, and are attacked or supported for their own reasons by contending groups, whether of the same gender or not. This particular construction of the royal tour works with the contradictory gender meanings offered by Princess Diana's clothes, and is then able to present a seductive image in which female desire can coexist with constraint, without jeopardizing the operations of power. As such it legitimates a specific gender ideology and a specific class message: that women can only be women when the traditional rulers rule.

We can summarize some of the main propositions about gender and its signifiers as follows:

1   Gender systems in society are sustained and mediated by gender components of logonomic systems and by sets of gender metasigns.

2   Gender metasigns are drawn from the basic semiotic resources of a given community, using transparent signifiers of power and solidarity to construct gender identities, gender prescriptions and gender ideologies. Since these signifiers concern general relations of power and solidarity, gender systems will not be immune from determinations by other dominant social structures, such as social class.

3   There will not be a single specification of gender (a single women's or men's image, language, or style) in a given society. The meanings of gender metasigns can refer to either the semiosic or the mimetic plane. They express both the interests of the dominant and their semiosic perspective, both power and solidarity. They can be inflected to produce the alternative meanings and interests of different groups.

Style as symptomatic

The first use of the word 'semiotic' was medical. Physicians attempted to read the signs of disease inscribed in bodies and symptoms, and predicted and prescribed accordingly. For social semiotics, analogies with medical models are notoriously liable to misuse. The metaphor of disease has been used too often to label people and behaviours in order to justify dubious and punitive 'cures'. Outside the medical profession, the ancient world had its own brand of social semiotician, who read the entrails of birds and other omens as signs and symptoms of the state of society, and forecast its fate. This whole body of science now seems totally discredited, revealed as fraudulent or misconceived, but its aims are by no means obsolete. The heirs of the ancient augurs are now called sociologists, who still report on the signs of viability and breakdown of social forms, though they use very different methods and assumptions, and work with a much better class of entrail.

As an example we will use Durkheim's study of suicide (1970). First published (in French) in 1897, this book is a classic text of sociology which at the same time reveals the character of that discipline as an unacknowledged species of social semiotics. Durkheim's social theory showed an acute sense of the forces he saw as splitting the unitary fabric of nineteenth-century society. Suicide is a particularly dramatic symbol of breakdown and collapse, so it was a convenient index for Durkheim to focus on. He then accumulated data which allowed him to correlate rates and types of suicide with kinds of social group. The dimensions he was primarily concerned with were power (order) and solidarity. On the basis of the correlations he found, he argued for a connection between rates and types of suicide, and a breakdown in a society's forms of regulation and/or cohesion. He labelled one type of suicide *anomic*, arising out of a breakdown in mechanisms of regulation, and a second type, *egoistic*, arising from a weakening of the bonds of solidarity and social cohesion. The third type seems anomalous: *altruistic* suicide expresses an excessive commitment to order or cohesion, though in conditions of crisis.

In Durkheim's account of kinds of social solidarity he made a distinction that has proved influential, between *mechanical solidarity*, where social bonds are strong but not complex or highly organized, and *organic solidarity*, where there is a high degree of differentiation and subordination. Durkheim saw organic solidarity as a higher, more developed form, using the evolutionary model which was so powerful a paradigm in nineteenth-century thinking. Because he feared disorder and the collapse of the existing society, he came to value order and cohesion, and their signifiers and supports, and this commitment points to the ideological basis of his theories. Yet these commitments are like an accent, a displacement of an interest which itself is not uniquely conservative. Societies historically do enter into states of crisis, when they are especially vulnerable to collapse and destruction by forces within or without. Conservatives or radicals alike are vitally interested in crises and the markers of crisis, whether their interest is to preserve a state or to overthrow it. Durkheim's study of suicide has deserved to be influential because the phenomenon he chose for study was a powerful transparent signifier of repudiation of the enabling conditions of social groups. His success still leaves a further task for social semiotics: to establish a systematic basis for a theory of signifiers of crisis and their diagnostic use.

Durkheim's theory of social structures was more developed than his theory of signifying systems, and once more we need to turn to theorists of language in order to complement social theory. A useful starting point here is the work of Basil Bernstein (1971). Bernstein's starting point was the existence in English of two types of speech, what we have called 'high' languages and 'low' languages, but which Bernstein called elaborated code and restricted code respectively. Bernstein argued for a functional relationship between these two kinds of language and kinds of social organization, both at the level of social classes and at the level of family organization. Elaborated code he saw as associated with high-status speakers on formal occasions, and with a type of family organization he labelled 'personal', in which there was considerable scope for redefinition of role relationships. Among the markers of elaborated code are complex syntax, subordination of clauses, elaborate noun phrases and verb phrases (full of qualifications and modalities), differentiated vocabularies, various types of transformation and above all, explicitness of meanings. Restricted code has the opposite qualities:

simpler syntax, restricted variety of linguistic forms, and implicit meanings. This was associated by Bernstein with a 'positional' family structure, where code relations are laid down and non-negotiable. Complementing his work on kinds of language, Bernstein also developed an analogous pair of categories to describe how different education systems organize and transmit knowledge. In 'integrated' systems, there are weak boundaries between categories, and individual items are constantly assimilated into new wholes; in 'collect' systems, items are regarded as discrete elements, to be accumulated in an orderly manner. Bernstein's study of these systems is concerned with both 'grid' (the nature of the classification system, strength or weakness of boundaries and boundary-maintenance, which we would see as concerned with the mimetic plane) and 'group' (relations of individuals to the group in structures of the semiosic plane). Mary Douglas (1970), an anthropologist, has taken over Bernstein's categories and extended them to apply generally to cosmologies and the codes that carry them.

Bernstein's work has been subject to misunderstanding and consequently has proved controversial, but what we wish to emphasize and draw from it is not in dispute. 'High' languages, in English as in other languages, do tend to be marked by syntactic complexity, specially by what can be termed 'hypotactic structures', that is, structures where clauses are subordinated in larger wholes. The phenomenon of hypotaxis can also be found on the paradigmatic plane, where differentiated vocabularies (organized in hierarchical form) mark the existence of hypotactic paradigmatic structures. 'Organic solidarity' as described by Durkheim is similarly characterized by hypotaxis, so that we can see hypotaxis in a language code as a transparent signifier of 'organic solidarity', that is, of a hierarchically ordered social structure. 'Simple' sentence structure is normally paratactic in form: the clauses are loosely linked without syntactic subordination, either in parallel or in series. The bonds within individual clauses are typically tighter than with hypotactic structures, while bonds between them are looser and somewhat less precise. In social terms this kind of structure corresponds to Durkheim's 'mechanical solidarity', and hence it is a transparent signifier of that mode of social organization. Transformational variety, in the syntagmatic or paradigmatic plane alike, is a transparent signifier of both freedom and power for those in control of them, as we have seen. The other dimension of these two codes concerns solidarity rather than power. Elaborated codes position participants at a distance from each other and from the world of referents, and hence must be explicit. Restricted codes can be implicit because they are context-bound, close to a context which links speakers and hearers in a common bond. So restricted codes express high solidarity, and elaborated codes the opposite.

Bernstein's work on education systems is concerned primarily with paradigmatic structures, the dominant modes of organizing and transmitting knowledge in a culture. Of his two codes, the 'integrated' is characterized by low boundaries and weak boundary maintenance, so that the form of the code is characterized by cohesion of the whole, though the whole that coheres in this way is formidably complex, and only an elite could grasp it. So we have a contradiction between the meaning of this code, as a transparent signifier of solidarity and cohesion, and its function, to differentiate between an elite and the rest. Similarly, the 'collect' code, with its high boundaries, signifies the individuation of knowledge and society. But 'collect' codes declare and enforce the lack of power of the learner, because of a hierarchy of knowledge in which beginners have strict limits, while at the top specialists are excluded from a grasp of the whole.

In these cases it is evident that we cannot read the signs inscribed into the codes in isolation from their semiosic context. The codes are constituted by social meanings that do not always reflect the situations and structures of the group concerned. This fact carries an important warning for any diagnostician of signs: meanings refer to and imply realities but are never themselves a guarantee of the nature and existence of that reality. The most scrupulous reading of signs must always be complemented by a scepticism based on an awareness of the inherent slipperiness of meaning in use.

Bernstein's work was concerned more with signifiers of power than of cohesion. The most important work on cohesion in verbal language is a study by Halliday and Hasan on cohesion in English (1976). This model has been used diagnostically by Rochester and Martin (1979), in a study of schizophrenic language, in which they demonstrate that the discourse of schizophrenics is markedly discohesive on the syntagmatic plane (connections that do not make sense), in the mimetic plane (references that do not make sense), and in the semiosic plane (discourse relations that are non-congruous). Schizophrenia like suicide is a persuasive transparent signifier of breakdown in the social order. Like suicide it involves breakdown in the dimensions of both power and solidarity. As an index of social crisis, it suffers from a number of difficulties compared to suicide. There is more room for dispute about the label in the first place, and the role of physiological factors in its development is also controversial. However, from the point of view of social semiotics it is clear that schizophrenic discourse collects together an exemplary set of transparent signifiers of discohesion and anomie which can be used diagnostically of those conditions, irrespective of the status of the medical category of schizophrenia.

We can set out a number of propositions to guide a diagnostic social semiotics, as follows:

1   The terms of a code itself can carry signifiers of power (order/disorder) and solidarity (cohesion/discohesion). The presence of these meanings in the privileged site of the code demonstrates their importance, though it does not guarantee their truth.
2   High or emphatic boundaries in the syntagmatic or the paradigmatic plane are transparent signifiers of solidarity and cohesion (within groups) and non-solidarity and discohesion (outside groups); and low, weak boundaries signify the opposite.
3   Absence or disruption of cohesive devices are transparent signifiers of repudiation of social relations: that is, of Durkheimian egoism.
4   Hypotactic structures, in the syntagmatic or paradigmatic plane, are transparent signifiers of complex, hierarchically ordered social structures: that is, of Durkheimian 'organic solidarity'.
5   Paratactic structures, in the syntagmatic or paradigmatic plane, are a transparent signifier of a less complex social organization, with more limited and stronger bonds of solidarity: that is, of Durkheimian 'mechanical solidarity'.
6   Absence or disruption of hypotactic and paratactic structures is a transparent signifier of the repudiation of kinds of social order and belonging: that is, of Durkheimian 'anomie'.
7   Transformational facility is a transparent signifier of freedom and power; and transformational constraints in the logonomic system signify the opposite.

These are broad principles meant to guide enquiry. There are innumerable particular forms of realization of them, in different codes and languages, from different societies and periods. To illustrate this variety we will look at a number of texts. First we will take a painting, reproduced in black and white as plate 4.2, a *Madonna and Child* by Cimabue, a Florentine artist who painted it in about 1280.

It is a typical painting of the period, Italian late medieval. Our reading of it applies to this distinctive style, not simply the individual text, and we make no attempt to an exhaustive reading either. Our concern is solely with markers of power and solidarity as signifiers of the social formation out of which this style grew. The text itself is marked by strong boundaries on the syntagmatic plane. The frame around the painting is emphatic, a simple angular shape covered in expensive gold leaf. Within this frame, the concern with boundaries continues. Haloes around the saints and angels not only enclose each in their own sacred space but separate their heads from their bodies. The chair the Madonna sits in is a massive barrier, and the saints below her are enclosed by architectural niches. The drawing style is linear, using lines rather than shading to indicate gradations in shape and mass. The represented social relations are similarly shown as fragmented. The society of angels has no internal structure: each relates loosely to the Madonna, or turns away. The saints below have no

Plate 4.2 Cimabue, *Madonna and Child, c.*1280: a signifier of an anomic, egoistic and
fragmented social form

unambiguous relationship to anyone. The Madonna does seem to be aware of the presence of the Christ child on her knee, but this awareness is not reciprocated.

The paradigmatic plane shows similar tendencies. Cimabue's colour range in the original painting is very limited, confined mainly to gold, plus red and blue. The colours are mainly flat, homogeneous colours, close to the focus of the primary colours. Only among the angel's wings is there some subtle shading, producing a range of pinks and blues. There is a similar kind of paradigmatic structure underlying the social categories. The social world is divided into sacred (saints and angels) and profane; and the profane are excluded from the presented world, so sharp is the boundary. Other categories are male–female (with only one female), human–angel. Each type is sharply differentiated from the others, but where there is more than one individual in a type (as with the angels and the male saints), there is very little differentiation, just as there is very little with categories of colour.

In both paradigmatic and syntagmatic planes, the ordering principles are strong but simple. The picture shows left–right symmetry, and upper–lower dominance. Both kinds of organization are paratactic, not hypotactic. Each coexists with the other, so this too is a paratactic feature. Similarly the angels are strung together vertically like beads on a string, just as the saints are organized along the horizontal plane, and the three spaces they seem to occupy are not related to each other or to the other represented spaces. The effect of the emphatic boundaries, added to the paratactic organization, is incoherence in the picture as a whole. In Durkheim's terms, it signifies a strongly anomic, egoistic and fragmented form of society.

It is important to note that these generalizations need to go beyond this one text, if they are to have any force. The features we have noted are typical of a style, not unique to this painting or to Cimabue. This typicality signals the presence of powerful logonomic rules which constrain Cimabue's freedom, and become an important meaning of his style. Giotto, a Florentine painter of the next generation, varied all these logonomic rules, and is regarded as a significant painter for this reason, so Cimabue's constraint was not inevitable (though the shift in the logonomic system across a generation is important here) and therefore is significant. Cimabue's reliance on Church patronage, and Giotto's support from secular patrons, are part of the specific social determinants on the qualities of style, which social histories of art attempt to illuminate. From a diagnostic point of view these considerations can be decisive. For instance, artists in the second half of the twentieth century have individually imposed on themselves specific constraints which are as thoroughgoing as those which operated on Cimabue and his contemporaries, but their 'minimalism', as the programme has been called, had an entirely different kind of source. Diagnostic readings cannot ignore the semiosic plane and the forces which constitute it, because it is always essential to be clear whose meanings are at issue, and who controls them.

The date and provenance of Cimabue's painting is known, and this allows us to see the relationship between these meanings and the society for which it was painted. Some writers have celebrated the harmonious world view of the Middle Ages, but late thirteenth-century Florence was certainly unharmonious and divided. It was a city-state in turmoil. Dante, to later ages its most famous citizen, was exiled in 1301 in a purge of his party, the White Guelphs, by their opponents the Black Guelphs. The combined Guelphs in 1266 had defeated the Ghibellines after fifty years of bitter feuding. Florentine factionalism was intense and manifest, the divisions in the body politic unbridgeable, and the overall structures of control weak. Until the Medici family established control in the next century, Florence was a battleground of competing factions and families. Underlying these feuds, however, was a massive development of banking and commercial activities that was to sustain the prestige and influence of Florence in the next two centuries, as a proto-capitalist centre. Whether or not it counts as a form of capitalism, it had most of the qualities Durkheim saw as leading to anomie and egoism. Suicide rates for the period are not available, but Dante, as a contemporary, saw suicide as a Florentine speciality, and linked it to the effects of commercialism. Cimabue's manner of death is not recorded, and there is no reason to suppose suicide, but this detail of personal biography is not important. Even in highly anomic and discohesive societies, most people do not commit suicide. Suicide rates are only used by Durkheim as an index of a much more pervasive set of qualities of the social order. Styles in art, architecture, literature and many other semiotic codes can provide further indicators. Some may prove more reliable than others, but even so, a range of kinds of evidence is likely to be better for diagnostic purposes than a single indicator.

With every text and every set of signs, it is essential to be precise about whose meanings are being scrutinized and hence, precisely who or what is being diagnosed. Our next textual example, for instance, does not define a whole society. It is an advertisement produced by a drug company in a booklet promoting a range of products for the treatment of schizophrenia. On the semiosic plane, then, the crucial relationship is between a drug company and psychiatrists, a commercial relationship between two kinds of professional, linked by a kind of patient who is classified as insane, unable to function as a social agent without medical help and medical approval.

The text as a whole consists of a double page with a drawing (with caption 'Fluphenazine. In the acute emergency admission') on the left and printed text on the right. The drawing shows a back view of a naked female figure, hugging arms in front. The figure's right side forms the vertical axis of the composition. In the top right quarter a white dove flies out of the frame; in the lower right stand two bottles of the drug; a hypodermic needle is angled obliquely through the lower right quarter. A horizontal zigzag triple band bisects the picture.

The text forms a block, set in well from the left margin to form a justified border, and with an unjustified margin on the right. The language used leans on technical medical terminology, with phrases such as 'the acute emergency admission', 'schizophrenia management', 'intramuscular administration', 'rapid clinical response', and so on.

This format of picture on the left and printed text on the right-hand side is used to organize the booklet throughout. All pictures are in pale pastel colours, which we have not reproduced, but also have a linear style. The text shows a number of contradictions, in terms of boundary strength and maintenance. Most of the picture has an emphatic frame around it, but this is broken by the dove's wings, and by lines in the lower right-hand side. The girl's body is sharply bounded on the left, but from the right her body boundary is penetrated by a zigzag and the needle and syringe, and the dove's tail is superimposed on her shoulder. The needle is opaque as it angles under her buttock, obscuring her, but semi-transparent as it crosses the bottles of Anatensol. In all these features of the text we have both strong boundaries and transgressions of boundaries.

We can also reconstruct the general form of the paradigmatic structures that organize this code, and here too we see both strong boundaries and transgression. The elements of the picture are both naturalistic (the girl, needle and bottles) and geometric (zigzags and other lines) and they come from both erotic and medical domains of discourse. The girl and the medical objects are both ostensibly physically real, but the dove is a symbol, either of the psychotic–poetic modes of thought of a schizophrenic, or of the freedom which Anatensol will give to patients. That is, the dove is a subjective–poetic image, but it refers either to the subjectivity of the patient or the subjectivity of the doctor. But the needle, phallic in shape, magnified many times in comparison with the size of the girl and angled suggestively across her naked buttock, is also charged with sexual meanings, and this compromises its classification as a medical object in a medical–scientific discourse. In the paradigmatic as well as in the syntagmatic plane we have markers of both separation and transgression. This affects how the reader can be inserted or constructed in the semiosic plane, because the picture draws on markers of both power and gender in an ambiguous construct. The patient is represented as female, naked, vulnerable and desirable to a male voyeur. Not all schizophrenics are young and female, nor are all psychiatrists male, but a specific gender relationship is constructed to signify a doctor–patient relationship in which power and solidarity are totally intertwined.

But this picture is on the left-hand side, separated by glossy white paper from the text which provides the technical information, creating a barrier between art and science, emotion and reason, transgression and control. The printed text is full of signifiers of power and control. In the print form itself, each letter is distinct and sharp edged, with white space between each word and each line, which signifies discohesion, compared to both the speech code (where sounds merge with each other in the flow of speech) and handwriting, especially cursive forms of script. The conventions of print tend to be paratactic, not hypotactic: word after word, line after line, neatly following each other. But this text is less orderly than is possible within print conventions. It is not justified to the right, so this margin represents a leaky border, like the borders on the right hand side of the picture. The spaces between words, lines and paragraphs are minimal, so the type tends to merge into a single block. It lists three specific points, each marked by a box, but these points are not strongly marked off from each other or the rest of the text. Markers of boundaries are weak, and so are markers of hierarchy.

The language of the text is clearly technical, with long words and abbreviations which act to exclude non-specialist readers. (A more detailed linguistic analysis can be found in Kress 1987.) However, there are still ' some curious features. The first three sentences are not complete sentences, according to standard English grammar. They lack a main verb as organizing principle, and are left as paratactic forms. The first sentence pivots around a dash, the second around three dots. The markers of parataxis do not stay consistent. Of the three points, the first is a 3-word phrase, a paratactically organized clause, but the second consists of two complex, hypotactically organized sentences, and the third of one hypotactic sentence. The different clause-type breaks the cohesion of the list-form and the text itself. Overall, both picture and text, and especially the combination of picture and text, carry many signifiers of discohesion and anomie, and contradictions which seem symptomatic of contradictory relations within the mimetic plane (doctor–patient relations) and the plane of semiosis (specialist–specialist relations). We may ask: if this is how the experts are, what are the patients like? Paradoxically, this text offers its own answer: the drug company constructs itself as an exemplary patient, in order to influence doctors to buy their products.

An analysis of a single text like this raises rather than resolves questions for social semiotics, since it is only at the logonomic level that we come to the study of social facts and forces which determine behaviour. Yet the interaction between the individual production of meaning and the broader systems of meaning that assert social control is not entirely predictable or unworthy of study. The text reproduced

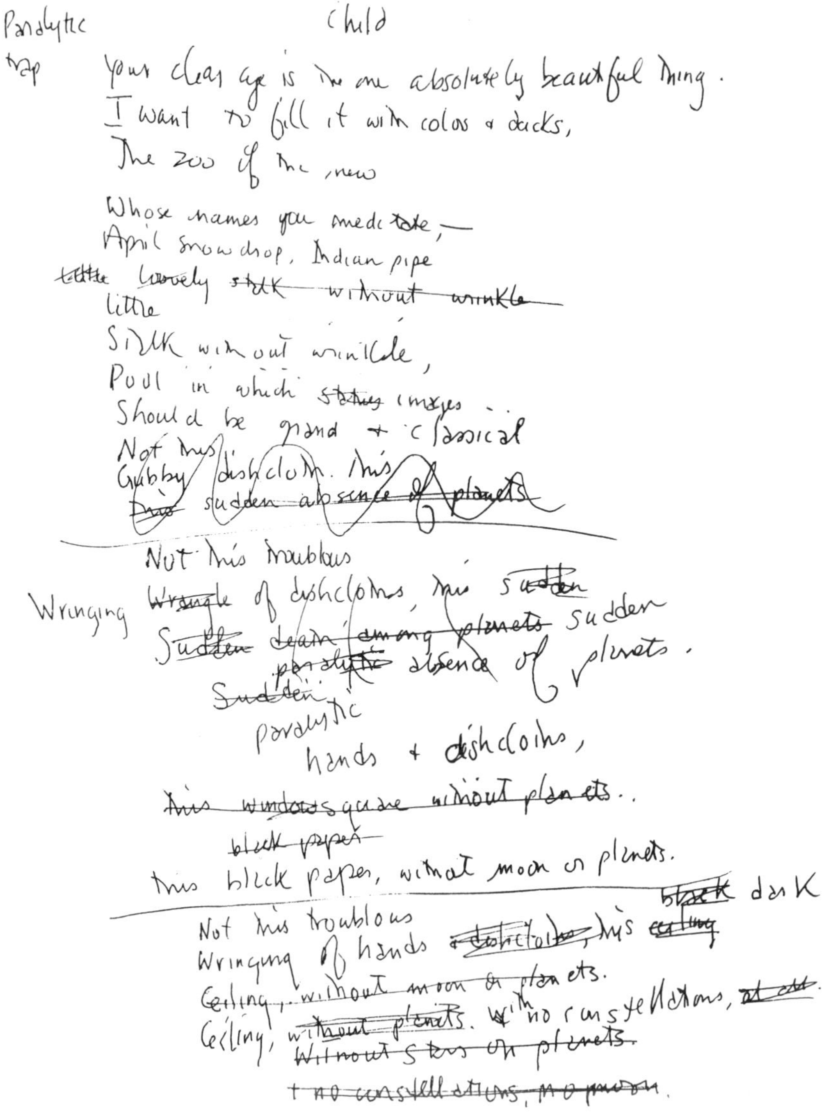

Plate 4.3 Sylvia Plath's *Child* (ms version): the syntagmatic correlate of anomie

as plate 4.3 was handwritten by Sylvia Plath ten days before she committed suicide. It was later published as a poem, in a book edited and published posthumously.

In this handwritten version, we can judge Sylvia Plath's 'style' in the etymological sense, in the action of her pen as it physically marks the page. In the title and first three lines, the writing is relatively clear – letters often separate from each other, spaces between words and lines. It is 'correct', incorporating the standards of writing which win approval in classrooms. As the text continues, however, these standards of clarity begin to be challenged by many deletions, with words and letters closer together, written at different angles, with no gaps between stanzas. Alternatives coexist, competing for the same structural place – it has two titles, 'child' in the centre, and 'paralytic trap' to the left, and the last stanza keeps restarting, leaving traces which are still not cancelled.

The despair this writing expresses was very real, as Sylvia Plath's actions were to show. The chaos that the text presents in this form would be unacceptable in a classroom, even though creative writing is often as messy as this. The poem was, however, published in the following format:

Child

Your clear eye is the one absolutely beautiful thing.
I want to fill it with colours and ducks,
The zoo of the new

Whose names you meditate –
April snowdrop, Indian pipe
Little

Stalk without wrinkle,
Pool in which images
Should be grand and classical

Not this troublous
Wringing of hands, this dark
Ceiling without a star.

The text in this form creates a very different impression. It is printed text, with every letter and word distinct from each other, with each line at a precise distance from its neighbours, and a space after each group of three. All these give an overall hypotactic order to the language which is stronger than was the case with the Anatensol text. This text maintains boundaries which were marked in the original, yet the sense flows easily over them, creating signifiers of both boundary and transgression, as the Anatensol picture did. The signifiers have stabilized the semiotic act by assigning it to a recognized genre, poetry. They also, at the same time, decisively remove it from the individual who produced it. The handwriting declared an individuality and lack of control which would be embarrassing to reveal. The poem, in print form, sanitizes it, by removing material traces left by the material social being, Sylvia Plath.

This text still retains some of her syntactic markers. In both forms the text decomposes from a coherent grammatical and hypotactic order in the first two lines to increasingly uncontrolled parataxis – the last eight lines of the print version are a string of phrases not easy to relate to each other, and most of the page of the handwritten text is like this. It is the syntagmatic correlate of anomie, more intense in the original but still recognizable in the published form. The original is marked by deletions, a process which the published form carries through to a purer degree by eliminating the markers which indicate that deletion has occurred. But the text in both forms is still marked by some deletions. The most important deletion is Sylvia Plath's own self-deletion. After the vivid ego in the second line (the strongly marked 'I' in the handwritten version) she eliminates herself from the surface of the text. It is her hands that are wringing, that are troubled and paralytic, and in the original it is her dishcloth and her death. This elimination of the self is a transparent signifier of suicide itself. So it is interesting to observe that the normal processes of editing and preparing work for literary publication only intensify these signifiers, while giving them the appearance of normality. The Anatensol text similarly deleted agents, both the agency of the psychiatrists performing their professional tasks and the activities of the patients before and after their treatment. (For example, 'management' and 'control' have the understood agent 'doctor', who is managing and controlling the 'crisis', which is what the patient has, rather than does.) These qualities in both texts are not idiosyncratic, and not normally regarded as symptoms of suicide or insanity. On the contrary, they are prescribed by the logonomic rules that underpin the language of power in many genres in contemporary discourse.

The study of style as symptom is not complete without mentioning the role of reception regimes. All three texts contain signifiers of discohesion and anomie that could be viewed symptomatically, as markers of social pathology. But one is an admired work of medieval religious art, one is a poem, and one is a piece of advertising. Each belongs to a genre where certain kinds of interpretation are ruled out, including most of the interpretations that we have given here. Works of art, especially religious, are said to belong to the domain of the aesthetic, which strongly rejects symptomatic readings of texts within its domain. The prohibitions against symptomatic readings of literary text were bent but not broken by the efforts of Freud and his followers. In general the literary establishment still polices its genres effectively

120

STYLE AS IDEOLOGY

enough. And the psychiatric establishment does not encourage the notion that psychiatrists and their successful commercial suppliers may themselves be good candidates for symptomatic analysis, though the idea is by no means unthinkable, among dissident groups in the profession (e.g., Laing 1969, 1971) and in forms of popular culture. Logonomic systems are by no means irresistible; on the contrary, the extent to which they hold sway or break down in a particular society is itself an interesting symptom of the state of that society.

5

Social Definitions of the Real

Towards a general theory of modality

In everyday communication it manifestly matters a great deal what weight we are to attach to an utterance. A statement may be said emphatically, without qualifications, and we know that we are being asked to believe that it is true. Or it may be hedged with 'I think', 'it may be that'. Perhaps it is spoken with a rising intonation like a question, and we know that the speaker is offering the statement more tentatively. Or it may be said with a laugh or an ironic sarcastic tone, and we know that the speaker does not believe in the statement at all. Words like 'may' or 'might' are referred to by linguists as 'modal auxiliaries', part of the *modality system* of language, and we will adapt this term to this whole class of semiotic phenomena. In non-verbal media the same kind of thing happens as in verbal language. Everyone knows that the camera cannot lie, but sadly photographers and users of photos can and do. Some genres are regarded as more reliable and trustworthy guides to reality than others. News footage, for instance, is regarded as more real than images from drama and fiction texts, and some kinds of fiction are seen as more fictional than others.

This kind of judgement is very widespread indeed in the practical social semiotics of everyday life. It is also crucial in determining the effects of semiosis, which only constrains action in so far as it affects belief. Contending parties seek to impose their own definition of what will count as 'truth' and 'reality', as a decisive moment in the battle for social control. As a result, terms like 'truth' and 'reality' have come to acquire a tarnished and dubious air; they are not objective absolutes to which anyone can appeal but premises created and exploited by specific competing groups. Since appeals to something like truth and reality are so fundamental in the social construction of meaning, social semiotics must be able to theorize the process. But since those categories seem to be intrinsically relative to the specific semiotic agent whose 'truth' or 'reality' it is, the notions seem unavailable for use in a semiotic theory that tries to explain them.

This is a dilemma which has paralysed semiotic theory and prevented it from developing a comprehensive and coherent account of reality and truth in semiosis. The two alternatives seem to be either a naïve realism for which truth and reality are unproblematic, or else a sophisticated idealism in which these categories are excessively difficult or unavailable. Our own solution to this problem, for the purposes of social semiotics, is to posit 'truth' and 'reality' as integral relations and places in the basic model of semiosis. As such they are never unmediated, never outside semiosis, always subject to competing forces in some semiotic process. In a social semiotics, modality is the term which describes the stance of participants in the semiosic process towards the state and the status of the system of classification of the mimetic plane. These include the categorizations of social persons, places, and sets of relations, which are from this point of view cultural places or values like any others. 'Truth' is therefore a description of the state when social participants in the semiosic process accept the system of classifications of the mimetic plane. 'Truth' is the state of affairs when the terms in the classificatory system, and the system itself, appear as 'secure', to borrow a term proposed by Trevor Eaton (1972 and 1978) to the participants in the semiosic process. 'Truth' therefore describes a relation of participants in the semiosic process towards the system of classification which is at play in the process. 'Reality' is the description by the participants of that part of the system of classification which is held to be 'secure' and which is at play in the interaction. At the time when participants are prepared to invoke the term 'truth', there seems to them a perfect fit between the system of classification and the objects which that system describes: a relation which seems at once transparent, natural, and inevitable.

Social semiotics treats all semiotic acts and processes as social acts and processes. What is at issue always in social processes is the definition of social participants, relations, structures, processes, in terms of solidarity or in terms of power. Semiotic processes are means whereby these can be tested, reaffirmed, altered. Hence questions of power are always at issue, whether in the affirmation of solidarity or in the assertion of power; whether in the reproduction of a semiotic system or in a challenge to that system.

'Truth' and 'reality' are therefore categories, from a semiotic point of view, which mark agreement over or challenge to the temporary state of the semiotic system. As categories they are no more problematic or intrinsically inaccessible to discussion and analysis than other semiotic categories, such as code, meaning, or participant. The practice of semiotics is of course itself inevitably a semiotic act, unable to declare absolute truths about absolute reality, while constantly doing so – as we are doing in this sentence. Social semioticians have no greater obligation to be troubled by this than any other semiotic agent.

Modality is, consequently, in play at all times, in every semiotic act. The affirmation of 'security' over the system of classification is an instance of the operation of modality, as much as the assertion of its 'insecurity'. Consequently all utterances (to use a verbal analogy) are modalized. What does vary is the use of modality either to affirm the 'security' of the classification system asserting its 'truth' or its status as 'reality', or to bring the security of the system into question, challenging its status as 'truth' or as 'reality': calling it 'fiction' rather than 'fact', for instance. Given that what is at issue is the question of 'affinity' or lack of affinity of the participants with the system (and thereby with each other) we can speak of a modality of high affinity (with the system) or of low affinity (with the system), or alternatively of 'high' or 'low' modality.

Modality expresses affinity – or lack of it – of speaker with hearer via an affirmation of their affinity about the status of the mimetic system. Affinity is therefore an indicator of relations of solidarity or of power, that is, relations oriented towards the expression of solidarity or the expression of power (difference). A high degree of affinity indicates the expression of solidarity between participants. A low degree of affinity indicates that power difference is at issue. Either power (difference) or solidarity may be expressed via a modality of high affinity with the mimetic system.

Modality points to the social construction or contestation of knowledge-systems. Agreement confers the status of 'knowledge', 'fact' on the system, or on aspects of it; lack of agreement casts that status into doubt. Of course, agreement and affinity may have been brought about by the relations of power-difference: that is, the more powerful may have been successful in enforcing their classifications on the less powerful. Once the classification is accepted, a relation of solidarity then exists around that area of classification. Difference of power and lack of solidarity may continue around other areas; hence the potent (and correct) identification of power and knowledge in semiotic systems of the kind we are dealing with. Modality is consequently one of the crucial indicators of political struggle. It is a central means of contestation, and the site of the working out, whether by negotiation or imposition, of ideological systems. It provides a crucial component of the complex process of the establishment of hegemonic systems, a hegemony established as much through the active participation of social agents as through sheer 'imposition' of meaning by the more powerful on the less powerful participant.

As with all signs, signs in the system of modality have their own history, which contributes to their meaning and effect. Signifiers of modality themselves are signs which bear the traces of prior contestations; they code the state of the mimetic system at one time. \Particular conjunctions of signifier with signified that make up modality systems are the outcome of semiosic processes, which register the state of social relations at a particular time. Modal signs are thus, like other signs, doubly determined: by the prior structure of signifiers, and by the socially/semiosically motivated conjunction of signifier/signified. In any analysis of modality the questions therefore are: what is the structure of the signifier (and its prior significance as sign), and what is registered by the conjunction of this signifier with this signified?

To help our theorizing and our description of this notion, and of the process, we will draw examples from verbal language, developing the key term 'modality', which we have taken from linguistics. In this usage, from which we start, modality refers to the status, authority and reliability of a message, to its ontological status, or to its value as truth or fact. Our approach owes most to the work of the linguist M. A. K. Halliday (1976), who extended the use of the term modality beyond auxiliary verbs (words like 'may' and 'might') to cover all those elements which have that function – whether as nouns, 'there is an element of doubt that . . .'; as verbs, 'I doubt that . . .'; as adjectives, 'It is quite doubtful that . . .'; or as any other form: 'perhaps', 'sure', 'kind of', and so on. Halliday's other fundamental contribution to a theory of modality was his insistence that modality is part of the interpersonal component of his functional grammar which corresponds to what we have called the semiosic plane (his other components being the experiential/ideational and the textual). Logicians who talk of modality generally assume it to be a property of propositions, placing it, in Halliday's terms, in the ideational component. Halliday's theory recognizes that modality is a matter of the relation of the participants in a verbal interaction, hence squarely in the domain of the social, and that modal forms are the traces of the activity of speakers acting in a social context.

Once this step is taken it becomes apparent that all utterances, all texts, given their social provenance, will always bear signs of modality; and given the semiosic function and origin of every item in a text, all items will be bearers of the traces of this activity and will therefore express modality. All signifiers with an appropriate structure can become conjoined with social signifieds, to produce modality signs. Very many aspects of verbal language, perhaps all, can then be seen as performing modal functions, structuring the relationship of the participants and their perspective on the status of aspects of the mimetic plane. This includes, for instance, questions, statements, commands (the traditional grammatical category of mood); tense ('past', 'present'); deixis (this/ that, here/there, the/a); so-called hesitation phenomena ('sort of', 'umm', 'er', 'kind of', 'you know', etc.). To exemplify some of these points, we will discuss the text of a brief interview. The participants are a male middle-aged, middle-class academic and an 'elderly' middle-class woman. The academic, Max, is recording some 'vox-pop' opinions on the questions 'What is language?' and 'What is it (language) made out of?' He has been to collect his car from the service station where it had been repaired, and after interviewing John and Syd, the proprietors, turns to a woman who has driven on to the forecourt to get petrol for her car. Here is the text of part of the interview:

MAX   A couple of questions very easy to answer for a radio programme
           we're doing. The first of the questions is *What* would you say
           language is?
WOMAN   Language ... well it's the dialogue that people speak within
           various countries.
MAX   Fair enough aaand *what* would you say it's made *out* of?
WOMAN   (*Pause, 8 seconds.*) It's made out of (*puzzled intonation*) ...
MAX   Hmmm.
WOMAN   Well I don't know you'd tell what it's *made* out of ... it's a
           person's *expression* I suppose is it?
MAX   I haven't got the answers, I've only got the questions (*laughing*).
WOMAN   (*Simultaneously – small laugh.*)
SID   That's not *bad* though.
WOMAN   Well it's an *expression*, it would be a person's *expression* wouldn't
           it?
SID   That's a good answer.
MAX   Thank you very much

We do not intend to be systematic here, and will restrict our comments to modality signs and their structures. (Detailed and systematic analyses of modality in verbal language can be found in our *Language as Ideology* and in sections of Fowler et al., *Language and Control*.) Max's opening is structured to pose the question in a particular way: not 'What is language?' but 'What would you say language is?' This more complex form of the question is addressed both to the status of the social relationship (male/female as gendered roles; 'middle-aged' to 'elderly' as socially constructed; middle-class to middle-class). ('If I were to ask you what is language, then) what would you say language is?' That is, the form of the question asserts a modality of low affinity in terms of the social position of the two participants: 'I might not even ask (because I cannot presume to impose ... and even if I were to ask, you might either not answer, or answer only hypothetically) what would you say ...'. The embedded question 'What is language?' is however presented with a modality of high affinity: the so-called present tense *is* (an indicator of high affinity) the classificatory/relational structure X *is* Y, both of which assert that there is a classification and that it has the status of fact.

The signifiers which are used here have a structure appropriate to the signified that they are conjoined with. So *present tense* as a signifier indicates proximity in time, and hence verifiability. It can therefore function as a signifier of a signified of a different kind of proximity, that is, social proximity, and hence of high affinity, 'truth', 'factuality', 'reality'. Temporal proximity can stand for social proximity, which can stand for ontological proximity = truth. Conversely, the hypothetical forms *if . . . then* and *would* are indicators of ontological distance, uncertainty, tentativeness, and can therefore serve as signifiers for social distance.

The modality structure reaches further, however. The interviewer, while using a question-form 'What is . . .?' is in fact issuing a command: 'Tell me what language is!' The imperative implies a structure of roles *giver of command/responder to the command*. That, however, is a social relation which the interviewer cannot assert; hence he uses the signifier of question (in the syntactic form of interrogative), with its role structure of *requester of information/provider of information*. This is a signifier constructed around difference of knowledge, which carries a signified structured around difference of social power.

The interviewer characterizes his questions as '*easy* to answer', whereas in the prior interview with the proprietors of the service station he had characterized them as 'Two questions that you can answer *briefly* . . .'. We speculate that what is at issue here is a modalizing of female knowledge as against male knowledge, notions of male activity ('You are busy, you can answer briefly . . .) versus female disability ('You are likely to be nervous, not used to dealing in definitions, this is easy (even) for you . . .'). The interviewer refers to himself as *we*, 'a radio programme we're doing', whereas in the preceding interview with John, the proprietor of the service station, he had named himself as *I*, 'a radio programme that I'm doing, John'. Again the first person singular pronoun is appropriate to express solidarity, while the first person plural pronoun is appropriate to express distance, of power, gender, or age.

Without any intention to be exhaustive, it may be useful to point out some further indicators of modality in the rest of the interview. The woman's pause is the first, obvious one; hesitation occurs where there is a need to think carefully because significant matters are at stake. Here a whole host of issues are involved, so her hesitation signals 'care in responding', itself a sign of social distance, of lack of solidarity. However, her decision to begin the answer with the restatement of the mimetic item at issue, 'language', is also significant in this context: she chooses to attend to the mimetic plane, where affinity is sought and might be established. She then gives her definition using a modality of high affinity: 'it *is* the dialogue that people speak . . .'. The interviewer's 'fair enough' is a modality of a lesser affinity – that is, 'we do not seem to agree, quite', though it is possible that this is motivated by the interviewer's wish to avoid casting himself as 'the authority'. The interviewee's pause and intonation are further modal signs, as is the '. . . how you'd tell . . .', which displaces the possibility of an answer from 'I', 'how I'd tell' to 'you', and employs the hypothetical 'would'. The tag-question 'I suppose is it?' asks the interviewer to affirm affinity, via a double modality operation. 'I suppose' indicates supposition, not knowledge, while 'is it?' requests the interviewer to confirm her supposition as knowledge, assigning him the power/ability to do so. The laughs of both interviewer and interviewee count here: the interviewer's 'this is just a game, a joke'; the interviewee's 'are you sure we can treat this as a game/joke?' Sid, one of the two males previously interviewed, asserts affinity 'That's not bad, though', in a form which starts from the assumption of lack of affinity on the mimetic plane ('it's likely to be bad') to half cancel this ('it's not bad, (even) though (this is a woman's answer)').

The woman's last answer indicates that for her the possibility of affinity has receded, both on the semiosic and on the mimetic plane. She starts with an affirmation of the modality of affinity '. . . it *is* an expression . . .', but then adds 'it *would be* . . . wouldn't it?' That is, she transforms the modality of high affinity on the mimetic plane, 'is', to a modality of low affinity 'would be', followed by the modality of 'wouldn't it?', which is lower than 'isn't it?' on both the mimetic and the semiosic planes. Sid's 'That's a good answer' attempt to assert high affinity, but that is no longer an option for her. The short exchange illustrates clearly two related points about modality. One is that modality is pervasive, appearing everywhere in an utterance or text, pressing all aspects of the verbal code into the service of modality. The second is the subtle way this both reflects and organizes the relationship of participants, responding to affinity on grounds of gender, class, age and setting.

The modality of a message, then, is not a single or simple truth value. It is nearly always a complex, even contradictory package of claims and counter-claims. In practice we have found that markers of modality often signify not only a final modality value, but also the sequence of the claims (Kress and Hodge 1979). In verbal language for instance, the order of modal auxiliaries implies the order of judgements, as the key to the overall modal value. These claims in the first place concern the fit between the mimetic content of the message and the reality to which it ostensibly refers. The claims range between the poles of affirmation and negation. All markers of modality signify forms of affirmation or partial negation. These markers are traces or signifiers of such acts which combine elements of affirmation and negation. As affirmation is a transparent signifier of solidarity and negation the opposite, a modality complex comes to signify not simply a relationship along the mimetic plane, between the message and a set of referents, but also a semiosic relationship between participants in the semiotic act. This leads to the fundamental proposition that modality values are a function of both the semiosic and the mimetic plane and are only explicable by reference to both.

Modality of visual media

The study of verbal language on its own has given to a socially oriented semiotics a model which in one respect can be misleading for the study of modality systems in general. Verbal language has, as we have shown, a highly articulated system of specialized modality markers, and context-specific rules for their use. Other semiotic codes use modality markers which are less clearly articulated, and less specific. And while it is not the case that the hearer/reader's reconstruction of modality markers is identical with that of the speaker/writer – social-semiotic systems are characterized by their heterogeneity, not by their homogeneity – nevertheless both the level of agreement over the meaning of verbal markers of modality in a given context, and the possibility of deciding on that meaning by means of verbal language, are greater in the semiotic system of verbal language than in any other semiotic system.

Nevertheless, the main points we have made about modality systems in the verbal code hold true in all semiotic codes. Readers of visual texts do seem to read the modality of such texts in a reasonably predictable fashion, and while the possible range of readings may be less narrowly constrained than in the case of the verbal code, it is constrained. Visual texts, no less than verbal texts, facilitate certain modality judgements and resist others. If we look at this process from the point of view of readers/viewers it is helpful to develop a more general category, *modality cues*, which include both specialized modality markers and also all the other bases for modality judgements in verbal as well as visual codes.

To illustrate the operation of modality in visual codes we will analyse some pages from comics: first two pages, one from *Beano* (plate 5.1), the other from *Dr Who* (plate 5.2). To conclude and summarize, we will look at some pages from a Western comic, a jumbo edition of *Heroes of the West* (plates 5.3–5.5).

Neither *Beano* or *Dr Who* would be judged a realistic text, but the modality cues which give a basis for these judgements are different in

© D.C. Thomson & Co. Ltd., 1981.
Plate 5.1 The world of Dennis the Menace

the two cases. To take *Beano* first, the drawing style is a cue which seems to indicate a 'play' text. We can label the style as 'unrealistic'. Some of the elements employed to convey that sense are simplified perspective, the flat colours of the original (not reproduced here), a compression of detail and some minor anatomical distortions. All these mark a gap between the given text and a presumed three-dimensional world that is signified by the comic. This gap is a generalized modality cue which serves as a marker as deployed in a specific semiosic relationship. For 'readers at large', those who do not have a relation of affinity with the mimetic sets of values at issue here, lack of realism, signals the text's fictionality, and the fact that they are not appropriate participants in this semiosic process. In a common-sense view, 'realism' in the visual code corresponds to 'truth' in the verbal code: a realistic visual representation is also likely to be seen as true. This is where the visual code has a large advantage over the verbal code. In the latter, representation usually involves a translation (except in rare cases) so that the effect of realism is much more difficult to produce. Hence for instance the higher status of television news coverage over that of newspapers. 'Readers at large' are therefore able to use lack of realism as an indicator of their lack of affinity with the set of mimetic values represented in the text, and hence their lack of affinity with the group which holds these values.

Of the figures, all of which are represented unrealistically, the 'good boys' are rendered more realistically, with less distortion than Dennis and his gang. Their eyes, ears and limbs are drawn in realist convention. Dennis the Menace on the other hand seems to have a nose superimposed on his mouth, and a single large eye with two pupils immediately above his nose. Gnasher, the dog, looks like a cross between an insect, a human and a ball of wool. In general, in this comic style the naughtier a character is the less realistic is the depiction, that is, the lower is the modality of affinity of the drawing style.

But as in our discussion of 'truth' and 'reality' in relation to the verbal code, so here too, 'realism' is established in the semiosic relation of participants. So while 'readers at large' are likely to judge the whole set of modality markers involved in this drawing style as signifying 'lack of realism', the specific addressees of this text are equally likely to assert their affinity with the text and its modality markers. For them as 'fans', the modality markers serve to signal their affinity with the mimetic values realized by this text. It is for them a world which exists as an antiworld to the 'realistic' world; and the code of which the visual modality markers are a part is an anticode, much in the way Michael Halliday describes the relation between language and antilanguage (see chapter 4). Readers of *Beano* therefore judge both the modality markers of the text and their significance, and also the distance signalled by them from the realistic world to which this text establishes an opposition. The *Beano* text permits its readers to establish relations of antagonism and difference from the absent but strongly implied world of the absent realist text.

This allows us to account for an apparent paradox. While Dennis and his gang are drawn less realistically, their motives and actions would seem more credible, or elicit greater affinity with readers of *Beano* than those of the softies – with their terror of words like 'ya' and their inability to lift a book. Use of a less realist style correlates here with greater affinity and credibility. But in the antiworld of Dennis the Menace, realism is the signifier of the opposed world, and therefore signifies affinity with the values of the opposed 'real' world, and a move away from realism signifies affinity with the values of the oppositional antiworld. The 'good boys' therefore tend to be drawn more realistically, to signify their alienness, otherness, as representatives of the world which is opposed by Dennis and his gang in their antiworld.

The comic therefore establishes both the mimetic values of its world, and a system of modality markers. This projected text which establishes the 'ground' of modality judgements, we will call the 'anchor text'. Readers of *Beano* know how to read this anchor-text: not directly, but rather as a function of the semiosic relations linking producers and receivers of the message, to each other and to other semiosic systems. Dennis is a realistic character for those who share many dimensions of this world, who are young, male, white and English. By a variety of means (including the Dennis the Menace fan club notice at the top of the page) readers are invited to identify with Dennis, which serves to link their own reality with his. These devices all help to attribute 'reality' to the text, and particularly to the central characters.

It is on to a base-line of this kind that the drawing style intervenes, labelling the whole action as a joke, not to be taken seriously, especially Dennis and his deeds. This acts as a weak negation of the message, but it is one which is easy to see through. What is negated is naughtiness, a mild form of hostility to authority figures – middle-class fathers and their middle-class sons. If the action of the comic was seen as an incitement to naughty action by *Beano* readers, the style would partially cancel it out, though not entirely. Beneath the partial negative of the drawing style the mimetic content is still visible. The style partly neutralizes it, but only partly.

The *Dr Who* strip has the opposite modality structure. The character and the scene represented are meant to be totally unfamiliar and out of this world in a fantastic landscape. But the drawing style uses precise detail and signifiers of three-dimensionality to signify a high degree of realism, and the artist has inserted some familiar objects into this unfamiliar world. Where *Beano* attempts to move away from the reality-

Plate 5.2   The unreal world of Dr Who

value of a realistic world, the *Dr Who* strip attempts to assign a high modality of affinity to its unreal world. But neither intends to impose the modality value signified by its style as a final value.

Modality markers, in visual as in verbal codes, are interpreted as a complex whose meaning is a sequence of modalities. A crucial stage in modality judgements rests not on modality markers, but on reference to a normative semiosic model, which includes assumptions about producers and messages, and about available sets of representations of reality. These assumptions are difficult to demonstrate, since they are neither in the text nor in 'reality' itself. Yet for a single culture, such as the one that produces both *Beano* and *Dr Who* comics, some broad specifications are sufficiently common for us to say that *Beano* gives an unrealistic view of a real world to its adolescent readers, and *Dr Who* the opposite: and that of the two, *Beano* is the more realistic.

The two strategies involve not only different relations to the readers' reality, but a different social organization in the semiosic plane. Dennis the Menace appeals directly to his readers: 'My club needs you!' A common orientation to a common reality incorporates readers into a solidarity group with easy conditions of entry, and the solidarity relationship implies a kind of truth. The content of the text, with its peer group solidarity against parents and non-solidary peers, might seem subversive, but the force of this subversion is weakened by the modality of the drawing style, and thus made safe. What is not at issue here is the affinity of the mimetic values for this group of readers. What *is* at issue in Dennis the Menace is the affinity of the mimetic values of this group of readers with the mimetic values of another group. The modality markers of the drawing style signal this problem. With *Dr Who*, the link between the represented world and the everyday world is obscure, and the high modality signals which encourage entry serve to intensify anxiety about the alien world. What is not at issue here is the affinity of the mimetic values of one group of readers with those of another. What is at issue is the affinity of the mimetic values for any group of readers. The modality markers of realism signal this problem. The society specified by the modality forms of *Beano* is a loosely integrated open group, but the society specified by *Dr Who* is an individuated elite. As with the structure of verbal modality complexes, the modality of texts like these signifies a sequence of modality operations which in turn signifies a form of social relationship.

Here we will briefly give a few further examples of the operation of modality in the visual code of comics. The comic book, the Jumbo edition of *Heroes of the West*, contains fourteen stories. Some of its heroes have claims to historical status, such as Wild Bill Hickock, Davy Crockett, Jesse James and Daniel Boone. Others are fictional, perhaps created for this comic series, or featuring only on this occasion: Curly Bill, Bob Allen – Frontier Marshal, the Cheyenne Kid and one female hero, Two-gun Lil. Finally, more difficult to classify, is John Wayne, hero of two stories. The conjunction John Wayne – Davy Crockett – Two-gun Lil is itself interesting, in suggesting a conflation of modalities in a timeless world of even reality-status. Only one story, 'Daniel Boone', provides a precise date: 'a sunny July day in 1776'. Only one story has a female hero, Two-gun Lil; only one other story has named female characters, 'Daniel Boone', which ends with the wedding of the three rescued daughters of the two male main characters, and concludes the volume.

Some focal mimetic categories are thus time/history/causality, and gender. The equation of realistic modes of representation with a modality of high affinity/reality/fact works here as in the two previously discussed comics. So the two stories involving John Wayne show him drawn in a style approaching photographic realism, signifying a close affinity between the comic text and 'real' films which 'really' star John Wayne, while not underwriting the reality of John Wayne as an actor nor the reality of the Western setting and plot. The story involving Davy Crockett shows him drawn in a far sketchier, 'unrealistic' style.

The modality cues draw on a small set of transparent signifiers. So a 'dense', detailed image can stand for realism or proximity, which can stand for present time, which can stand for factuality. An image lacking in detail and denseness can stand for unreality or distance, which can stand for past time, which can stand for fictionality. In the three extracts from stories that we reproduce here, the Davy Crockett story (plate 5.3) comes from the mid-eighteenth century, the Wild Bill Hickock (plate 5.4) story from the mid-nineteenth century, and the Two-gun Lil story (plate 5.5) can be read, by contrast with these two, as timeless, or as 'contemporary', through its possible temporal contiguity with the John Wayne stories. The three form a series in terms of visual modality, from the least 'dense', least realistic Davy Crockett story, to the more detailed, more realistic Wild Bill Hickock story, to the realist drawing style of the Two-gun Lil story.

Historical distance is thus quite clearly signified by the modality of the drawing style. Davy Crockett is given the visual modality of 'mythological figure' emerging through or out of the mists of time. But the drawing style signifies more than this. The same set of signifiers express a complex relationship between modality values and primary categories of the mimetic plane. We will look at two of these: the categories nature/culture, and gender categories of male and female.

The Western genre assigns specific meanings to the opposition nature/culture in constructing its characteristic mimetic universe. Produced for contemporary urban readers whose world is oppressively civilized, it offers them a past world that is closer to 'nature'. But it occupies a marginal space in relation to these categories, the world of the frontier, the site of a struggle between men (white, male) as carriers of culture versus nature, represented through a hostile environment, through Indians as 'savages', and badmen as those whose natural qualities of greed have not been tamed. This semiosic and mimetic ambiguity gives rise to ambiguous modality values for signifiers of both nature and culture. The natural is a universal timeless value that has been temporarily suppressed, or it is a fantasy. The cultural is contrived and fake, or it is 'like us'. The equivocations can be seen especially clearly in the 'Davy Crockett' example. Indians as things to be shot are represented in vague outline, barely distinguishable from trees or bushes, but Davy Crockett, in his coonskin hat (= nature) is more real than General Jackson. In this particular story, after the unreal Indians are slaughtered, their chief, Red Stick, is depicted (in a detailed, realist mode) deciding to escape and retreat to the woods (nature). The troops (culture) try to find them there, 'but Davy knew that it was hopeless'. He leaves this polarization of nature and culture, and the final frame shows a woman with two children waving to a returning Davy Crockett. 'Now that the uprising was over, Davy could return to his first love ... the Tennessee country ... and his family ..... Being an Indian fighter is all right, but there are some things in life that are more important than that!' This closure not only restates an ideology of domestic life, it also gives it a modality value as fully real, as the marker of reality which frames the fictions of the story itself. Thus ideology is built into a modality scheme, and the modality scheme naturalizes an ideology.

Gender is a more difficult category to track in this genre, since it is often significant in a characteristic absence. The mimetic balance (one out of fourteen stories has a female hero, and only two name any female character) reflects the semiosic conditions: these are stories about males to be read by males, concerned to construct a masculine identity in isolation. But there is one story which raises the issue of gender by its disruption of the normal patterns of the genre: 'Two-gun Lil'. This is not only different in having a female hero and a female villain. It has distinct qualities of style which signify both the gender of its subject and along with that the modality assigned to gender within the genre.

We will focus on two sets of transparent signifiers. One is the frame-size. 'Two-gun Lil' averages 7.5 frames per page (compared to 'John Wayne' at 6.5, and 'Davy Crockett' at 5.5). The smaller frame size signifies intimacy, intimacy the values of the domestic, the feminine. In terms of the modality of the genre itself, this is high affinity, low status. In contrast, large frames signify the epic, the public, the

Plate 5.3 Davy Crockett through the mists of time

Plate 5.4 Wild Bill Hickock on the danger trail

Plate 5.5   Two-gun Lil raising the issue of gender

masculine, as low modality (most unlike the world of the readers) but high status. The other difference is the drawing style. In 'Two-gun Lil', the style is linear, with clear, unbroken lines which represent people, objects and relations unambiguously. In 'Davy Crockett', boundaries are blurred, there is a heavy use of shading and overlapping, and blocks are broken up by seemingly irrational intrusions of lines or blanks. This difference serves to classify gender within the genre – with feminine equated with clarity, precision, rationality, and culture, and masculine with imprecision, energy and irrationality. It also gives a complex double modality, both to the style of 'Two-gun Lil' (as more realistic mimetically but lower affinity semiosically as against 'Davy Crockett'), and also to the more usual style of the genre.

We have illustrated our discussion of modality in visual media by reference only to one genre, comics, showing that within this genre there are further distinct genres, each with their own modality characteristics. Clearly the situation gets even more complex when we consider other visual genres: art (painting and sculpture), film, TV and print media of various forms. (For a discussion that includes TV, see Hodge and Tripp 1986.) Here we will summarize a number of general principles which can be applied to a wide range of visual media.

1   Many features of visual texts as transparent signifiers of semiosic activity (relations between producers and receivers of texts, texts and referents) act as modality cues, signifying the status of the text or parts of the text as high or low affinity.

2   Visual texts imply a mimetic content which as 'anchor text' has a modality value based on its affinity with the experience of whoever judges its modality. Given the different ways receivers can be positioned in relation to mimetic content and to texts and producers, the modality value of a text is not fixed, but depends on receiver position and orientation.

3   Since signifiers of modality are constructed from ideological categories of the semiosic and mimetic planes, modality and ideology can interact, ideology assigning modality values and modality legitimating ideological values. Conversely, a repudiation of the ideological values of a text or genre will include a drastic reclassification of its modality.

4   Different genres, whether classified by medium (e.g., comic, cartoon, film, TV, painting) or by content (e.g., Western, Science Fiction, Romance, news) establish sets of specific modality markers, and an overall modality value which acts as a base-line for the genre. This base-line can be different for different kinds of viewer/reader, and for different texts or moments within texts, but these differences themselves acquire significance from their relationship to the genre's basic modality value.

Modality at risk

In examining the complex relationships between forms of modality and the semiosic context, the theories of Gregory Bateson (1973) on schizophrenia provide a valuable framework. Bateson saw schizophrenia as in effect a pathology of modality systems, in which schizophrenics are unable to correctly label even their own thoughts and communications, to say nothing of those of others. He was thus led to develop a general theory of modality to explain this phenomenon. In this task he looked first at 'play' in humans and other species, such as monkeys. In these species, behaviour such as threat can seem dangerous, yet be responded to by other animals as 'play', as not-for-real. Governing this response pattern is a set of signals – expressions, gestures, ways of performing the action – which label the action with the modality of play. Bateson did not use the term modality to describe these signals. His term was 'metacommunication', seeing this as communication about the communication itself. In extending the scope of a theory of modality Bateson took the step of seeing this as a property of non-human communication that is basic to communication systems in a way that is not so obvious if the starting point is linguistics and modal auxiliaries.

Reflecting on schizophrenic communication, Bateson hypothesized a disruption of the metacommunicative function as a crucial determining feature. He saw the characteristic metacommunication pattern of schizophrenics as in fact a well-motivated response to a kind of family interaction which he called the double bind. In the schizogenic family, he concluded, the patient grows up exposed to parental communication which is full of double messages of love and hate (solidarity and non-solidarity). ›But the patient does not simply experience this as ambivalence. The typical pattern of this parental communication is that the words will say one thing (e.g., 'I love you') while other metacommunication signals will say the opposite (e.g., cold tone of voice, withdrawal of the body). Instead of helping to label the verbal message consistently, the metacommunication cancels the verbal message. But if the child tries to interpret the verbal message as its opposite, metacommunication signals indicate that that is wrong, too. In this situation, metacommunication proves so distressingly unreliable and contradictory that the child learns to do without it, developing a different system instead.

There is still an unresolved controversy about the causes of schizophrenia which raises a general issue for social semiotics. One school of thought insists that schizophrenia has physiological causes (see, e.g., Namba and Kaiya 1982). They may be proved right some day, and identify specific chemicals or genes that produce schizophrenic symptoms. Even if they do, however, schizophrenia will remain a useful site for the study of modality at risk. Alcoholism is a comparable phenomenon. No one doubts that alcohol is a drug with specific physiological effects, producing distortions of reality. But alcoholism takes different forms in different societies (see e.g., Everett et al. 1976). Alcoholism in different cultures develops specific modality structures attached to various patterns of social relationships, and these processes and effects can be profitably studied by social semiotics without at all denying the role of alcohol as a material substance. Bateson's importance is not that he discovered the cause or the cure of schizophrenia (he didn't), but that he demonstrated the nexus that exists, for both schizophrenics and non-schizophrenics, between forms of communication and specific patterns of interaction, with a pattern of modalities at the centre of this set of effects. In the terms we have used, he showed that modality can be an effect of the semiosic plane projected on to the mimetic plane. A pattern of social relationships can be the motor for definitions of reality and truth. Schizophrenic texts illuminate these normal modality processes and relationships precisely because they take them to extremes.

The text we will analyse from this perspective is a sample of schizophrenic writing which was included in a book about schizophrenia.

> Do I see cake Do I do the reverse of acting
> Yes Do I feel sensually deceived
> thoughts in mental suggestion in increase of
> senses in suggestion
>   senses deceptive
>   in in deception deception deception
>   deception
> vanilla lemon as lemon vanilla as the beginning
> of in in suggestion suggestion suggestion
> suggestion of the suggestions as the
> beginning of in suggestion
> lemon vanilla as inceptibility of the
> reason as lemon as in suggestion
> suggestion suggestion suggestion of
> the suggestions
>   insuggestion
> Do I see I do in suggest

(Arieti 1981: 76)

This is explained by Dr Arieti (1981: 77) as follows:

This is a typical example of word-salad and stereotypes. The first impression we get upon reading it is that it is utter nonsense. We are also impressed by the repetition of some words. Let us try, at least, to grasp the spheric meaning.

The patient is preoccupied with a phenomenon that he cannot understand: Are his senses reliable, or does he undergo mental suggestion? The world he is experiencing is chaotic, fragmentary, uncertain. Almost all the things he observes lead him to two alternative conclusions or symbols that have become prominent to the point of embracing everything else: sense deception or mental suggestion. In other words, is he the victim of his own senses, which deceive him, or is he undergoing mental suggestion, coming either from himself or from the external world? Almost everything comes to be perceived in terms of these two stereotyped concepts: deception and suggestion. He undergoes strange phenomena. 'Do I do the reverse of acting?' That is, 'Do I do the opposite of what I would like to do?' However, a few things remain like islands of reality that are not yet submerged by the invading ocean of deception and suggestibility. 'Do I see cake?' he asks himself; that is, something tangible, concrete. And later he sees lemon and vanilla, colorful and pleasant objects that stand out in the sea of confusion expressed by abstract words. Mental suggestion seems to win out over sense deception. The patient seems to recognize that the trouble is suggestion, and, as a matter of fact, the repetition of the word suggestion has a suggestive quality.

This text is an authoritative guide to the 'sense' schizophrenic writing makes, and for the moment we will draw on it. As Arieti reports it, this 'sense' reads like a profound reflection on the problematic status of truth and reality, attempting a resolution that pins its faith in physical sensations. But this sense is not immediately evident, and it is the apparent lack of sense that probably strikes most readers about the text. It has the random surface sequence that Arieti calls a 'word salad', as a characteristic of schizophrenic language and thought. But if these words are not random, if they have a sense and that sense is something like what Arieti says, then we must read this as a heavily transformed text. For instance, to interpret 'senses deceptive' as Arieti has done we can project a fuller form 'the senses are deceptive'. This is a relational form with the modality of a general truth. But this relational form can be derived in turn from a prior transactive form, 'the (my) senses deceive someone (me)'. We cannot guess what modality this transactive might have had: 'the (my) senses may/might/perhaps/sometimes/will/ have deceive(d) ...' Similarly 'in deception' can be interpreted as a transformation of 'X (may) deceive(s) Y'. Other transformational processes that seem to have occurred include a fusion of 'suggestion' and 'indigestion' to form 'in suggestion', which in ordinary language would seem a pun, carrying the implication that the processes of suggestion may be as physical, and unpleasant, as indigestion.

It is possible to rewrite the whole text in this way. The result would be a text that made sense at every point, a repetitious meditation along the lines indicated in Arieti's summary. This sense would partly be our own construction, an artefact of a prior assumption that this text does make sense, this kind of sense. Someone who had made the equally *a priori* assumption that this is just mad talk would not bother to perform these transformational reversals, and might well disbelieve the validity of our reading. So our reading has no absolute status. But it shares this with all acts of interpretation, and all the linguistic processes it invokes are very common in normal English.

If our reading is right, this text differs from non-schizophrenic English in two major ways. One is that transformational processes, mainly deletions, have made the sense almost inaccessible. This 'sense' is what we have termed the anchor text, corresponding to the backyard world implied by 'Dennis the Menace'. Our interpretation assumes that this schizophrenic conceived and could have written a transparent mimetic form of that text, which signified a version of reality clearly and directly. He has, however, almost totally obscured whatever was in this anchor text by innumerable intervening transformations, leaving us to guess at it with difficulty. But the transformations have not only affected the clarity of this anchor text. They have also eliminated almost all the markers of modality that are obligatory in English sentences. After the first two lines there are no full verbs, until the last line. The verb in English is the major site of modal auxiliaries, and of tense markers which also have a modal function. The resulting text is almost without modality markers that would indicate how it is to be read and how significant or important it is to its writer. The effect is the equivalent, in grammatical terms, of the flat intonation and indistinct pronunciation typical of schizophrenic speech. Significantly, the writer starts and finishes with a series of question forms, but does not use the question mark which labels them as questions.

This set of transformations has a double effect, serving a contradictory purpose. By obscuring his meaning, this schizophrenic has broken contact with the psychiatrist, thus expressing an extreme form of non-solidarity. But a text is still offered, giving the psychiatrist a chance to break the code (as this one believes he has done, at least in part). So the text has a crucial ambiguity, strongly excluding those who cannot understand but including those who can, in a small, intimate elite. The result is like combining the deformed surface of *Beano* with the obscure modality of the anchor text of *Dr Who*. Whereas the *Dr Who* modality strategy creates a committed cult of followers, the schizophrenic lives in a fan club of one. The suppression of modality markers contributes to a reader's disorientation, concealing the status of the communication; it leaves the text unlocated in both the semiosic and the mimetic plane. Both qualities support Bateson's contention that the semiotic forms of schizophrenic language are ideally adapted to express a complex and fundamentally ambiguous set of social relationships. Qualities of the language which are ostensibly concerned with truth and reality are only explicable if they have been co-opted as means to communicate about the social relationship itself.

Modality and control

Social control rests on control over the representation of reality which is accepted as the basis of judgement and action. This control can be exercised directly on the mimetic content that circulates in a semiosic process, or it can be exercised indirectly, through control of modality judgements. Whoever controls modality can control which version of reality will be selected out as the valid version in that semiosic process. All other versions can exist briefly but are deprived of force in the longer term unless a group refuses to let that force be negated. The sanction of modality ultimately has its source in the agreement of a group of people.

Sansom (1980) has studied modality processes in one kind of group, Aboriginal fringe dwellers in Darwin, Australia. Among the mob of Wallaby Cross, a locality on the outskirts of Darwin, there are, in Sansom's account, two major generic modalities. One is characterized as 'the word' (or 'a straight story'), the accepted truth, the official version of reality. This is contrasted with 'what somebody bin say', general opinion or rumour. The process of establishing 'the word' is long and rule-governed. First there is 'checking up la detail', in which witnesses accumulate evidence for a composite version. During this process, a single story emerges, much more compact than the component narratives, and it has powerful social sanctions. Sansom describes one incident where one of the camp women delivers 'the word' to the camp boss, who on this occasion had offended camp morality. He listened in silent submission, totally isolated and alone, without a defence in language, in spite of his status in the camp (1980: 132). In Wallaby Cross society, when a version acquires this status, it becomes forbidden to tell a different version, or to seem to act on the basis of a different version. Details which once had currency cease to exist. Someone who was not present at a happening will not be given independent eyewitness versions: only the impenetrable 'word', a statement which has the absolute modal power it has because it is deprived of its transformational history, of the process by which it came into existence, and the different versions which have been trimmed and reworked into their place in the 'word'. Only in the memory of eyewitnesses will any discrepant experience be retained. For these eyewitnesses and participants there will be two kinds of truths that may coexist, but they will have no doubt which truth has social currency and effect. The price for dissent will be exclusion from the community itself – a powerful sanction in Wallaby Cross, where the solidarity of the mob is just about all that life offers.

An analogous process occurs in the contemporary mass media, as they mount campaigns on behalf of specific interests, against sections of the community. As an example we will look at the general campaign during 1981 against leading left-wing figures, such as Ken Livingstone, Labour chairman of the Greater London Council (the GLC) and Tony Benn. This campaign seemed extremely effective at the time. Livingstone and Benn were painted as ogres, single-handedly responsible for electoral defeats of Labour. Covering the election campaign in a relatively sympathetic report one *Guardian* writer reported as follows:

The Labour Party's local organizers admit that Mr Livingstone is something of an electoral liability. 'We cannot deny that he is an issue in the elections', says Mr John Braggins, the party's constituency agent.

But he is confident that personal appearances by Mr Livingstone in the constituency will allay voters' fears. 'He's a very nice, ordinary person, he's not an ogre', Mr Braggins said.

When Mr Livingstone appears at a public meeting it is not his opinions on the IRA that he talks about but London's fight for survival under a Conservative government which he claims is intent on stripping local authorities of their freedom. (*Guardian*, 28 October 1981)

In the last paragraph, Mr Livingstone's argument, his version of reality, is given, prefaced by 'claims' (not 'says', or 'argues'), after mention of some 'opinions' (not 'ideas', or 'observations') that he is *not* giving. The previous paragraphs establish Mr Livingstone within his group, his own 'mob'. The 'word' of the local organizers is assembled by a process that is as inaccessible as the 'word' of the Wallaby Cross mob. The quotation from the Labour Party agent that follows admits only that Mr Livingstone is an 'issue', not a liability. Mr Braggins reports Mr Livingstone's attempt to establish his 'word', and his modality, through personal appearances; unlike the Camp Boss who was isolated and reduced to silence by the camp 'word' he has not accepted the media's 'word'. In the incident reported by Sansom, crucial witnesses brought against the Camp boss included his wife and his daughter. By a similar technique, Mr Livingstone is seemingly repudiated by his own allies. With his friends against him his words seem to come from a mere individual, whose words have no status as a result. Yet there would have been many who would have agreed with the criticism he is said to have made of the Conservative Government.

The same process can be seen, more crudely, in a more popular paper, covering a different election: 'Foot blasts Red Ken over poll trouncings' (plate 5.6). This article concerns a by-election, in which the Labour vote dropped by 14 per cent, the vote of the Conservative candidate defending the seat dropped by 19 per cent, and the Liberal/ SDP candidate gained a spectacular victory, having lost his deposit in the previous election. Beneath the headline is a small photograph of Livingstone's face, captioned 'Blamed: Livingstone'. Alongside is a

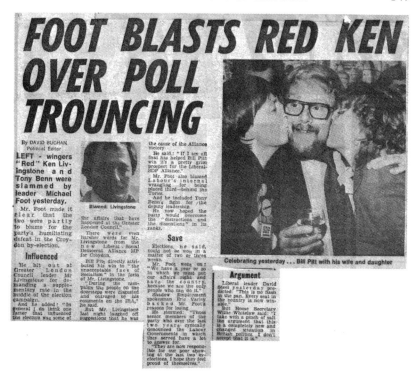

Plate 5.6 Modality transformed

much larger photograph of the victorious candidate, being kissed by two ladies: 'Celebrating yesterday ... Bill Pitt with his wife and daughter'. Livingstone is isolated with a worried frown. Pitt is being kissed by two ladies, his wife and daughter. The headline attacks Livingstone in two ways. 'Red Ken' labels him as socially insignificant ('Ken' rather than 'Mr Livingstone') and politically subversive ('red'), and 'blasts' indicates very strong criticism. The 'blast' as it is glossed below is: 'In general I do think one factor that influenced the election was some of the affairs that have happened at the Greater London Council.' Again what we have is prominence given to the reliabiilty of an individual (Livingstone), whose status is challenged by what is reported as a savage attack by a Labour leader, speaking therefore on behalf of that group of people. In practice, Foot's 'accusation' is unspecific, with many indicators of low modality: 'In general', 'I do think', 'one factor', 'some', all weaken its force. Foot's statement is heavy with modalities at its beginning, which seem partly to negate the criticism and therefore to reaffirm solidarity. The newspaper report ignores these modalities, and takes the disagreement that Foot had specifically distanced and then translates this content into a surface form that talks of violent physical action.

The newspaper headline has done two things. It has eliminated Foot's modalities – the weight Foot attached to his criticisms, and to his relationship with Livingstone – and it has transformed message-status (modality) to social relations (violence). This is exactly the opposite process to that of schizophrenic language, where social relationships are translated into implicit modality markers. But in both cases, explicit modality markers are removed, and the content of the message is displaced from the centre of attention, and its real modality is made problematic. 'Poll trouncing' has its modal markers removed by transformations, and thereby, as a noun, becomes an unquestioned fact. Labour's share of the vote in the election certainly slipped very badly, but the Conservative vote slipped even more. This second fact does not appear in the headline or in the article that follows. The headline has economically established one 'word', and disestablished another, while it has focused its main attention on a transformed modality, the status of Mr Livingstone.

Orwell's famous satire of politics and language, *1984*, focused on this technique, widely used in his day as now. In his fictional state, Ingsoc, the media deployed two figures (neither of whom certainly existed): Big Brother, benign ruler of the society, and Goldstein, the arch-heretic. Orwell describes the ritual curses directed at Goldstein, to reinforce his status as an isolated and discredited speaker whose views were therefore automatically wrong. Big Brother's statements, conversely, had a totally positive modality. They were utterly reliable. The hero of the novel, Winston Smith, was employed in making sure that Big Brother was always right, by rewriting historical records, so that the past would always conform to the present words of the Leader.

This is a process similar to that which Sansom describes for fringe-dwelling Aborigines, who similarly remove any competing historical record that would challenge 'the word'. For fringe-dwellers the process of establishing 'the word' involves the group and is conducted in public, governed by rules accepted by all. In Orwell's state, and in contemporary media production, 'the word' is established by media corporations without reference to the group which is asked to accept it as 'the word', without rules that are known explicitly by the wider group to govern the transaction. Yet under these conditions a phenomenon becomes even more visible, which must be present in Aboriginal society also. Orwell labelled it 'doublethink'. Owing to contradictions and changes in political life, the statements by Big Brother became untrue periodically and had to be attributed to Goldstein, and vice versa. Black becomes white and white becomes black. So although 'Big Brother' remains the modal marker of 'the word' for Ingsoc society, some statements acquire a contradictory modality because in the past they had the Goldstein marker. 'Doublethink' is the general condition of knowing that a statement is both true and not true, both true to experience and true to 'the word', to the social definition of reality. We can summarize this part of the argument in the following three points:

1   Social control requires the control of modality systems. Modality factors are therefore a major focus of semiotic activity and struggle.
2   Primary targets in strategies of modality control are a single incontestable version of reality, and a single classification of categories of semiosic agents as legitimate or illegitimate.
3   When personal experience conflicts with socially validated truth, the result may be not simply coercion of thought, but also a radical collapse of the modality system into Orwellian doublethink.

Difference and the construction of communities

Much of our argument so far has been that in the social definition of reality, 'truth' is not what is right simply because it is right, not what has been 'proven' beyond reasonable doubt. The issue of truth is bound up inextricably with issues of power and solidarity in a specific group. Truth is both mobilized and put to the test in every semiosic exchange. Difference thus becomes the primary motor of semiosis – different versions of reality to be resolved through semiosis, coalitions to be created, antagonisms to be overcome or prevented, or activated and declared. Because of the complex dialectic that surrounds difference, truth and reality have a double face and double function, as either an effect or a determinant of social relations.

Some of our discussion has focused on the macro-level; in the preceding section we examined how 'the word' is established in larger groups. But the process of establishing 'the word' in and for a community always necessitates and depends on the actions of actual individual social agents, engaged in countless semiotic processes. Here we wish to show in some detail the operation of these processes at this micro-level. Without a clear account of semiosic processes at the level of the individual social agent, the analysis that we have put forward so far will remain without its essential underpinning.

A model developed by the psychologist Fritz Heider (1958) is helpful in mapping the often complex processes whereby coalitions are constructed in the name of truth, or truth is produced by coalition. Heider's theory applied mainly to coalitions of individuals, but Newcomb (1974) has adapted it to mass communication systems. Heider considered relationships between each member of a group of three people or entities in schematic terms as either positive (+) or negative (−). He then distinguished between two kinds of relationships, 'balanced' (in which the signs added up to 0 or plus) and 'unbalanced' (in which the signs added up to a negative). Heider and others have found so strong a tendency towards 'balanced' relationships that people will change signs in 'unbalanced' relationships to achieve 'balance'.

We can note that a simple plus or minus may be too simple, in some cases, to describe complex relationships, and there may be problems even in assigning a value. But accepting this simplification for the moment, we still need to understand why it works, in so far as it does, and what it is that is working. If we take a typical 'balanced' triad, as in figure 5.1, we can see in general terms what is happening. In political terms, A has an alliance with C, and both are opposed to B. The plus is a crude marker of solidarity, so that a new entity, AC, is constructed opposed to B, created by the opposition to B. If we look at an 'unbalanced' triad, as in figure 5.2, we can see its political difficulties. The bond of solidarity binding A to C creates an entity AC which has both a positive relation to B (through A) and a negative one (through C). Where AC's cohesion is confirmed by the hostile presence of B, in the 'balanced' form, it is split in the 'unbalanced' form. The same

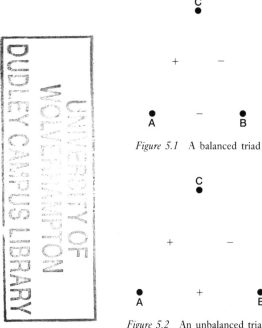

Figure 5.1   A balanced triad

Figure 5.2   An unbalanced triad

is true of the solidarity group of AB in the second case. An obvious solution is to change one of the signs, so that either AC or AB becomes a cohesive group opposed to the one remaining, who becomes 'it' in the dynamics of the triad.

Following this analysis, we can apply the same principle to any number of entities. So long as the alliances and oppositions lead to a consistent pattern of groupings, it will be stable, and the larger conglomerate groups will be held together both by bonds of solidarity and by common objects of antagonism. Where there is no consistent, simple binary pattern, unstable alliances will be the norm. But where some of the relationships are weakly specified, they are likely to be transformed to create the possibility of consistency.

This is precisely what happens in communication when there is underspecification in crucial semiosic elements, especially where certain kinds of receiver are unsure about the producer/receiver relationship or about mimetic elements in the represented world. In mass communications, or wherever the producer–receiver relationship is abstract, the producer can produce a positive semiosic relationship (in brackets in figure 5.3) by creating a mutually positive world. Where there is real difference in the defining worlds at issue we have a four-term structure (as in figure 5.4). There is obvious instability here. Either the difference between WP and WR must be resolved, or it will be the basis for antagonism. Efforts to resolve differences can come from either P or R or both, turning the opposition between the two worlds into an alliance by both retaining and masking contradictions.

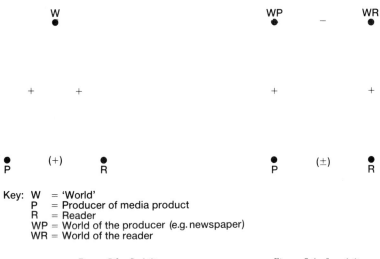

Key: W = 'World'
     P = Producer of media product
     R = Reader
     WP = World of the producer (e.g. newspaper)
     WR = World of the reader

Figure 5.3 Stability   *Figure 5.4* Instability

To illustrate these processes at work in a specific instance in the mass media, we will take examples from one issue of the mass circulation *Sun* newspaper: Thursday, 24 September 1981. We will begin with page 3. The page is dominated visually by a scantily clad 'Sun bird', as is normal practice for this newspaper. This example has Linda Lusardi holding a stethoscope to a bingo ball, looking directly at readers/viewers and smiling. Above is the caption 'Bingo Belles' and inset is the further caption 'No. 9 . . . doing fine'. To the right is the main news item. Headed 'Handy Andy flies in to rescue a sailor', it tells how Prince Andrew's helicopter rescued a sailor who had been swept overboard. It has two photographs: one larger one of Prince Andrew, and a smaller one of 'John', the sailor.

The two stories seem unrelated to each other, and to other items which take a more obvious political line. We will argue, however, that these two texts are moments of a complex strategy of constructing a community and aligning it on the side of a contentious form of truth. The notorious 'Sun bird' is usually supposed to be just a cynical device for selling newspapers, by exploiting sexist attitudes towards women and nudity. Undoubtedly, it does have that purpose. But it also has a modality function as well. The nudity, the model's direct eye contact and smile and the sexual innuendos of the accompanying text ('If this is what the doctor orders, give us more!') all attempt to establish a strong solidarity relationship between a gendered reader and a gendered producer (writer/photographer/newspaper), both male.

The effect of this text doesn't stop here, however. The community it constructs remains in existence to frame the response to other items in the paper. The main 'news' story on this page concerns Prince Andrew. There are two photographs accompanying this text. Prince Andrew is pictured turning his head and eyes, smiling – a less gusty laugh than the model's, but otherwise there are the same codes transmitting similar messages. The rescued sailor is pictured lower than Prince Andrew, a smaller photograph in less sharp focus, so that although he is smiling more broadly, the reader's relationship is less close with him. The headline text carries a different set of relationships. 'Handy Andy' establishes a mutually close relationship between the writer, the reader and Prince Andrew. The text that follows is in formal language, as is signalled by the use of the Prince's title. The three-way relationship between reader, writer and Prince is more distant and deferential. But alongside that text is the picture of Prince Andrew smiling in a relaxed and friendly fashion directly at the reader. The reward for being a *Sun* reader is to be Linda Lusardi's lover and a friend of the Prince.

This model will be replaced by another 'Bingo Belle' in the next issue, perhaps never to appear again. Prince Andrew and other members of the Royal Family, however, will appear again in *The Sun* and in other popular dailies and on TV, and the structure of the relationship will be reinforced even though the specific content of this story, his heroic role in a rescue, is forgotten. The community created by a newspaper text is not abstract, or without continuity or reference to social existence outside the text. Cumulatively the Royal Family is established as the close friend of every individual in the nation, so that not simply an image but a relationship is replicated throughout the community, in which readers feel more closely related to the well-known members of the Royal Family than they do to the unknown people in their street and throughout the country, whose lifestyles and interests in fact are much closer to their own.

The Sun's treatment of Labour politicians, especially left-wing leaders like Tony Benn, follows the same principle, but is here used to establish an intense but hostile relationship. Plate 5.7 is a photo and article from the same issue of *The Sun*. The photo of Benn is cut down so that it is the same size as that of the rescued sailor, smaller than Prince Andrew's, looking to the side with a grim expression. The article is not overtly hostile to Benn, merely reporting a confrontation with another Labour politician, Denis Healey, as they contest a battle to be deputy leader of the Labour Party. It is a contest in which the reader could take either side, but the picture establishes a strongly negative relationship with Benn. Workers or members of the Labour Party might not know who was their friend among the Labour Party leadership, but Benn's photo seems to be declaring him an enemy. The sets of relationships projected within the world presented by the media and across the boundaries of that world with readers form stable patterns which are anchored by the relationship with the reader. We can diagram the two relationships we have looked at, as in figure 5.5. In triangles of this form, the sum of the signs $(+/-)$ must be positive for the relationship to be stable, that is, for it to project a single relationship of harmony or antagonism, in which everyone can be simply classified as friend or enemy. In the case of Prince Andrew, he saves John and John is grateful: a solidarity relationship in the mimetic plane. John seems an ordinary person like us, smiling from the newspaper, and Andrew's friendliness is, as we saw, even more strongly indicated. This group can be expanded infinitely with people who like Prince Andrew (who are therefore like us, so that we like them). With the Benn–Healey conflict, we have a structure of oppositions built around the axis of the Benn–reader relationship. If that is negative then everyone who dislikes Benn (Denis Healey, or *The Sun*) forms a cohesive group, united by their common dislike. The structure would come under stress if there was a treble negative: for instance if Mrs Thatcher and Mr Benn, fierce opponents of each other, were also presented as equally repugnant to

Plate 5.7 The discrediting of Labour's left

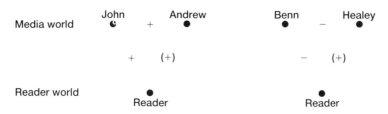

Figure 5.5 Two solidarity relationships

the reader. This structure of antagonism, one, for instance, where the electorate is completely disenchanted with all politicians, projects a social world in which there can be no stability, where the reader is offered no possibility of an alliance. Such structures do appear, at different times in differing societies, structures of 'us versus them', where all readers are (constructed as being) entirely alienated from the ruling group, or all politicians. Papers like *The Sun* normally do not offer structures of this form. There has to be the possibility of a positive and *The Sun* will provide it if it cannot be found anywhere else. That, after all, is a major ideological and political function of newspapers.

The three stories together form a sequence which has a double effect: creating a solidary community of *Sun* readers and from this basis affecting attitudes to political figures and issues, ultimately assigning them specific modality values. We can map the sequence as in figure 5.6. The Lusardi and Prince Andrew items (and many others) together construct a solidary *Sun* community, the preservation of whose unity requires the exclusion of Benn. The size of the community which excludes Benn, and which waits to welcome the reader into its capacious bosom, implicitly expands to leave Benn seeming virtually on his own. Difference is resolved partly by being displaced and exaggerated. The technique is similar to that of the Party in *1984*, where Goldstein is displayed as the unifying isolated object of hatred in the 'Two Minutes Hate' organized by the party.

It might be useful here to relate our argument to frequently recurring debates about media bias, especially around election campaigns. These are usually arbitrated on the basis of methods of content analysis, a method which relies essentially on quantitative criteria of various kinds. Our argument is designed to show that this elaborate apparatus must then take account of specific modality effects on content as in the article on Benn. From one point of view, the article could be described as objective, or even favourable to Benn and the left, since most of it reports statements by Benn and his supporters, 44 lines, against 13 lines giving a contrary viewpoint by John Golding. However, not only is modality weakened by words like 'claimed' and 'thought', it is inverted

1 Page 3

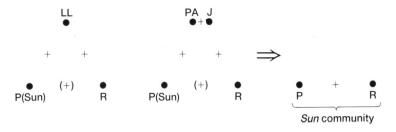

2 Benn story

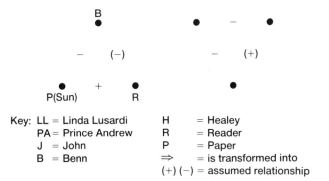

Key: LL = Linda Lusardi   H   = Healey
     PA = Prince Andrew   R   = Reader
     J = John   P   = Paper
     B = Benn   ⇒   = is transformed into
                             (+) (−) = assumed relationship

Figure 5.6 The technique of community-building (with exclusion)

for those who have been persuaded to see Benn, and hence his allies,
as anti-authorities. A key statement is 'they upheld Mr Benn's claim
that Labour Party members were not involved in the shouting-down of
Mr Healey at a Birmingham meeting at the weekend'. Modality markers
are used here in the customary way to control the response to this
claim. At its core is an incident presented without modality markers,
the 'shouting-down' of Mr Healey. This core acquires the status of
uncontested truth. 'Were involved' introduces one claim which is
labelled as in contention. It is specifically negated, but the agent of the
negation is given and situated polemically: Mr Benn.

The body which upholds this claim, the Labour national executive,
could be taken to have made a decisive intervention, if they were well-
known, independent of Benn, and trusted by *Sun* readers. Instead, in
so far as Benn has a known negative value, the national executive
becomes discredited by association with him. Readers who are
conditioned into an anti-Benn stance, especially if they have no reliable
alternative sources of information, will know what modalities to assign

and what to believe: obviously there *was* an incident, and Labour extremists were involved. The greater the protests by Benn and the left, the more firmly will this be believed. It is a powerful strategy. And it has a further bonus: the creation of doublethink. Because readers perceive the paper to be offering objectively, without comment, what they feel to be untrue, they have the unsettling feeling that they do not know what can be trusted. But Benn and the Left are attributed with this assault on modality itself, guilty of forcing the honest *Sun* to print their devious lies. And the more plausible Benn's statements, as recorded by *The Sun*, the more insidious they would seem, and the greater the anger they would generate. In this analysis, it seems, Benn couldn't win.

Part of our analysis here could be tested empirically. We would expect a significant proportion of *Sun* readers to regard Benn's claims as lies, and Benn and the Left as untrustworthy, a greater proportion than would be the case with readers in, say, Australia or America. But we can gain some idea of the effects of a media campaign such as this by looking at the overall results of the deputy leadership election which was its focus. Throughout the campaign, the majority of the media strongly favoured Healey, presenting Benn as an electoral disaster. A poll of ordinary Labour voters published just before the election showed 60 per cent in favour of Healey. Yet in the actual vote, conducted amongst Labour party members in constituency branches, Benn won by a landslide, 82 per cent against 18 per cent.

These results are diametrically opposed. They graphically illustrate a number of important features of modality strategies. First, the negative construction of Benn did seem to work, for a substantial majority of Labour supporters, people who might consider voting for Labour in an election. It is easy to see why. *The Sun* alone had a readership of over 5 million each day, day after day. Allied to other media it was able to make a repudiation of Benn seem a consensus truth. Constituency members, however, were remarkably solid for Benn. Since they were exposed to the same media campaign as the 'ordinary' Labour voters, it is clear that they reacted differently to it. Not only did they resist it: the signs are that they inverted its messages. It is important to understand how this could happen. One relevant factor is that the constituency parties are 'grass roots' organizations, with alternative communication networks, which sustain an alternative community. They were therefore able to negate the *Sun*'s line, by the same kind of logic and tactic as the *Sun* itself used: 'What a rag like the *Sun* supports must be dubious and what it criticises must be right.'

This instance shows one way in which a media campaign or concerted educational campaign can be resisted. The resistance must work through real alternative networks that bond a strong community, aware of its own identity and its hostility to the society or group which is mounting the campaign. But it is also important to note that the anti-Benn media did not lose everything in this campaign. The final result of the election vindicated Benn's supporters in their belief that they could resist the media. However, it also created a modality-split within the Labour party which fed on and exacerbated the conflicting interests within it. The split focused on Benn as a marker of truth and of group identity. Those who did not support Benn did not simply oppose the election of Benn and his supproters, they felt that rational argument and the resolution of difference by rational argument was no longer possible. When opposing groups within a larger social formation believe themselves to be operating in terms of different modality constructs, argument becomes a source of incomprehension and discohesion.

This raises one further point about usual perceptions of the effects of media campaigns. There are numerous studies which attempt to measure the effects of media on or in a specific campaign (see, e.g., Price and Paisley 1981). The assumption here is one of a quite direct relation between a text, or a series of texts, and shifts in the ideological alignment of readers, and of their social practices. Similar arguments are used in relation to debate around the appearance of violence on television, of the availability of pornography, and so on. Simply put, the assumption is that seeing violence is likely to make you more violent in your next difficult interpersonal encounter. Our argument in this book suggests much more gradual shifts, slow adjustments to logonomic regimes, to modality systems, to discursive positioning, to realignments, and reconstruction of social subjects and social agents. As we write this in 1986, Tony Benn has become an irrelevance in Labour politics, let alone in politics at large in Great Britain. We do not wish to say that *The Sun* campaign in 1981 or before and since has had that 'effect'. Hegemonic processes do not work in simple ways. But we also wish to insist that *The Sun*'s campaign against the left of the Labour Party has had its effects, together with very many other texts, from many other sources. Texts are social objects, and the production of texts involves social processes. Texts as social processes have social effects. That is how we assess the effect of the mass media in this as in other areas.

At the same time, the media campaign we looked at against 'Red Ken' Livingstone in 1981 adopted the same strategies with seemingly the same success for a while, but it did not ultimately prove so successful. By the time the Thatcher government finally abolished the GLC (Greater London Council), Livingstone had won the credibility battle. We will not attempt to explain here how this happened, except to point out that Livingstone was able to deploy a variety of alternative modes of communication to create a strong alternative, oppositional community. The point to stress is that in the battle for social control through competing definitions of truth and reality, there is not a single inevitable outcome. Resistance is possible, and modality strategies that prevail in some instances may fail in others, always because of specific, analysable reasons. A group that sustains its solidary bonds will be impervious to hostile assaults on its truth, though if its conviction of a common truth is eroded, its solidarity will be put at risk. This may seem like a circular argument. In practice it follows on from the interdependence that exists between modality systems and functions and social relationships as they are constructed and mediated through semiotic activity. This interdependence constitutes the most important single point that social semiotics needs to make about modality and the social definition of truth.

6

Transformation and Time

Semiotics and history

Men make their own history, but they do not make it just as they please; they do not make it under circumstances chosen by themselves, but under circumstances directly encountered, given and transmitted from the past. The tradition of all the dead generations weighs like a nightmare on the brain of the living.

K. Marx, *The Eighteenth Brumaire of Louis Bonaparte*

History is so important to Marxism that its central doctrine is called *historical* materialism, yet as Marx's comments show, Marxism also has an ambivalence towards history. History is the dead weight of past generations, the presence among the living of constraints from the dead, regrettable but not to be ignored. The transformation of the present would be so much easier if we did not need to bother about the past. Marxism attempts to understand the past precisely in order to break its nexus with the present, while realizing that that is impossible.

There is a similar contradiction, less clearly recognized, in semiotics. As we have seen, Saussure did not in fact deal a death blow to diachrony, and the eagerness of semioticians to attend its prematurely announced funeral is symptomatic. In spite of the official obsequies, diachrony did not disappear. Peirce's notion of semiosis as process emphasized movement and time. He also offered a history of culture in terms of successive 'habits of thought', essentially the same project as Foucault later undertook, in his 'archaeology' of successive epistemes. In structural linguistics, historical inquiries lost great momentum but again did not entirely disappear, and the claims of history are beginning to be recognized again. Chomsky's theory of transformations restored one aspect of diachronic process to the centre of the linguistic stage, and this provided a new interest both in the history of language, and in children's language, though Chomsky's interest in children's language was more concerned with the anti-historical category of innateness. Outside semiotics and linguistics, history still has an honoured place in academies, in 'history' departments, in literature, art and philosophy departments, as well as in museums, tourist industries, popular culture and rhetoric. Still further afield, Einstein was integrating time as the fourth dimension into physics at precisely the same moment that Saussure seemed to be removing it from semiotics.

Social semiotics, then, cannot ignore or equivocate with history and time, nor can it smuggle this dimension in through some back door. It must do more than take account of the diachronic dimension, it must accept it as a necessary and integral part of social semiotics. The solution to the problems of history in social semiotics – where it begins, how it is structured, and how it bears on the present – is to dissolve the boundary between diachronic and synchronic in favour of a single unitary field. Every semiotic structure inevitably exists in space and time, and every semiotic process takes place in those dimensions. The time taken to read a single picture or a word may seem negligible; so may the time taken by a brief conversation. But to ignore the temporal dimension is to introduce a distortion, and such distortions have a cumulative effect. Precisely because time is removed from the study of the sequence of texts that constitutes the evidence of history, history itself cannot be connected to the present. Its meanings become potent but unassimilable, leaving the meanings of the present all too glib but mysteriously lacking in power. The problematic relations of history with the present disappear when the semiotic field is seen as always and only constituted by relations in a space–time frame, together with transformations of those relations. Within this unitary field, 'history' offers structures and transformations of a formidable scale, which can helpfully be explained by referring to simpler, smaller-scale structures of semiosis. History also makes available some elemental large-scale structures and processes which help to explain the nature and tendencies of innumerable individual acts of meaning and interpretation. History is ideologically constructed temporality, at whatever level, on whatever scale. Time in semiosis is always history.

Towards a materialist theory of transformations

We will begin with a site of transformations where the transformations are familiar and visible, and clearly important to interpretation. Everyone writing an essay knows that the final form has drawn on previous drafts which are transformed by stages, some of which partially survive to trouble the smooth surface of the finished text. These earlier drafts did not come out of nowhere. They draw on items from other texts, some of them recorded through citations and footnotes, others not acknowledged and yet others lost from memory. All of these texts had (or still have) a material existence. The transformations we are talking about here are not mysterious and intrinsically unknowable. But it is also the case that for most of the time we do not have available to us all of the texts that went towards the final text. We have to guess, to construct the history that makes sense of this text. Our judgement of the text includes our sense of this history, and what transformational work its author seems to have done. A writer whose works bristle with references has transformed an impressive range of works, even if the conclusions don't get far. A writer who is thought to have assimilated and reworked a body of complex ideas is regarded either as an 'original' thinker, or else as wrong-headed (depending on the judgement of the original body of ideas).

Because we have to guess so extensively, we are liable to be deceived. Authors can elide texts they have read and pretend to have read others that they haven't. They construct a pseudo history for their text which may guide our own construction of its history, or which we may suspect and resist with a counter-history of our own. A materialist theory of transformations does not need to deny this process of projection and counter-projection. On the contrary, these processes are themselves material facts, embedded in the social processes of struggle and negotiation, incorporation and resistance that are characteristic of semiosis. These processes, transformations and the projections of transformations, are found with signs, texts and messages in all codes. Every act of decoding rests on a theory of transformations and some strategy for reversing transformations. A materialist theory of transformation regards transformations as social/material processes, linking socially/historically situated texts, in processes which have historically and socially located agents.

It may be useful here to make one other point concerning our use of the concept of transformation. In semiotics, the most detailed analyses of transformational processes were those provided in the earlier work of transformational generative grammarians, in the period between 1957 and 1970 approximately. That work assumed that transformations were processes which operated on specified structures, producing specific structural changes, and new resultant structures. In the case of syntactic structures these could be, and were, relatively well specified, at least at the initial and final stages. In many of the cases which we discuss in this chapter, and in this book, no such clearly specified structural descriptions exist, and nor do we or can we provide them. That is, the material is both more complex, and infinitely less well described than language is. Our hypothesis is therefore (1) about the existence and status of such processes, potentially at least open to description in further work in semiotic analysis, and (2) an assumption that, although complex, the processes are actually performed constantly by social-semiotic agents in the course of everyday living.

To illustrate, we will take a cartoon by Patrick Cook (*National Times*, 13–19 June 1986), reproduced as plate 6.1. This cartoon marked the exit from politics of Premier Neville Wran of New South Wales, whose last years in office had been marked by scandal after scandal. This background is essential to understanding the point of the joke, which has an amazed bird watching its shit bounce off without a trace. This image is a transformation of the vulgar verbal phrase 'the shit sticks' (something that many of Wran's enemies hoped would happen, and his friends feared had happened). In this case it's clear that the joke works basically by means of a series of transformations. These act on an open set of texts describing Wran's stormy premiership (it doesn't matter to the joke which or how many of these incidents are remembered). They also act on a specific verbal phrase, transforming it from one medium into another – although that verbal phrase was itself a transformation

Plate 6.1   A politician as his own monument

of a highly charged physical image into words, so Cook has in some respects simply reversed that earlier transformation.

The bird doesn't simply repeat the phrase from its earlier political context. The phrase 'the shit sticks' has been transformed into its opposite: 'Amazing! None of it sticks!' 'Amazing' implies an earlier form 'I am amazed by this', from 'This amazes me', which implies in turn an earlier 'I expected (that shit would stick)'. 'None' is a strong negative, which implies a long sequence, somewhat as follows: 'I expect shit to stick', 'This shit doesn't stick', 'Nor does that and that and that . . .', 'None of it sticks'. The word 'None' implies a lot of examples of shit, none of it sticking. It is possible to treat 'None' as just another word added to the original sentence, not a major transformation. However, what we have is a relationship between at least two texts, one of which has the opposite meaning to the other. 'None', in this interpretation, is a single word which, however, signals a series of transformations, acting on a series of texts. Negation in general, then, must be seen as a transformational process, a relation between actual or hypothetical texts.

But Cook's minimalist text is dense with meaning because of a whole series of implied transformations. For instance, the line drawing pretends to be a representation of a statue of Wran, a transformation from a three-dimensional to a two-dimensional shape. This three-dimensional text is a key stage in the meaning of the cartoon. Without recognizing its necessity, it is impossible to see the joke. But no one is meant to suppose that this statue actually exists. The status is a pseudo text, projected by pseudo transformations. We may suppose that Cook must have more or less imagined it: we know we aren't being asked to suppose anything more. Part of the joke is to imagine the statue; another part is to deconstruct this image. The transformational work we are invited to perform is complex and seemingly contradictory, but the contradiction is itself part of the meaning of the joke.

The motivation for this transformation-that-isn't, and hence its meaning, could come, we guess (guesses are essential in decoding transformations) from an article by Colleen Ryan in the same issue of *The National Times*, which commenced: 'Neville Wran's last year of government in New South Wales will be remembered for monuments – projects designed to outlast a man's political life and which might have lent immortality to his reign' (p. 3). Cook's cartoon seems like a comment on and transformation of some parts of that text. So the statue-that-never-was is a substitute for various other monuments which will exist, but at considerable expense ($A 900 million, according to the article): a monorail, a tunnel under Sydney Harbour, and a casino. These projects could be justified as public-spirited works. Cook's transformation of them (if that is what it is) into a statue of Wran implies a judgement on them, that they are simply Wran's ego writ large – the same judgement that is made explicitly in the Ryan article. Transformations are not statements, but in this case we can see clearly what is true in many other cases as well: assumed transformations imply statements and the meanings associated with them. Transformations are not only operations on structures of meaning. In drawing readers into an exploration of (possible) paradigms of statements, that is, explorations of mimetic systems, transformations project series of meanings and, by a kind of shorthand, become meaningful themselves.

Cook's implied comment is a complex and subtle one, brought out by the precise transformational work he has done and has asked readers to reproduce. For instance, the representation of the head is indistinguishable from Cook's normal caricature of Wran. The cartoon text, then, has a double source: a statue (which doesn't exist) and a man (who does). The casual drawing style, full of deletions, allows both to be projected. The ambiguity is itself significant. Just as the public works are represented as equivalent to a statue, so the statue is represented as equivalent to the man. Wran is his own statue – or, Wran is already a monument, a public phenomenon, not a real flesh-and-blood person. We can schematically represent the processes as follows:

$$\left.\begin{array}{l} \text{Text A (Wran as politician)} \\ \Downarrow \\ \text{Text B (Wran as statue)} \\ \Downarrow \\ \text{Text C (Public works as statues)} \end{array}\right\} \Rightarrow \text{Text D (Cartoon)}$$

This maps both the processes of change (whereby the successive texts are significantly transformed) and also the survival of each of these texts in the final text D, which deliberately signifies each of the earlier texts.

The pedestal beneath the Wran statue has indecipherable writing on it, which we can guess is Wran's name. This is a kind of deletion transformation. Deletion transformations are among the most common in semiotics. This example shows that the meaning of a deletion transformation is not given by the fact of deletion alone. The meaning includes a projected agent and motive. In this case, we are given a number of implied agents and motives. If we see this as a representation of a statue, then it is presumably time and the weather that has eroded the name. So part of the meaning is that this cartoon is situated in the distant future, when Wran's name has been forgotten but his statue/monuments still survive. Even with this interpretation we have a double meaning: either (1) shit won't stick when Wran's name has faded from history or (2) even after his name has been lost, the Wran magic will prevent the shit sticking. But the deformation of the name has another agent, Patrick Cook, whose deletion of the name expresses hostility, we may guess, the same hostility as is expressed by the deletion of Wran's three-dimensional humanity. It is important to stress that deletion of itself doesn't mean hostility, though that is a common core meaning which deletion has. The meanings we have derived from this particular act of deletion have been complex and specific to the text. They are guesses, not facts. The interpretation of texts is always a matter of guesses, not facts. But some guesses are richer and/or more plausible than others. A transformational reading of a text is often hypothetical to some extent, but this is by no means a reason why semioticians should avoid attempting it.

Semiosis in time

The succession of transformations that link a specific text to prior texts takes place in time, real or hypothetical. Equally important, acts of semiosis take place in time also. The flow of semiosis can be understood as itself a series of transformations, organized by logonomic systems or escaping from their control. A transformation is defined as a structural change, from structure A to structure B. The structures at issue in semiosic transformations are the structures linking the semiotic participants to each other and to the series of messages and meanings they are producing.

To examine transformation within discourse a good starting point is with dialogue. The following passage is taken from *The Dreamers*, a play by the Aboriginal dramatist, Jack Davis (1982). The characters are Aboriginal: Dolly the mother; Meena, her 14-year-old daughter; Shane her 12-year-old son.

SHANE   What's the capital of London? Meena! What's the capital of London?
MEENA   Aw Mum, he's gotta be joking.
DOLLY   Why?
MEENA   Didn't you hear what he said? How dumb can you get?
SHANE   OK, I just asked a question.
MEENA   Now listen, Shane, London is the capital city of England.
SHANE   Oh (*Pause*) Where's Eden-berg?
MEENA   Where?
SHANE   Eden-berg.
MEENA   I dunno, give us a look.
SHANE   See. You don't know everything.
MEENA   Edinburgh, stupid – the capital of Scotland and Ireland. The country is spelt I-R-E-L-A-N-D, not I-S-L-A-N-D.
SHANE   (*resentfully*) I dunno. (*He throws the homework book down, unfolds a comic and begins reading.*)

DOLLY   Meena, take that rubbish out and put it in the bin. Come on, there's enough flies in here already.

MEENA   Aw, Mum, make Shane do it. I gotta finish a ten-page assignment on Aborigines tomorrow.

If we take this text as a sequence of utterances we are faced with a seemingly insoluble problem of explication. Why do the individual utterances follow in the order they do? Or what does it mean that they have this order? However, if we take semiosic structures as primary, we have a clear answer to the second question, and a framework for addressing the first. The opening moves of the dialogue (Shane's and Meena's first lines) can be represented as in figure 6.1. The relation between the semiosic structures which constitute the two utterances reveals itself as a complex transformational one, in which various elements of structure A are transformed in B. In any dialogue, it is normal for the participant roles to be transformed. The system of pronouns marks one site in texts where this transformation is carried out regularly, as 'I' becomes 'you' and vice versa (see Benveniste 1971 for an important discussion of pronouns in discourse). This reclassification of the participants is so normal and continuous that we usually don't notice it, but it is a crucial transformational process none the less.

In this exchange, however, the transformational process is more complex and extensive. Shane in fact asks the same question twice. The main difference between the two comes from the addition of 'Meena!' which attempts to transform Meena's significance in the semiosic structure, by a change from a question (in which Meena

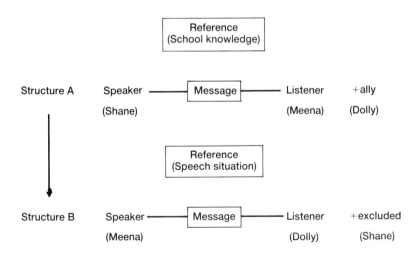

Figure 6.1   Semiosic structures: a complex transformational relationship

among others might have the required knowledge) to a command (for Meena to give the answer). Dolly the mother is present in the semiosic situation, though seemingly invisible in it at this point. A minimal account of the semiosic structures includes the referent and its social construction and meaning. Shane is doing schoolwork, and the question comes from this domain. In fact school carries its own semiosic structures into this Aboriginal household. Shane is repeating a school type of question. By doing so, he seems to occupy the place of the schoolteacher, a position of power, and puts his sister into his own position, of ignorant answerer. But the transformation is a double one, because it is Meena, like the schoolteacher, who knows the correct answer, or Shane supposes she does. The subject-matter of the question is part of this complex social process, through its status as school (and hence non-Aboriginal) knowledge about non-Aboriginal culture. Given the status of Aboriginals like Shane and Meena in white Australian society, the nature of the question has a further transformation of both of them into honorary Whites, who are being acculturated into English culture.

Meena's reply, however, isn't what Shane predicted or tried to construct. She transforms herself to speaker, as requested, but addresses her mother, thus transforming Shane into an object of discourse, not a participant, a 'he' in her text, not a 'you'. She also negates the topic of the conversation, replacing school knowledge with a metacomment on the status of the previous utterance. Her utterance is a statement, not a question, establishing a relation of equality and solidarity with her mother, which excludes her brother. Membership of this solidarity group requires a specific body of knowledge, white school knowledge, which may not be shared by Dolly (and isn't, as it turns out). What matters is the social categorization of the topic, in the ongoing process of the conversation. The fundamental terms of this categorization are power and solidarity. The ambiguous function of knowledge comes from the fact that it can define both. Shared knowledge (and the process of sharing it) confirms solidarity. Control of knowledge, on the other hand, signifies and underpins relations of power.

The next utterance, by Dolly, involves a further semiosic transform-ation. Instead of matching Meena's statement with a congruent one, she asks a single question: 'Why?' This transforms her from an ally to a questioner who is not incorporated into the community constituted by White school knowledge, who occupies a place much closer to Shane than to Meena. Meena tries to recuperate her transformation of Dolly by asking 'Didn't you hear what he said?' as though Dolly's question showed only that she hadn't heard what Meena had just said, not that she rejected Meena's school knowledge and her status as honorary White. But Dolly says nothing, a further negation of Meena's attempted transformation. Dolly's nothing has a significance that comes from her place of authority, as mother, in the social structure, which remains essentially the same from beginning to end.

The transformational sequence we have just looked at doesn't make full sense in its own terms. We need to understand other social structures in order to understand this conversation. First there is the structure of the Aboriginal family, with the mother able to control her children, who slowly and reluctantly still obey her. Then there is the structure of Australian society, and the place of Aborigines in it. All participants essentially take both these structures for granted throughout this short stretch of conversation. It's tempting for the analyst to see these structures as invariant and unchanging, a permanent and fixed background to the semiosic transformations. However, they are not in fact outside time: they simply move according to a different time scale. Ten years previously, when Meena was 4 and Shane was 2, the family relations would have been different. In ten years' time, they will be different again. The dialogue occurs at a transformation point, for the children and for the family relationship. Meena and Shane are close to adolescence, a stage marked in traditional Aboriginal culture by mediating rituals to mark a specific transformation. White Australian culture has a less marked set of rituals mediating this transformation, but it occurs.

The relations between Aboriginals and Whites also are not static, though the time-scale for transformations here is very different. Two hundred years ago, Europeans had not invaded Aboriginal Australia. One hundred years ago the relations between Aboriginals and Europeans, and hence the social significance of Aboriginal and English knowledge, was very different. What the relations will be in another hundred years time is impossible to predict. But none of these transformations takes place outside time or outside history. What must be insisted on, on the contrary, is that transformations on all these time-scales – at the levels of the exchange, the human life-span, and the historical epoch – are equally part of history, part of a single diachronic whole, just as in a clock, the spring may seem still as the second hand moves visibly around, yet they are both part of a single system.

The text we have looked at shows traces of these other histories. We can describe in everyday language the relationships of the three levels of diachrony, as they work in this instance, and for many purposes such a description is adequate. This Aboriginal family is at a turning point, as far as the two children are concerned. Both are faced with new roles in the near future, involving new areas of power, but also, potentially, new areas of weakness, in a labour market where Aborigines are still discriminated against. Gender roles will also break the solidarity bond between them as brother and sister. One option does exist: to take advantage of the opportunities now offered by White Australian society to a select number of congenial, Europeanized Aborigines. This access to power, however, has a heavy price: the rupture of bonds of solidarity with other Aborigines. The dialogue shows, in miniature, precisely this struggle being acted out. Meena is trying out the role of White Aborigine, repudiating Shane for his ignorance of White culture, while trying to retain solidarity with her Aboriginal mother, by pretending that the mother also has undergone the same transformation. The assignment she is trying to do, which she hopes would absolve her from her duties as an Aboriginal daughter, happens to be a project on Aborigines, but this simply reinforces her alienation from her family and people, since the school curriculum transforms them into objects, seen from a White point of view. Shane, in contrast, is defined as a failure because of his lack of knowledge of White culture, and discouraged (by Meena, on this occasion) he picks up, not a spear or a boomerang, but a White comic.

This dialogue is a fiction, but it illustrates the dynamics of innumerable incidents which cumulatively make up history. Analysing it more formally, we can see how it articulates with that history. The short exchange contains a set of contradictory transformations of the relations of these three people. To illustrate, we will take the versions of the relationship between Dolly and Meena. The starting point is one where Dolly has a relationship of power (>) and solidarity (+) with her daughter. There are moments when one or other of them constructs the relationship as one of equality (=) and solidarity on the grounds of age; as Meena's superiority but non-solidarity to her mother (on grounds of her identification with White status); or as her new equality and solidarity with her mother (by a transformation of them both to Whites).

Base relationship	Set of transformed relationships	Site of transformations
	D + − M (M: Young ⇒ Old)	Age
D + > M ⇒	D − < M (M: Aboriginal ⇒ White)	Race
	D + = M (M and D: Aboriginal ⇒ White)	Double race

All these transformations are found in the single exchange, coexisting within it. The situation is the same as Saussure noted in diachronic linguistics, where alternatives coexist for a while, at the level of *parole*, in what he called a synchronic state. But though these alternatives coexist, at this stage in the life of this family, in this stage of culture, one cannot read off the overall direction of longer-term changes from a study of a small arbitrarily chosen bit of text. This directionality will come from the blocking of some transformations at either or both extremes of a transition period. The forces that lead to the blockage can not be seen unambiguously in a single exchange: they are clearly visible only in a longer diachronic span. Twenty years ago, for instance, the transformation Aboriginal ⇒ White would have been very difficult for an Aboriginal. Now it is relative more easy, though still difficult enough. As a result, the single transformation (Meena: Aboriginal ⇒ White) is more likely than the double transformation (Meena, Dolly: Aboriginal ⇒ White). Such a differential transformation is likely to split the generations and break the solidarity of the Aboriginal family.

What a precise transformational analysis of a stretch of language can show is a fuller set of possibilities for change than are realized in a specific social transformation. Meena, for instance, is shown here hypercorrecting for White culture. Only with 'Edinburgh', which she makes the capital of Scotland *and* Ireland, does she make a mistake, which White Australians of her age might also make (though probably not an English schoolgirl of the same age and ability). However, later in the play she is shown coming home late, from a date with her Aboriginal boyfriend, having left school and abandoned the difficulties of White culture for Aboriginal solidarity. That is just one possible individual history. Even that is not definitive, since at a later stage in her life she might, given different circumstances, opt for White culture, or at least a measure of it. And even if she seemed to opt for a position like Dolly's when she married, she would still have the option of taking a different position if a daughter attempted to co-opt her, as she did with Dolly.

Synchronic syntagms and frozen time

To posit only three levels of diachrony is of course only a simple approximation. There are innumerable levels of the diachronic, innumerable scales within which discourse makes sense. The exchange we quoted would have taken about one minute. In spoken language individual utterances take a shorter time, and individual words in English take on average about half a second. But words themselves are made up of individual sounds, phonemes, which are produced at about 12 per second, with an upper limit of about 20 per second if intelligibility is to be possible. The point of mentioning these figures is to note that at these levels events move so fast that they seem instantaneous and static, though brief, just as at other levels events move so slowly that again they do not seem to move. The difference is one of degree. But these differences of degree crucially affect the acts of production and reception of meaning; and the same is true for all other kinds of sign.

To illustrate, we will take a single word, still from the dialogue we have quoted. Shane says 'Meena!' between his two questions. This word could stand alone. It is, therefore, a syntagm, since without syntagms there is no meaning. In the spoken form, it seems not to have a structure in time, or so the written form suggests. Because of this quality, we can call it a *synchronic syntagm*. But it is, nevertheless, still not independent of time. The word 'Meena', immersed in normal speech, would take about half a second to say. As an exclamation, it could take a full second – twice as long. The extra time is taken up with an extension of the phonic substance, and in particular of an intonation pattern, which takes place in its own time-scale. A number of patterns are possible: either Mèena, (heavy emphasis on the first syllable, falling tone, imperative); Mèéna (rise and fall; command plus question); or Meéná (double rise; question or plea), as well as a large number of other variations. The combination of word and intonation pattern acts equivalently to a linear syntagm unfolding in time: 'Meena, I order you to tell me/please tell me/could you please tell me.' But these forms all unfold in time. The single utterance 'Meena' seems to present a syntagm in a single moment, which is then extended so that the syntagm can be read.

The conventions of writing in fact present it as a diachronic syntagm: 'Meena + !', though this becomes a synchronic syntagm again when taken in at a single fixation of the eye. The system of writing introduces an asymmetry between production and reception here, so that a syntagm can be synchronic as it is produced, but diachronic as received, though this depends on the specific reader, or the conditions of reading. The distinction between synchronic and diachronic syntagms is relative, not absolute; it is a condition of acts of production and reception of meaning, in physical space and time. But precisely because it does have this material reality, the distinction powerfully affects judgements on the status of a message. Syntagms which seem synchronic, outside time, appear to be more valid, since the relationship they assert seems established as identity in a single time and place. So 'Meena!' asserts power more persuasively than 'Meena, listen to me!', since it seems to suggest that the very nature of the name is to be included in an imperative.

Synchronic syntagms can be deployed in space – as with writing or painting or photography. They can also exist as a combination of two media – as for instance in the sound-track and the images in a film, whose conjunction Eisenstein has called 'vertical montage'. But synchronic syntagms can even be produced in the same time and the same medium, as is happening with 'Meena!', where the two systems of intonation and phonology, both carried in the medium of sound, coexist in significant conjunction. The same phenomenon occurs in painting and film where colour codes and representational codes coexist. The phenomenon is widespread in human semiosis. In fact we can go further and say that human message systems are typically multisemiotic, consisting of many kinds of synchronic syntagm, which have the contradictory quality of seeming so transparent as to be almost not perceived as messages, and yet are peculiarly difficult to analyse or to resist.

Montage as transformation

In order to extend this discussion to a general semiotic principle, we will consider visual media. Eisenstein's pioneering theory of film (1968) focused on montage as the primary syntagmatic principle of cinema: sticking pieces of film together to create specifically filmic meanings. It is true that a full account of the language of film must include many other juxtapositions – compositions within the frame or *mise-en-scène*, or 'vertical montage' as Eisenstein labelled juxtapositions of image and sound-track, or scenes and episodes. Yet Eisenstein's stress on shot-montage is still the right one for a social semiotics of film, because each strip of film will normally have been shot from a single camera occupying a single space and time; and that positioning signifies the social relations which constitute the utterance. So a montage of shots is a transformational sequence of the same kind as the sequence of utterances in spoken discourse, involving semiosic transformations in the same way. Its precise history is crucial to its interpretation; and it interlocks in the same way with other diachronic structures and transformations, operating at other levels.

To illustrate, we will take (plate 6.2) two pages from a *Wonderwoman* comic. The principles that we apply would apply equally to a shot sequence from film or TV. On the first page there are five frames, on the second only one. In each frame, a point of view is clearly indicated, as though for a camera. This seems to position the reader in the same spot as the artist, fusing their viewpoint so that they have a single relationship to the action. The sequence between the first two frames is a complex transformation, involving more than just a reversed point of view. Page 1, it must be remembered, is page 1. There is no other introduction: this *is* the introduction. Page 2 provides the information that more usually begins a story in this genre of comic. So the reader of this story starts cold. She probably knows about Wonderwoman (we say 'probably' at this stage: in fact, the exact relationship, and the different constructions of these readers, mustn't be taken for granted). Her primary relation to the comic is as consumer to product, with a mediated relationship to the producers/artist. It is this structure which is decisively transformed by the initial frame.

Plate 6.2 The synchronic and diachronic syntagm of Wonderwoman

The initial caption, 'Observe . . .', is an imperative, placing this free consumer in a subordinate position, required to obey without question or understanding. The angle of vision is from slightly above, a transparent signifier of power, and from inside the scene of the coming narrative, a transparent signifier of participation. But the frame is narrow, excluding the surrounding scene and the context that might explain what is going on. There has been no 'establishing shot'. The

artist presumably knows much more than the reader, and far from sharing this knowledge he is withholding it, able to manipulate the reader via this asymmetry. Far from an identity, as is signified through the viewing position, there is a relationship of power between artist and reader, and deliberate non-solidarity.

The second frame positions artist and reader even higher, to seem even more powerful; but now this viewing point is further from the scene, with the centre of the action moving away from, not towards the viewer. This transformation, then, from frame to frame, is a further exclusion of the viewer from the action, into a position of even greater power but also of greater ignorance. And this position is chosen by the artist, not by the reader, so its effect is even more coercive. Readers experience their powerlessness especially at the moment of maximal power, as signified by the viewing position.

Frame 3 is the result of a transformation of the viewer-position from extremes of pseudo power to a position that is at eye-level to the kneeling Wonderwoman, to the side, and further from her than from the other woman who is now identified as a queen. The queen's speech gives more information about what is going on, but invokes a hidden history, involving Diana's 'honor', and a judgement on it to be made by a goddess of love. Is Diana's crime, in the eyes of a love goddess, to have accepted love or to have refused it? The name Aphrodite signifies Greek mythology, a whole area of discourse that is valued highly by high-status speakers in European culture. Most twentieth-century adolescent female readers in English-speaking cultures will not know that Aphrodite was the Greek goddess of love. However, in this invocation they are given this information. Just as the visual angle switches from a remote superiority to a closer equality, so correspondingly the degree of shared knowledge is expanded, though there is still distance and power. In the fourth frame, the point of view is now just behind Wonderwoman, level with her head as she kneels, listening to Aphrodite's double message (I do whatever you want, if you do what I tell you). Wonderwoman is labelled, not as a superhero but as a daughter (the word is in dark type) who is seemingly being tested for obedience of some kind. The possibility of identification, withheld thus far, is now offered at maximum strength for girl readers with powerful mother figures, who, up to this point, have accepted the mysterious test imposed on them by the comic writers.

The passage from frame 5 to frame 6 requires the page to be turned. The picture shows Wonderwoman breaking the chains and asserting her superhuman strength. But the montage-effect is equally startling. This frame is not only five times the size of the previous frames, it also includes the information that was withheld from the previous narrative. A box above gives the defining information about her, information which normally commences a story. The title of the story to follow comes at the bottom: 'Heritage'. So does the identity of the production team: four men and one woman; Nansi Holahan, whose name is stuck in the bottom left-hand corner of the box, is given the less than central job of 'colorist'. The viewing point for this frame is at a level with the central fire, and also with Wonderwoman's head as she still kneels. The expanded size of the frame allows Wonderwoman to be seen in greater size and detail, as though in close-up, and the context is also more explicit, as in a long shot. The result is simultaneously a sense of greater power and greater intimacy. Wonderwoman is seen at her own level, looking from the direction of the fire which is identified with Aphrodite.

One semiotic transaction that must be studied, with this comic, is that between its authors and its target audience: English-speaking adolescent female readers. The authors, as we have seen, are primarily males, self-transformed to occupy a female viewing-position in an all-female world, offering a female fantasy to females. We as analysts are males, without even a female colorist on our team, so we asked an 18-year-old girl to read these two pages, and give her comments.

Oh I don't like it, Wonderwoman being degraded. Being dutiful's alright but she shouldn't grovel! But after that (i.e. page 1) I'd just pass on, forget it (i.e. the opening) because that's how Wonderwoman really is you know, dominant and all that.

From these comments we can outline the progress of the reader's response. She clearly came to the comic with a strong initial structure of expectations about Wonderwoman, expecting to identify with her – but as someone powerful, not weak. She registers the comic's attempted transformations of this structure, at least at the level of content, but resists them, feeling alienated from the comic itself. So she reaches the transformation of the transformation, at page 2, with a sense of relief: it has cancelled out the attempted transformations of the previous page, and she proposes to forget it ever happened.

In fact the situation represented on the first page is closer to her personal experience than that of page 2. This reader still lives at her parental home, though she works for the public service. She is middle class, intelligent, attractive, and can afford to dress stylishly; she enjoys earning money, and has some work ambitions, but doesn't regard herself as ready to leave the family home yet, especially not to settle down and marry, either with her current 'steady' boyfriend or anyone else. She is four years older than Meena, and in different circumstances, but she is probably about the same distance from marriage, at a similar transition point. The experience of helplessness, ignorance and submission carried by both semiosic structure and content of page 1 of this comic represents one pole of her current position, an exaggerated version of the childish subservience she is outgrowing. Her words 'I'd just pass on, forget it' are as appropriate to the transformation point that she is involved in in her life as to her reading of the text. As with the Aboriginal dialogue, so here the personal history of this participant, seen in transformational terms, interlocks with the transformational processes of the semiosic act. And again, the short piece of text offers a wider range of structures and transformations than is clearly visible in her everyday life.

Her personal history itself has the form it does because of a wider social history. The numbers of women in the work-force, the greater autonomy demanded by women, the new levels of consciousness generated by the women's movement, are all parts of this girl's circumstances that constrain and shape her history. One part of this general movement that leaves its traces in this text concerns the gender identity of the authors of the text. These males have achieved a gender transformation, to occupy a female position, and from this position they appropriate distinctively female experiences. Yet the girl reader did not strongly object to this transformation. Wonderwoman herself is a partial transformation in the other direction. As Wonderwoman she is a princess, but as a woman she is Diana Prince. Generically she is a transformation of Superman, but in the text itself she is compared to classical males as well as females: 'beautiful as Aphrodite, wise as Athena' but 'stronger than Hercules, swifter than Mercury'. With the women she doesn't compete, sharing only a solidarity of excellence; with the men she competes, and excels on their own grounds of strength and speed.

This point raises the much wider issues of the relation between gender and generic form, an issue which is receiving increasing attention in the context both of feminist theory and of women's writing (see, for instance, Cranny-Francis 1987 a and b). The fundamental question is whether existent genres code patriarchal values so firmly that the substitution of characters of female gender for those of male gender may leave the underlying system of values quite intact, in a sense entrenching them more firmly. Our position is that while this is a complex matter, nevertheless, if genre does code social-semiotic relations of participants, then new social relations, including new/ different valuations of gender roles, will require the development of generic forms which adequately and appropriately code these relations. At the same time, switching gender positions in established roles will have its effects on any one generic form, and, via that, on the set of social relations projected by the genre.

The classical references point to a curious aspect of the semiosic structure itself. They constitute 'knowledge of the classics', a recognized domain of knowledge, which has played its role in the history of English culture. In England up till the nineteenth century, Greek and Roman culture was the preserve of the ruling elite, and a marker of class membership, excluding even members of the commercial middle classes, a point Matthew Arnold made with great force. But in the twentieth century there has been a revolution in the curriculum, and a different body of knowledge is now the marker of 'culture' and of membership of the ruling elite – just as royal titles like princess and queen no longer identify the leadership of the ruling elite. Our girl reader, in spite of a respectable level of education, couldn't remember independently what Aphrodite and Athena were goddesses of, but this didn't trouble her. She neither expected to remember nor felt the need of this knowledge, though she knew enough to recognize (or believe) that the classical reference was correct. So a real though remote transformation in the structures of knowledge is repeated by the semiosic strategy of the text, which transforms classical mythology not into contemporary (high) culture but into popular culture. She felt that this knowledge separated her from the writers of the comic, but that it was an unproblematic transformation which she could reverse if she wished, and thus recover not simply a past stage of culture but a connection with a former cultural elite. It is, of course, a more facile transformation than Meena was engaged in, in her attempt to enter into Anglo-Australian culture from an Aboriginal background. It has the effect of uniting a progressive tendency in the culture with a regressive one, again showing a wide range of contradictory transformations, alternative histories, at the level of discourse.

As we have seen, diachrony can move too fast as well as too slow for the fact of process to become visible. Our girl reader invoked one important example of this when she said, of page 2, 'that's how Wonderwomen really is'. The picture shows Wonderwoman in a characteristic action, breaking chains. More precisely it shows her with arms apart, chains broken, with speed lines and indicated sound-effects showing what has happened. The picture is still, yet the meaning of the syntagm is movement. Since the image is static we can treat it as a synchronic syntagm, yet it is understood as a syntagm of movement, a diachronic syntagm. And to decode it, the eye must move, diachronically, from part to part to build up details of the syntagm. In one sense the whole page is a synchronic syntagm, seen as a whole at a glance, yet because it must be read and because the reading takes place in time it is also a diachronic syntagm. But Wonderwoman is a synchronic syntagm in another sense. The text in the box at the top gives a list of her qualities, but the girl reader clearly did not need this list to know what Wonderwoman 'really is'. Wonderwoman is a complex bundle of meanings, which can be put into syntagms in time and space, and must be acquired in that form. But with practice and repetition these syntagms compress together to seem almost instantaneous. And the more instantaneous they seem, the more intrinsic they will appear to be, and hence more self-evident, more unchallengeable. Because the girl reader did not remember specifically the time in which her syntagms about Wonderwoman were formed, her impressions seemed to her to have an absolute status, and the diachronic syntagms of page 1 were powerless by contrast.

So we can see that time, the diachronic dimension, is never irrelevant to semiotic analysis. Time may move too fast or too slow to be easily seen or incorporated into the terms of analysis, but time is always relevant to interpretation, and to ignore it always involves distortion. There is no fixed boundary between synchronic and diachronic; there are only diachronic phenomena, moving at different rates on different scales, which for some purposes can be treated as static but only provisionally and for strategic reasons. Discourse is a site where meaning plays between participants in a semiotic exchange, whether this is speech or dialogue, comic or film, ritual or game. Discourse analysis, then, can reveal the processes which constitute such exchanges, where the social action of flow of time is in some ways especially visible, where transformational possibilities can be allowed freer play before being pressed into the service of history or its absence. But this can only happen when the intrinsically social nature of discourse is a fundamental premise, and where the discursive events are set into a complex but unitary diachronic scheme.

Reading history

Social semiotics can no more do without an account of history than it can dispense with a social theory. But strategies for reading history have a formidable history of their own, and there are many influential theories and methods of history to choose from today. On the one hand we must beware of inventing the wheel, but we cannot avoid the obligation to situate social semiotics in a wider historiographical frame. So in this section we set ourselves a specific and limited task. We will focus on only one major issue of historical method, and we will confine ourselves largely to some concepts and methods from the study of language. In this way we hope to establish some principles that can be applied more generally to the historically oriented tasks of social semiotics.

The issue we will be concerned with is the problem of continuity and discontinuity in history. Foucault, himself a major historian of discourse, has argued (1971) that this is a dominant theme in contemporary historiography. In many kinds of intellectual history he sees a concern with discontinuities, ruptures and breaks, with crises and revolutions in systems of thought, discontinuities so great that the systems of thought and meaning before and after the break are incommensurable. His own work as a historian of ideas is a case in point. So too, to mention only two other influential names, is the epistemology of the French Marxist, L. Althusser (Althusser and Balibar 1977), and the philosophy of science of the American, T. S. Kuhn (1970). Yet Foucault also notes the presence of continuities in historical work, or rather of discontinuities at different levels, in different series. The relationships between continuity and discontinuity and the status of the discontinuities are problematic. There is an excitement in claims that a crisis has occurred, a watershed reached, that a revolution has happened; yet the continuities seem to flow under and over these radical breaks, casting doubt on their dazzling absoluteness. More important for social semiotics, the most radical of these claims include the idea that the 'revolution' has altered basic modes of thought and possibilities of producing meaning. That is to say, these theories ultimately rest on unstated or unexamined premises from a historical semiotics.

To begin to sketch in the basics of a historical semiotics, we will go back to the nineteenth century. Comparative philology, the tradition in which Saussure was trained, had striking successes in its assault on historical problems, so impressive that many people in an age obsessed with history saw this discipline as providing a model for all forms of historical enquiry. Saussure's work marks a break, a discontinuity, after which this kind of claim would cease to be common. But the achievements of this historical discipline remain, worthy at least of being looked at again by social semiotics.

The achievements were concentrated in two areas, each relevant in a different but complementary way to the issue of discontinuities and continuities. The most spectacular achievement was a version of a theory of discontinuities. Analysing sound changes, especially in European languages, linguists demonstrated the presence of 'great' sound shifts. These were changes that affected not simply individual words or sounds but the whole phonological system of languages. They showed massive regularity and occurred with surprising speed, across whole series of language communities. These were revolutions, but invisible revolutions. Their discovery was formulated in the nineteenth century in a series of 'laws' of language which were hailed as a vindication for a new historical method. Yet alongside the discovery of these large-scale laws and dependent on their formulation went another kind of work: the tracing of the origins of individual words as part of historical lexicography. This work fed into the compilation of dictionaries which are still an impressive resource, as exemplified by a modern dictionary like the *Oxford English Dictionary*. This second scholarly enterprise was not so spectacular in its claims, and in fact it had an opposite tendency. Where the laws of sound change proposed massive regularities around discontinuities, historical lexicography assembled innumerable continuities, the slow vicissitudes of change in words and meanings over time. Although dictionary fashions have changed in reaction against the nineteenth-century tradition, and although few scholars were willing or able to push this enterprise much further, the work has remained available.

We do not want to suggest that the changes in historical linguistics happened without reason. On the contrary, Saussure's unhappiness with diachronic linguistics, as we saw in chapter 2, stemmed from problems in his conception of the nature and scope of linguistics itself, problems which his whole tradition shared. At the centre of these problems was the divorce between the study of language and the study of social forces. Without this connection, it was impossible to examine the reasons for linguistic change, since these reasons are primarily to be found in social forces. So it was only in terms of a sociolinguistic theory that these problems could be addressed and resolved. Here the essential pioneering work was carried out by W. Labov, whose work (1978) not only became a dominant force in sociolinguistics but also laid the basis for a new form of historical linguistics which social semiotics can draw on for its own purposes.

As we saw earlier, Labov worked mainly on language variation as it correlated with social stratification. But he also investigated the mechanisms that account for that variation. He enunciated clearly the essential premise for diachronic studies: the mechanisms of language change must be assumed to be the same for small-scale contemporary phenomena as for large-scale changes in the past. From a semiotic point of view, we can extend this premise to cover all semiotic forms. Labov did not in fact invent this premise. As he says himself, it was a basic premise of the 'Neogrammarians', an active school of linguistics contemporary with Saussure, who himself knew their work well. As Labov repeats it, this principle sounds obvious enough, and so it is. Its temporary suppression across the Saussurean fissure cannot have happened because it is unthinkable in any intrinsic sense. We must look elsewhere for the reasons why it was, for four decades, virtually unspeakable in academic discourse.

Labov used Chomskyan transformational linguistics, but like Saussure he concentrated especially on sound changes and he mapped them in ways similar to Saussure, meticulously describing sequences of transformations with specific sets of conditions and constraints. Where Saussure had only three stages – stage 1, with form A, stage 2 where forms A and B coexisted, and stage 3, where only form B survived – Labov expanded Saussure's stage 2 into five steps. At the first step there is free variation, arising out of an indeterminacy in the system itself. The second step occurs when this variation becomes systematic, associated with a particular group or social situation. As a result of this association, which initially may be unconscious, according to Labov, in step 3 the variation comes to have social meaning as a group marker or indicator of situation. In step 4 the marker is systematically developed and generalized, as part of a distinctive phonological patterning, an 'accent'. By this stage the marker has a recognized meaning, both for the group itself and for the whole community against which the group is defining itself. In step 5 a set of markers is exaggerated, along the same continuum, and becomes a stereotype, a focus of linguistic prejudices from the outside community. By this point, the group using the marked form is in Saussure's stage 3, but the community as a whole is not. The different forms coexist, comprehensible and meaningful to all members of the speech community. Their meaning and rationale is to express and control social relationships.

The most important implication of this for a theory of ruptures is that they never really happen. Yet they undoubtedly seem to happen, and this seeming is important. Behind the appearance of a rupture must be a major transformation and serious opposition between groups, and that in itself is important. This is why theorists of rupture have so often been the most illuminating historians. This transformation must exist, to different degrees, in the previous system, and the transforms must coexist with the original form, in a meaningful relationship, which can only serve its social function if the transformation is comprehensible to the group marked off by it. The group identified with and by the transform must therefore understand the original form plus the transformational process that has altered it. It is less axiomatic that the previous group can easily reverse the transformation, but a form of it is part of their own system. The cause of the barrier between the two, then, must be primarily social, not cognitive. If a group distinguishes themselves in terms of a major transformation, it is not because they do not understand the others, but because they do, and repudiate them. A new style, of language or thought or behaviour or appearance, functions as an antilanguage (in Halliday's terms), assuring identity and difference, declaring its ideology and protecting its secrets.

To see periods of art or culture as monolithic blocks divided by deep fissures of incommensurability and incomprehension, then, is a mistake, but it is a significant one. It repeats the hegemonic act whereby history is rewritten by a dominant group, which attempts to elide the very opposition which completes its meaning. Yet it incorporates into that history a recognition that the ruling group was once a revolutionary group. Kuhn's history of science as a succession of incommensurable paradigms has fallen into the error of accepting the rewriting of history that he observed is the normal practice of dominant groups. In Marx's phrase 'The ruling ideas of each age have ever been the ideas of its ruling class' (Marx and Engels 1970). A history of successive 'ruling ideas' or dominant cultural forms gives the dominant not only the victory they won, but the obliteration of those whom they defeated.

Apparent ruptures exist as massive generalized transformations, which are typically reversible and have always been prepared for. A history of ideas or semiotic forms which proceeds in terms of successive epochs across moments of rupture is in effect accepting claims of the dominant group and its forms to be the whole of society and its culture. They turn struggle in time into a difference across time, and by this illicit transformation into diachrony they make the actual diachronic processes more difficult to follow. They mark a major social change, because only a major social change could produce an apparent rupture, but the nature of this change then becomes harder to see. The rupture is not a cognitive barrier. The analogy with verbal language, which has been used to suggest that semiosis and thought will be incommunicable across such boundaries, in fact argues the opposite. A successive stage may appear to be very different, but it will never be unintelligible. The closest micro-level phenomenon in general semiotics is the sequence of fashions. The hemlines may go higher or lower than the unfashionable would want to wear, or hair may be longer or shorter, but those who refuse to go along with the trends know precisely what meanings and what group affiliations they are repudiating. All such changes can be analysed in terms of both continuities and discontinuities, characterized as *slides* or *transformations*, and the choice by an interpreter of either model is itself ideologically significant.

The other resource and model offered by historical linguistics is the tradition of etymology. Raymond Williams's *Keywords* (1976) has made good use of this tradition, showing its potential productivity (see also Hodge 1984). His impetus, like Labov's, came from the needs and structures of the present, not the past. He observed that the vocabulary he himself used, as a cultural analyst and a member of a group of intellectuals, was subject to shifts of meaning and discontinuities whose origins could be located precisely in society and history. The full dictionary entry for such words consisted of a set of meanings, not a single meaning. Though the list as a whole might seem incomprehensible, the pattern makes sense historically. Major shifts of meaning, the emergence of new terms into writing (he assumes that they probably entered speech somewhat earlier) always derive from and illuminate events in social history. But though there are quantum leaps in meaning of this kind, their rationale is clear in contemporary terms. They are leaps, but not ruptures. And the former meanings often survive, to complicate the lexicon and to gesture at history.

In order to build etymological studies into a general semiotics, we need to understand semiotically speaking just what words, as studied by Williams, are; or more precisely, just what structures are at issue in the transformations Williams is tracing. Saussurean semiotics encourages us to think of words as elemental signs, corresponding to a segment of reality cut up according to language-specific rules. This is clearly inadequate for most of the words Williams studies. For many of them he offers, following normal conventions, definitions in proposition form. So although other similar words, synonyms, can be used to point in the direction of the definition which gives the meaning (or meanings) of a word, we can posit, as a basic semiotic premise in this area, that the meaning of a word is minimally a mimetic syntagm (or set of mimetic syntagms) implied by it. A word is the carrier of a compressed message, a synchronic syntagm. The importance of words, for historical semiotics, is that the messages contained implicitly in words were repeated many times, and assigned a high validity. As embedded in other syntagms, they are often so potent as to take over the syntagm. In this kind of framework the study of words is a study of key cultural texts. Working in conjunction with a rigorous comparative historical method, it can extend a spotlight far back in time to reconstruct complex structures and processes of meaning that otherwise would have long disappeared. And it can be applied to recurring fixed synchronic syntagms in other media, such as formulae, themes or clichés in art, film, architecture or ritual.

We will illustrate the method by looking at one word, 'culture', which Williams has analysed. In *Keywords*, he devotes six pages to it. He gives its root word, the Latin *colere*, whose literal meaning was 'to cultivate', from which 'colony' and 'cult' also derive. His analysis traces the emergence of abstract meanings the word has come to have, so that now in the late twentieth century we have four main sets of meaning according to Williams: the original physical act of cultivation, and also three transferred senses, referring to artistic culture, general processes of the intellect, and the whole way of life of a people. The strong emergence of these last three he dates to the middle of the nineteenth century, though he sees a long period of preparation going back to the sixteenth century. If there is a 'rupture' involving this word in English, then it is to be located in the mid-nineteenth century. We can be even more precise. Matthew Arnold's *Culture and Anarchy* of 1869 mobilized two of the three new meanings, and Edward Tylor's *Primitive Culture* of 1871 gave wide currency to the third. A theory of ruptures might also note the passing of the Electoral Reform Act of 1867, which doubled the British electorate at a stroke, to Arnold's dismay, and Darwin's *Origin of Species* of 1859, which influenced both Arnold and Tylor, disturbing the one and inspiring the other.

However, a semiotic archaeology would also have to point out that this structure of meanings already existed in the Latin word, available to English and other European intellectuals who knew Latin (as Arnold and Tylor both did). The history traced by Williams occurred much as he records it, but it was constrained by another history which we also have to understand, and a full reading must follow the articulations of these two histories.

We will start, then, with *colo*, the root word, fixed by the words that radiate out from it. The Lewis and Short Latin dictionary gives four main classes of meaning: till or tend; inhabit; bestow care on; worship or flatter. The first two are seen clearly as the primary meanings, the second two as sets of transferred meanings. The first meaning in Latin is the most common form, the starting point of the series. It is clear that the one word refers not simply to an action in itself, but to a *process*, with typical agents and objects. It is this full mimetic syntagm, a transactional model, which gives its minimal meaning. The action is farm work: tilling, tending crops, etc. The understood agent is a farm worker or peasant. The object is a class of entities on which the labourer works: soil, trees, fruits, and so on. The other physical meaning is 'inhabit'. In the full general structure in which it occurs this is a non-transactive model. Although it can take an accusative case in Latin – for instance, a home or fields – these are understood as locatives, and the agent is no longer a worker but an owner. The transferred meanings simply involve transformations of implied objects of non-physical action: worship (the gods), flatter (nobles), or cultivate (virtues).

In Latin, an agent is usually inseparable from the verb form (e.g., *colo* is 'I cultivate'). Classes of agent and sometimes of object are similarly assumed. The primary transformation that explains most of the meanings is a set of two related transformations of the assumed agent from peasant to owner or intellectual, and of the object to abstract qualities regarded as 'worked over' intellectually. It seems likely that the group that initiated this transformational possibility would be an intellectual class dependent on a landowning class; but the records are not full enough for us to check this guess. What is certain is that this transformational set continues to be active in fixing the meanings of *cultura* and other derivatives. *Cultura* is then produced by the addition of a number of elements, $+ t$, $+ ur$ and $+ a$. We can set out this set of transformational processes as follows:

$$\left\{ \left\{ \begin{array}{c} \textit{Agent} \\ \text{Peasant} \\ \Downarrow \\ \text{Owner/} \\ \text{intellectual} \end{array} \right\} + col + \left\{ \begin{array}{c} \textit{Object} \\ \text{Material} \\ \Downarrow \\ \text{Intellectual} \end{array} \right\} \right\} \Rightarrow cul + t + ur + a$$

So, before it is borrowed by French, English or other European languages, *cultura* has its own history, clearly inscribed into its set of meanings. It doesn't simply correspond to a single stretch of reality; it represents a set of possible transformations of a process, with a further set of judgements attached, with the whole package, transformations as well as additions, forming a dynamic meaning-complex. When it first appears in English, French and German, it seems to have lost most of its complex additions, but what it acquired, in the history traced by Williams, is mostly the systematic recovery of the original complex.

But this doesn't leave the English history of the word empty of significance. The lines of force may have been laid down in Latin, but not all the options are taken up, and even its reinscription into English is a social act. When we look to actual discourse, we see innumerable specific transformations which arise and disappear, more numerous than will enter a lexicon as public meanings, though the boundary is often arbitrary. In Arnold's *Culture and Anarchy*, the key word is, inevitably, used in innumerable contexts which transform it in many ways that have no clear Latin parallels. To take a passage almost at random:

I must remark that the culture of which I talked was an endeavour to come at reason and the will of God by means of reading, observing, and thinking; and that whoever calls anything else culture, may, indeed, call it so if he likes, but then he talks of something quite different from what I talked of. And again, as culture's way of working for reason and the will of God is by directly trying to know more about them, while the Dissidence of Dissent is evidently in itself no effort of this kind . . .

Here 'culture' is at first a process consisting of intellectual work, with a deleted agent who is easily recoverable (people like Matthew Arnold), and then transformed into a personified entity, who is doing the same kind of thing as the deleted agent earlier. The objects, however, are slightly different and this affects our specification of the agent. 'Reason' makes the agent a philosopher or intellectual; 'will of God' makes him a kind of priest. The two together, then, transform him into a single being who combines the two roles and resolves the opposition between them (an opposition opened alarmingly wide by Darwin's work of ten years earlier). The opposition that Arnold is addressing and resolving didn't exist in that form in Roman culture, so it was not part of the meaning of the Latin word. Nor, in spite of Arnold's efforts, did it become a recognized part of the meaning of the English word. But it is out of the flux of such transformations, occurring in profusion in discourse, that new meanings arise and are fixed; and the fact that they do so is itself significant.

One advantage of the English history of 'culture' is the availability of materials to reconstruct the history of the discursive formation within which its meanings are embedded. Matthew Arnold's individual use of the word was undoubtedly influential, but that was partly because he articulated so adequately the viewpoint of a particular section of the middle classes, as he was conscious of doing. That section was the middle class products of the public school system (in which Dr Thomas Arnold, headmaster of Rugby, was a distinguished figure). Matthew Arnold's ability to appropriate and reproduce the transformations implicit in the Latin word was no mysterious coincidence. He was a classical scholar, and classical scholarship was a major marker of membership of the group he represented. The classics (including a knowledge of Aphrodite, Athena, Hercules, etc., sufficient to write many issues of *Wonderwoman*) were a large part of the cultural capital purveyed by the public school system. The ability to use the term and its transforms so freely and assuredly, then, marked group membership as clearly as knowledge of the elite content (again much of it from Greek or Latin), or a tone and accent of educated superiority, which Arnold also possessed.

In these terms, Tylor's central use of the same word in a different sense in 1871 – only two years later – marks not a rupture (as we have seen, all the possible meanings were available before, and continued in play afterwards) but the presence of a new force in direct conflict. Tylor, later Sir Edward Tylor, appointed first professor of anthropology at Oxford University at the ripe age of 64, was the son of a wealthy Quaker brass worker. As a Quaker he was a 'dissident', one of the class scornfully excluded by Matthew Arnold from any understanding or interest in 'culture' or culture. Arnold was right about Dissenters such as Tylor in one respect: as a Quaker he was debarred from entering a university. Yet he was still able to acquire a formidable grasp of that withheld cultural capital, and helped to found a new discipline and a new set of meanings for the word 'culture' itself. His new meaning was not, therefore, just a new meaning, but a challenge to an existing hegemony.

Arnold and Tylor represent two alternative sets of transformation associated with the word 'culture', enunciated from two different speaking positions in the society. Arnold takes the transformational potential of the Latin *cultura*, its core transformation of peasant or material worker into intellectual work(ers) of various kinds, which he associates in nineteenth-century English society with educators, intellectuals and clergy, including also – and this is a distinct contribution – poets and other artists. But for Arnold, the transformational route back from intellectual to material work is precisely barred. So 'culture' is firmly opposed to the work that defines working classes, even though Arnold professes to want to offer 'culture' to the masses.

Tylor's definition, on the contrary, extends the scope of the original transformation, and uses it to establish a chain of equivalences. For him, culture is both material work of all kinds and also intellectual work. The transformational link, instead of being broken as in Arnold, is opened up. Since it is applied to 'primitive' cultures, it includes activities of pre-agricultural peoples, and insists on their fundamental continuity with the various forms of life of modern man. This transformation as a meaning is specifically declared as a basic premise in his style of anthropology: 'There seems to be no human thought so primitive as to have lost its bearing on our own thought, nor so ancient as to have broken its connection with our own life'.

Tylor, however, has also transformed the Arnoldian speaking position. A Dissenter excluded from the right to use the word 'culture' or to claim access to its substance, he has transformationally entered that place – just as he ultimately achieved a chair at Oxford, a knighthood, and signifiers of full membership of the British establishment (Arnold himself received no knighthood). Yet he doesn't renounce the egalitarian commitments that marked his identity as a Quaker and Dissenter, but continues to proclaim them, legitimized by being spoken from this position. His position, with the inclusive sense given to the word 'culture' that functioned as a kind of badge, was carried into the twentieth century by the new discipline of anthropology. The transformation he achieved was a double one, then, of the syntagms implied by the word, and of the speaking position itself.

Taken in general terms, the transformational sequence of 'culture' has the form of the Hegelian dialectic, and the resemblance is illuminating. The progression is as follows:

Culture A $\Rightarrow$	Culture B $\Rightarrow$	Culture C
Material work:	Intellectual work:	Intellectual *and* material work:
Original meaning	Negation of A:	Negation of negation or transcendence:
	(Arnold)	(Tyler)

However, to make this dialectic progression meaningful, we must also note that culture *A* survived vigorously alongside culture *B*, as an oppositional meaning sustained by an oppositional group. And though it may look as though culture *B* achieved dominance at a certain point – especially if we look at the writings of the class that then dominated literary production – culture *A* and the group defined by it continued to exist. So culture *C* had been prepared for throughout the period dominated by culture *B* and it represented both a return of what was repressed but never eliminated, and also an incorporation or assimilation of it. But culture *C* continued to exist alongside the other two basic forms, each of which continued to generate further families of sub-meanings. Although in narrow structural terms there is an absolute rupture in the transformational progression from culture *A* to culture *B*, and a less absolute but still important break between culture *B* and culture *C*, in the society itself and in its bank of potent meanings there is always only a shift of balance in a larger whole which does undoubtedly change, but which has equally important continuities.

Williams's work on words was for him only a sideline to his major work as a cultural historian, yet it provides a model and motivation for a fully developed historical semiotics. Like Labov, but even more insistently, he sees a reading of history as indispensible to a reading of the present, and he sees social forces as the motor for semiotic change. He goes beyond Labov and Saussure in treating 'key words' as themselves complex messages in their own right, not simply elements in other syntagms – though it is precisely in the flow of discourse that they acquire and develop their meanings, as even Saussure knew. The tracing of synchronic syntagms of this kind – and different accents in speech, different motifs in art or dress or etiquette follow essentially the same laws of development – offers new possibilities for semiotic archaeology.

Decoding a classic

One kind of semiotic object that must be addressed by a historical semiotics is the 'classic' text. In most societies there is a set of cultural texts whose official task is to represent the past to the present. For Foucault, this class of privileged text is designed to generate endless commentaries. The word 'classic' comes from a Latin word meaning 'classroom'. A classic is a text to be studied, a message from the past chosen for its semiotic density and also for its suitability on ideological grounds. It is part of a system to legitimate the status quo, a system which must at the same time prepare prospective members of the ruling class for rule. This double function gives an ambiguous value to the classic. There is a further complication, from the point of view of a ruling class. There are severe limits on their ability to invent classics. Classics can be endlessly re-edited, reinterpreted and submerged by commentaries, but something of them still remains. A moment's inattention might be sufficient to give some group the opportunity to let their meanings irrupt into the present again, with meanings the more potent the longer they have been suppressed.

Classics in the literal sense were written texts, but the same functions are served by texts in other media. Certain buildings are carefully preserved and restored as public monuments. Museums and art galleries display various artefacts and works of art, and store others for scholars to use. In modern societies, the institution of education controls some of the discourses which make sense of this range of objects, though not all. Groups from schools visit museums, but adults also go on their own. In countries with many surviving monuments, tourism offers a more populist discourse on history, partly parasitic on educational discourse but with its own distinctive emphases. To cite just one instance, Stonehenge attracts huge numbers of tourists each year, yet neither it nor its conjectured history is a large item in the school curriculum. The mass media offer their version too, through cultural programmes, institutionalized as for instance in Britain's BBC2 service, and through authoritative restatements like Sir Kenneth (later Lord) Clark's television series *Civilization*.

This set of classics falls in the area of what Matthew Arnold called culture, enough at least to be judged elitist; a culture by and for the ruling class. In literary criticism the concept of the 'literary canon' has been criticized as the construct of a specific ruling caste. Bourdieu (1984) noted the patterns of attendance in French museums, which show a largely middle-class composition, and he invoked the notion of 'cultural capital' to explain it. 'Cultural capital' is an enabling background, consisting of modes of reading and sets of assumptions that allow a person to enjoy and appreciate works in a museum. According to Bourdieu this capital is distributed on class lines. Even if it only provides labels of class identity, this division is potent enough, since it allows a seemingly public and common set of objects to reinforce class divisions at the same time as they proclaim a unitary national culture and national identity. But Lukacs (1963) has argued that the 'masterpieces' of the bourgeois literary canon do much more than this: they offer an understanding of society that was exceptional for their epoch. Marcuse (1964) saw a critical dimension, a dialectical quality in great art, which he felt was lacking from what he called one-dimensional popular art. These two positions are not incompatible. 'High' culture could function as both class label and mystified repository of powerful knowledge. Something like this double position is what we will argue in this section, though we see the status of this 'powerful knowledge' as so problematic, even for a ruling group, that it will never be freely and simply available even to the culturally trained.

To situate this discussion in a particular context, we will take the period of European culture labelled the Renaissance. The precise scope, nature and significance of this period is disputed by historians of art and culture, but its currency and potency in contemporary thought is not open to question. Sir Kenneth Clark's *Civilization* inevitably included an account of the Renaissance in his authoritative version of high culture and its history for a mass audience. In the book of the series (1969), the chapter devoted to this moment is headed 'Man – the Measure of all Things'. It begins:

The men who had made Florence the richest city in Europe, the bankers and wool-merchants, the pious realists, lived in grim defensive houses strong enough to withstand party feuds and popular riots. They don't foreshadow in any way the extraordinary episode in this history of civilization known as The Renaissance. There seems to be no reason why suddenly from out of the dark, narrow streets there arose these light, sunny arcades ...

Sir Kenneth as mediator of high culture to the masses gives with one hand and takes with the other, exactly as Bourdieu might predict. He invokes a grand explanatory version of the meaning of history, in which this episode is pivotal. He knows something about the economic and social context, and rapidly sketches it in. But the point of both history and context is their irrelevance to an understanding of the Renaissance, which was not 'foreshadow(ed) in any way' and seemed to have 'no reason' for its emergence. Instead of a transformational framework linking Renaissance art and culture to its present and its past, Clark's Renaissance is insistently dislocated. It functions solely to carry its message to our own grim, defensive age. Clark sums up the message as follows: 'The dignity of man. Today these words die on our lips. But in fifteenth-century Florence their meaning was still a fresh and invigorating one.'

The 'Renaissance' as a complex ideological sign then becomes a signifier of 'civilization'. Its function here is apparently to include all of 'us' (modern men) in a common category of those who are excluded from this fresh and invigorating age, though Sir Kenneth's world-weary tone signifies his membership of an elite who at least knows and understands what has been lost. Within this framework, individual masterpieces, classics of the Renaissance, are glimpsed briefly by the camera or alluded to in the book of the series, and they come to signify the Renaissance itself, since there is no time and no other framework to allow them to have any other meaning.

Clark's text contains a predictable list of names of Renaissance 'masters': Michelangelo, Leonardo da Vinci, Donatello. For our illustrative reading of a classic text we will focus on one text by one of these masters: Donatello's statue of St Mary Magdalene (plate 6.3). Donatello as a sculptor is famous enough to make it into Sir Kenneth Clark's shortlist, though he is not as well known as Michelangelo and Leonardo. Of his works, the statue of Magdalene, carved in wood some time between 1450 and 1455, is regarded as an impressive and innovative work for its time, but it is not mentioned or filmed in Clark's text. Its relationship to Clark's ideological version of the Renaissance and to his chosen set of classics is significant but oblique, and this obliquity allows us to see more possibilities for the analysis of a classic text.

Plate 6.3 Donatello's *Magdalene*: a transformational work

To see this statue in isolation, as a static sign, however complex, is to occlude the possibility of reading it historically or even reading it at all. Its meanings are to be found in the set of transformations in which the statue is involved, in the various histories, short and long, which intersect it. It doesn't have an autonomous meaning, which can be deciphered and then related to history. Its history *is* its meaning. Or rather its histories, because there is a plurality of these diachronic chains: so many that it is hard to know where to begin the task of explication.

One of these histories, however, is nearly indispensible: the discourse into which the statue was first inserted. Just as words gain meaning only in discourse, so also a statue as a sign is intrinsically dialogic. For the analyst, the task is to recover the relevant discourses, in so far as that is possible. For a statue, its original setting was one decisive discourse. Donatello's statue, designed for the Baptistery in Florence, was a complex response to a building which itself was replete with messages from many voices. Its functional meanings grow out of that context. Outside of that context the statue can have other functions and meanings, but those can only exist as a suppression of these other functions and meanings, or as a transformation of them. So in the twentieth century it can have a tourist function, drawing people to Florence. It could even be used as a hat-stand. A historical semiotics will not *a priori* declare these other functions illegitimate or wrong, or see the original function as absolutely privileged. What it must do, however, is to see the sequence of functions as a series of real acts by specific agents, who are responsible for the transformations of function they perform.

The picture (plate 6.3) gives some idea of the original context for the *Magdalene*, which is a wooden statue about 1.98m high, on a low pedestal. It was placed in a central panel between two columns along the south west interior wall of the Baptistery in Florence, an octagonal building, in the Romanesque style. The altar is in the west wall, reversing the normal ecclesiastical practice of having the altar at the east end. The walls and floor are faced with polished polychrome marble. The domed ceiling above is dominated by a large series of mosaics, executed in the thirteenth century in the Venetian style. Above the altar is a huge image of Christ. In the segment to his left, (immediately above the *Magdalene*) is a picture of the saved being resurrected. To his right, the damned are shown suffering the torments of hell. The five remaining segments of the octagonal roof are divided into five bands. The highest band has huge angels. The lower four have parallel narratives, drawn from the Book of Genesis, the Story of Joseph, the Story of John the Baptist and the Story of Christ. Each begins with birth or creation, to the right of Christ, and ends at the left, just above the *Magdalene*, with either a triumph (Joseph and Christ) or a catastrophe (the flood, St John's deposition). The first dialogic relation we will look at here concerns the giant mosaic. This had been in position for 150 years before Donatello commenced his statue. It is an immense work, with large areas of gold background. Whatever he thought of it, Donatello could hardly ignore it. He too was a decorator of the Baptistery fabric, and his statement could not avoid interacting with the image already in place. Since the mosaic is so clearly a text in the pre-Renaissance style, Donatello's relationship to it is a specific instance of the transformations that constituted Renaissance style in general. Donatello's sculpture transforms the mosaic in virtually every element in the basic communication model. The artist of the mosaic is a collective figure, all individual differences having been irrecoverably deleted; for instance, Cimabue 'is thought' to have worked on it. Donatello is an early example of that significant figure of the Renaissance, the named artist producing work that is recognizably individual. The collective artist of the mosaic is also situated differently in relation to the viewers. Its figures, larger than life size, floating metres above the populace, signify power, a total identity with the power of the Church, the physical fabric and the social institution itself. The artists have sacrificed individuality for access to this position of power, and they leave no scope for its unity to be challenged. Donatello's statue, on the contrary, is at ground level, only a little raised, and it can be approached close up, walked around, assimilated. It asserts intimacy, not power. And because it does so working against the discursive structure imposed by the dome, it challenges the social unity created by the mosaic. The statue is spoken in the Church, but it isn't the Church who is speaking, and the meaning itself is addressed to individuals on an equality with itself.

The content of the statue also represents a transformation. The subjects for statue and mosaic come from the Bible, but there is a striking difference in the degree of realism of the two. This is generally recognized as a marker of the Renaissance style, and Donatello's statue shows it in a marked form. The different modality expresses a radically changed relation between artist and viewer, one of identity and equality, not difference and power. The components and implications of Donatello's realism are too various and complex to be taken for granted in schematic generalities. We will take one picture from the roof mosaic, the *Adoration of the Magi* (plate 6.4), for more specific contrasts. Donatello's sculpture is accurately three-dimensional. The *Adoration* is not only two-dimensional (except for the curve of the roof) but it does not code depth or time consistently. People and things depicted do not correspond to an easily recoverable reality, physical or social. Where is the setting? Inside or outside? Is it day or night? A star shines in the

Plate 6.4 Thirteenth-century mosaic: context for the *Magdalene*

unblinking golden sky/landscape, to signify night, but no shadows are cast in this metallic world. The tower behind the group of people gives contradictory spatial cues, the arches and top sometimes seeming to recede into the pictured space, sometimes going the other way. But there is no visual illusion or trick here, only the impossibility of such illusions. The people also are two-dimensional, psychologically as well as spatially. The faces are blank, and a whole range of semiotic codes that could communicate social and emotional messages have been largely eliminated: gestures, expression, clothing, intonation, or, to sum it up in a word, the semiotics of accent. Our point is not that figures are not shown as individuals, but that the multiple codes through which dissent and difference could be communicated, by groups as well as individuals, are rendered as unspeakable by the mosaic conventions, which in turn codes social conventions. The primary function of the code is control, achieved by drastic, irreversible transformations of social and physical reality. Like a typical antilanguage, it creates an antiworld, where the predominance of the social meanings of exclusion and control leads to a severe reduction in meaning potential.

By contrast, Donatello's statue is 'expressive', using a whole set of codes which have been eliminated from the art of the mosaic. The body is emaciated, the face gaunt, a message in the same way as the thinness of an anorexic is a message. The modelling of the body redundantly repeats the same message, through the tendons standing out, the bones of the sternum clearly outlined, and enough of the chest visible to imply withered breasts concealed by the ragged garment. The hair falls on the shaggy coat, thick, matted and almost indistinguishable from the animal fur. Donatello has reproduced signifiers of the ascetic saint's self-violation and self-hatred.

This plenitude of transparent signifiers accounts for the realism and emotional power of Donatello's statue. It also allows his own set of transformations, as radical as the mosaic's. His Magdalene stands on a vestigially indicated rock. The rest of the world of people and things has not just been flattened and distorted, as in the mosaic, but eliminated. The statue stood between two masonry columns, against a background of patterned marble, an effect seemingly comparable to that of the gold background of the mosaic. But there is a crucial difference. Donatello's deletion of the background is signalled, and it is reversible. The single rough rock projects a desert landscape, the hands are lifted in solitary prayer, her eyes are sunken and unseeing, and she is totally alone. The imagined context is recoverable, and if it is recovered, it marks a sharp contradiction to the environment she is actually in, which is a richly decorated and very public place. This invisible but strongly evoked world she carries with her is not simply a contrast to the wealth around her, it is a condemnation of it, if we remember what St John the Baptist represented in his time, a fierce critic of the contemporary Jewish state (Herod) and church (the Pharisees). The Baptistery is dedicated to St John the Baptist, who was also patron saint of Florence.

Donatello has made a number of other transformations. The Magdalene's figure is not purely realistic. In contrast to the ravaged face and bony chest, the hands held up in prayer are slim and elegant and ungnarled, and the legs that emerge below the shapeless garment are also slim and shapely, without the distended veins and strained tendons Donatello could so easily have represented. The Magdalene, then, is both young and old, beautiful and repulsive, subject and object of loathing and desire. This set of contradictions also applies to Donatello's use of biblical sources. In the Bible narrative, Mary of Magdala is not depicted as old. She stood alongside Mary the mother of Jesus, below the Cross, and in John's gospel she alone saw the risen Christ. She wanted to touch him but he warned her not to. In the

Church tradition she is a reformed prostitute, become the lover of Christ. Donatello has taken the ambiguities of this figure and pushed them to a limit, by representing her as old, ascetic, ravaged and yet still beautiful.

There is another transformation Donatello has introduced. His Magdalene stands in a Baptistery dedicated to St John the Baptist. In the years 1450–5, a period of personal crisis for him, the only other statue he carved was a statue of the Baptist. His Magdalene wears a shaggy pelt which was normally associated with the Baptist, signifying his extreme rejection of culture as corrupt. Above her is depicted the life of the Baptist, and she stands below pictures of his end, staring at the baptismal font in the centre of the building. She is not simply the biblical Mary Magdalene forty years after, she is also St John the Baptist transformed. The structure of the transformations involved can be indicated as in figure 6.2. She is not only old, she is bisexual (as was Donatello's famous *David* of thirty years earlier). Asceticism of the type displayed by John the Baptist is shown as a career open to women too – as it was in Donatello's Italy. St Catherine of Sienna is the most notable example; she died in 1380 aged only 33, emaciated by punitive fasting and self-discipline, but so politically potent that rival groups stole her head and body as soon as she was dead, so that they could appropriate her charismatic power. Closer to his time but less militant was St Catherine of Bologna, Abbess of the Poor Clares (1413–63). Bernadino of Sienna was a male in the same tradition, dying in 1444 and canonized in 1450. Savoranola continued the tradition forty years after Donatello carved his statue, and was burnt for his efforts in 1498. For three hundred years before the Reformation the Church threw up a succession of charismatic ascetics, who were either canonized like St Francis of Assisi or burnt like Savoranola, but who together

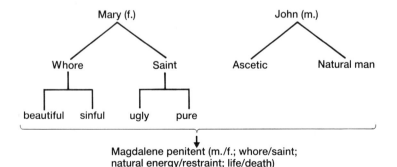

Figure 6.2 St Mary and St John: transformation to the *Magdalene*

made up a continuous radical tradition that foreshadowed militant Protestantism.

Donatello's own political position is hard to assess, since he left no writings and was apparently circumspect in other ways. His father, a wool carder, had been expelled from Florence for his part in an unsuccessful rebellion against Medici rule. The son not only survived, but was strongly supported by Cosimo Medici, who may even have commissioned the *Magdalene*. But Vasari reports that Donatello retained an independence from Cosimo and other patrons, and Florence led by Savoranola briefly expelled the Medicis forty years later, in 1494. The citizens marked the occasion by placing Donatello's bronze *Judith Killing Holofernes* in the main square. This statue, celebrating a biblical heroine's execution of a tyrant, ironically was commissioned by Cosimo, and produced at much the same time as the *Magdalene*. The latent radicalism of Donatello could be recognized by contemporaries, even though he worked within a Medici patronage system and was undoubtedly constrained by those conditions.

Donatello's statue achieves a radical break from the meanings of the previous form, yet it also coexists with them in the same building. The connection is closer than might appear at first. The narratives around the roof go from right (birth) to left (death, triumph). Magdalene is placed at the left extreme, under representations of the resurrection of the just, though she is not yet dead. The four narratives around the roof run in strict parallel, so that they can be read vertically (connecting an incident from Genesis with incidents concerning Joseph, St John the Baptist and Jesus) as well as horizontally, to create complex typological transformations. So Jesus is shown rising from the dead, immediately above St John lying in his tomb – dead, but destined to be resurrected through Christ. Thus John is both like and unlike Christ, living and dead. Joseph, shown in triumph, is like Christ triumphant, and above him Noah enduring the Flood, entombed in the ark, is like John the Baptist, soon to be resurrected. Donatello's transformation of John the Baptist into Mary Magdalene is the same kind of process. Her body faces towards the right, following the narrative line of the roof heading towards death, glory and judgement. However, her face turns back away from the altar and the figure of Christ, away from the consolations of the traditional narrative. The contraposto twist, later to become a signature of mannerism, here expresses an ambiguity towards the religious tradition, a crisis of faith. But to do so it uses the forms of that tradition, transformed in idiosyncratic ways.

In our far from exhaustive reading of this statue we have located a series of transformations which together give it its 'Renaissance' quality. These transformations establish a dialogic relation with the previous tradition, achieving a deliberate break. This break is not mysterious and absolute. Its components are all explicable and motivated, and exist in some form in the previous system. We are looking at a new accent, not a new language, and Donatello as an agent of the change remains totally fluent in the previous form. The same basic set of transformations underpin Renaissance art, Protestant religion, and radical politics, three different spheres of culture and society which saw major changes in Europe between 1300 and 1600. Donatello's transformational work takes sides in all three areas, sharing both the underlying affinities, and also the primacy of the political or social meaning. The transformations in art and religion express a fundamental political attitude, not vice versa, just as forces in society provide the motor for changes in verbal language. Donatello's work deserves to be studied, deserves to be a classic, because it engaged directly in the critique of the old forms which established the new accent, the new tradition.

What we have done is not wholly different from what is sometimes done by art historians, and the materials accumulated by various scholars are valuable in establishing the discursive context of a 'classic' text. Historical semiotics no more makes scrupulous scholarship redundant in the fields of art and culture than in the field of verbal language. Yet there is a curious blindness towards necessary connections which seem to be established by scholarship within existent disciplines. The *Magdalene*, for instance, is now exhibited in the 'Museum of the Works of the Duomo', alongside other sculptures, by Donatello and others, sculpted for Florence's cathedral and Baptistery over a period of three hundred years. The new context establishes new syntagms, new meanings, but also effectively suppresses the original semiosic context which made it a classic text. Scholars know where it originally stood, but seem not to know why it mattered or what it might have meant.

This is the typical kind of transformation achieved by the traditional museum. Individual items are displayed in isolation from their dialogic context, with labels to act as cues for those with enough knowledge to supply something of a framework. In this way the effect which Bourdieu criticized is achieved. The works in a museum are only legible for those who know the gist of the discourse which once surrounded the works, or some alternative history, alternative discourse which can serve the purpose. Without this 'cultural capital' even famous works, the classic texts, are opaque. This makes them especially vulnerable to incorporating into a different version of the constituting dialogue, a different version of history. One of the ideological effects of the modern museum is to create a market for a text like Sir Kenneth Clark's *Civilization*.

The ideological nature of a popular history like Clark's may be acknowledged as blatant by some who would still insist that history itself must be seen as inherently a construct, rewritten on water by successive generations, with no measuring stick to judge each different version. We believe that such a view is excessively pessimistic. History is indeed a site of struggle, and no historian is totally disinterested. Yet historians as ideologues are not entirely free, nor are sources totally malleable. In this dialectic, classic texts play a crucial role, since competing commentaries keep alive their dialogic character, and museums of various kinds (including schools and universities) preserve their material forms, to challenge grosser attempts to neutralize their force. Decoding classic texts is as crucial an enterprise as the elite culture claims after all. However, to do it properly requires systematic study of many kinds of non-classic text, which the same elite excludes from its own definition of culture.

7

Transformations of Love and Power: the Social Meaning of Narrative

This chapter addresses a double theme: the family as focus of social meaning and semiotic process, and narrative as a major carrier of social meaning. The two topics are often kept in distinct compartments, seen as the province of different analytic traditions. Sociology of the family has been a topic for 'hard' sociology, involving empirical data and statistical analysis. Theories of narrative, however, have been dominated by literary forms of semiotics. Even where it has invaded anthropology via myth analysis, narrative analysis has tended to look for formal patterns, aiming to transcend the specific social contexts and their distinctive forms of social organization. But in practice, patterns of family organization are inevitably sustained and negotiated by means of a myriad set of narratives, so that the social processes and social meanings at issue cannot be understood without powerful forms of narrative analysis. Conversely, the meaning and function of many narrative genres are so closely bound up with the institution of the family that this becomes a primary site for us to explore the social meanings of narrative itself. This set of relationships make sense in terms of diachronic processes, primarily transformational operations of diverse kinds. Transformations of love and power constitute various family groupings and link these to other structures within a social formation. The narratives that carry and mediate these processes are themselves linked by transformations to each other and to the nexus of social meanings clustering around the family, whatever specific form the 'family' may take under different social conditions. A theory of narrative of this kind is an integral component of what Poster (1978) has called a 'critical theory of the family'.

Semiotics of the familial text

In contemporary sociologies of the family, this institution is assigned a crucial role in processes of change, though usually a conservative one. The family is seen as the agent of primary socialization. It is the site of the first decisive confrontation between individuals and the society they have been born into. Through the family, a society reproduces not simply physical bodies but also social persons. Sociology recognizes differences, within this institution, either between different social classes and ethnic groups or across time, for instance in the slow process of the formation of the 'modern' or 'nuclear' family as it exists under capitalism. But there is an overall impression of the family as an immensely stable and stabilizing force, changing only slowly if at all, resisting pressures for change outside itself.

This impression of stability, however, needs to be put against a recognition of the intrinsically transformational processes which underlie it. At any one time in a given social group, the structures of the family can be described through a set of roles and rules that govern the proper behaviour of individuals and constituent families. This model may have such currency over time or across a social formation that it can seem an eternal verity, an unchanging pattern descending from above. Such a model is always presented as a synchronic syntagm, a set of relationships outside the flow of time and process. But this impression is a normal ideological effect of the use of synchronic syntagms. The eternal verity of the family has to cope with the ubiquitous presence of change, as new individuals are born and incorporated into specific places, and then redistributed into different places as they or others grow weaker or stronger, sexually active or quiescent, or dead. Given this endless change, the illusion of absence of change can only be achieved by homeostatic transformations, transformational reversals of the existing processes of change. So the apparent absence of change, far from being a given, is itself one of the products of transformational processes, which must be precisely regulated and controlled if the trick is to be pulled off yet again. It is fashionable to see the family in contemporary capitalism as being in a state of crisis. It would be as true to say that crisis is something that the institution of the family has never been out of.

In contributing to the study of this process, social semiotics needs to be clear about the scope and limits of semiotic explanation. On the one hand, individual concrete families are made up of actual people, including biological parents and siblings. But this set of bodies only functions as a social unit because of the social meanings assigned to it and to its various constituents. These meanings are communicated by a large number of texts, as we have said. But it is important to insist that the family as a set of meanings is itself a kind of text, or more precisely an overlapping set of texts which we will term *familial texts*. Children making sense of others in their social environment are constructing a familial text, one which is likely to be different from whatever they might be able to say about it. They are themselves assigned a pre-existing meaning in the familial texts that confront them so coercively with impenetrable closure, texts whose meanings are potently reinforced by actions and behaviours of others essential to their survival. The familial texts are hinted at by innumerable, barely comprehensible other texts in other semiotic media. They present children with their greatest semiotic challenge before they have even begun to crack the phonological code; before they have entered into verbal language.

The familial text that children first construct is deeply learnt, and it provides the starting point for a chain of transformations that make sense of every other major social relationship. Ideologues in many societies at many times have exploited this transformational chain, explicitly linking structures of power in the state with structures within the family, invoking the authority of the father (e.g., the monarch as father of his people), in defence of the mother (land). We are not suggesting that the power of the state is derived from or reflects power in an autonomous family structure. On the contrary, the familial text that confronts a child within its family experience as an absolute text, outside its powers to comprehend or control, is the product of a series of transformations which will be substantially the history of social determinations of the family, not the other way around. Children work on and with these given structures in a variety of ways, in the process of negotiating a place for themselves. If they then deploy transformations of familial texts to make sense of later relationships of power and solidarity, they will come up with a complex and contradictory account of social reality. There is not a single, predetermined set of meanings to do with gender and power within the family, and nor could there be an inevitable extrapolation from family to state or to any wider social grouping. So the patriarchal model of the family, to cite just one important instance, should never be seen as a self-contained social fact, but rather as an ideological transformation of an existing flux of familial texts, a massive intervention on behalf of one class of author. If it seems a closed, incontestable text, then that is the result of the efforts of these ideological agents. Links between this construct and patriarchal constructions of politics or work are likewise transformations which must be achieved and sustained by specific agents for their own reasons:

they are not inevitable and 'natural' consequences of patriarchy within the family.

There are two theorists whose work has been important for understanding what we have called familial texts: Freud in his psychoanalytic theories (e.g., 1965, 1971) and Lévi-Strauss in his account of the structures of kinship (1963, 1969b, 1976). Freud's controversial contribution is his theory of the Oedipus complex. In his formulations, he sometimes makes this sound like a universal psychic fact. In practice, his discussion treats it as a crucial set of meanings, the construction of the parental dyad made from a specific position, at a particular stage. The 'Oedipus complex' is primarily the son's text, about his parents and their relationship to himself. In Freud's theory, this 'complex' will probably be connected with an actual event, which carries the meaning of the complex for the son. That is, in the terms we have been using, a diachronic text is intrinsically related to a synchronic form, the relationship itself, so closely that each acts as the transform of the other, although the synchronic form, the 'familial text' as we have called it, is in a sense prior, waiting for the appropriate event to trigger it off, or even inventing an appropriate occasion.

The Oedipus complex, however, does not normally exist prominently on the surface of mental life, according to Freud. The son specifically repudiates it, transforming its values to a new form, one in which he incorporates the father into himself. But the Oedipus structure coexists with its inversion in the mind of the son, constructing a double self, which Freud labelled 'super ego' and 'id'. In Freud's account, the Oedipus structure is also subjected to many other transformations, which construct many other people in terms of the Oedipus structure as kinds of mother, father or son substitutes. Freud sees the process as going on continuously throughout life, producing other relationship texts (for instance in politics and the work-place) and other major narrative forms (for instance in religion, art and literature).

Freud's theory of the transformational processes that constitute the family and link the family with other institutions is exemplary as far as it goes. But it has two major limitations which must be addressed if his account is to be incorporated into a theory of social semiotics. He gives his Oedipus complex no history and no social context. The Oedipus text is the son's text. Freud made a number of attempts to adapt it to daughters, none satisfactory. It is produced in reaction to the texts of powerful others, most immediately the mother and father, whose own relationship is constrained by external social forces in ways that Freud normally did not examine. These external social forces and conditions of existence will vary in different societies or from different positions within the same society. Long before the son's Oedipus complex could function to make sense of his own social relationships, those social relationships will have formed that complex. The Oedipus complex should not be treated as an irreducible and absolute text, which must ultimately underlie all forms of family structure at all times. Freud's theory is much more subtle and powerful if it is seen as a theory of the transformations of specific familial texts, rather than as the discovery of a universal familial text.

Lévi-Strauss's work on kinship has a more ambiguous position in relation to semiotics and to the rest of his work. His work on myth is recognized as a major if controversial contribution to narrative analysis. His theory of kinship, however, has been less well received. Semioticians tend to ignore it, regarding it as social anthropology, not semiotics. Social anthropologists agree, but they judge it a dubious social theory, over ingenious and universalistic, not at all helped by what they see as strained analogies with language phenomena. We do not minimize the difficulties in the form that Lévi-Strauss gives to his theory, but we will argue that it contains some original and powerful contributions to social semiotics which well repay the study.

Lévi-Strauss offers a useful correction to the Freudian framework, because as an anthropologist he is concerned with pre-literate societies, not with contemporary capitalist families. The object of his theory is a kind of kinship system called the avunculate, i.e. a system in which the maternal uncle (Latin *avunculus*) of a boy is assigned an important role. In such systems, Lévi-Strauss claims, two rules apply universally. Firstly, the relationships between father and son and uncle and nephew were always inverse. Thus, if the father–son relationship was good, the uncle–nephew one would be bad, and vice versa. Secondly, the brother–sister relationship was always the opposite of the husband–wife relationship. Lévi-Strauss illustrated these relationships in the form of kinship diagrams which are standard practice in contemporary anthropology. We reproduce, as figure 7.1, an example of one such diagram. In this the son has a positive relationship with his father, as in the post-Oedipal stage in Freud's account. This seems to be achieved at the expense of projecting a negative meaning on the uncle, who thus represents the Oedipal father. But the other part of Lévi-Strauss's equation is less easy to explain. In the contemporary ideology of family life it is unthinkable that the marital bond should be weak (in spite of divorce statistics to the contrary). But this has been a systematic feature of the marital relationship in many societies, at many times. Any adequate account of the structure of the family has to be able to theorize its conditions and consequences.

Lévi-Strauss produces the mathematics of this possibility but not a plausible transformational theory of it. If we invoke Freud, or anthropologists of the family such as Mead and Bateson, we can see the large gap in Lévi-Strauss's scheme. He leaves out the mother–son

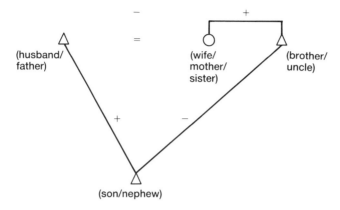

Figure 7.1   A kinship diagram as a familial text

relationship, which in Freud's theory would be transformed to brother/ sister and husband/wife. It then becomes interesting to explain why there should be a widespread social rule to the effect that the positive form of the mother–son relationship cannot be transformed to both substitute relationships, or why there should be an obligation to dislike one category of woman as well as an obligation to love another.

But Lévi-Strauss does have an explanation of the social basis for this pattern (and the gender bias he has built into it). In all societies, he claims, it is men who give women in marriage, which he sees as a transaction involving three elements: a receiver (the husband), a donor (the maternal uncle/wife's brother or some equivalent) and a commodity (the wife). The brutally reductive terms enable us to see, perhaps more clearly than Lévi-Strauss did, exactly who is the author of the structures he is describing. Lévi-Strauss does insist that what he is describing is a symbolic structure, not an unmediated social fact, and this is a crucial advance from the point of view of social semiotics. But he failed to recognize that 'symbolic structures', like Freudian 'complexes', are socially produced by specific social agents. That is why we will call them 'texts', not 'structures', and why we will attempt to trace them back to their social points of origin. The data that Lévi-Strauss draws on is mostly derived from the work of male anthropologists working with male sources and informants, describing familial/kinship texts from that vantage position. His own structural maps, in the form of circles and triangles, equals-signs and brackets, pluses and minuses, show the typical features of classic structuralism, the qualities that have given structuralism a bad name. These maps should be regarded as transformations of a chain of previous texts, going from the anthropologists' summaries/transformations of their informants' summaries/transformations, and so on back to the masculine familial texts that they purport to describe. In this process, men are turned into triangles, women into circles, and the whole complex semiosic process has been eliminated without a trace. Even so, we should not underestimate the value of what Lévi-Strauss has allowed us to do. The structures he describes may be excessively abstract, formal and simplified, but that reductiveness was arguably necessary before anyone could begin to read them as a kind of text.

We summarize some propositions about familial texts as follows:

1 Individuals develop schematic models of their relations with others in the form of *relationship texts*, synchronic structures which assign values to relationships within a particular group. Where the family corresponds to an important institution within a society, we can call this set of texts *familial texts*.

2 Familial texts represent a stage in a transformational process, and analysis must trace such texts backwards to earlier stages in order to understand the contradictions and possibilities of later stages.

3 Familial texts must be understood both as constructs from a specific social place, and as compound texts which incorporate the texts of significant others. Normative texts, which give the familial ideology of the dominant (in terms of gender, age and status) will still incorporate traces of oppositional texts, in the form of discrepancies or contradictions, just as alternative texts will incorporate versions of the texts of the dominant.

4 Familial texts are constrained by the material conditions of family life, and their different forms cannot be understood without reference to these material constraints.

5 Familial texts will be transformationally linked to other synchronic relationship texts making sense of other kinds of relationship, and to innumerable narratives, i.e. diachronic syntagms representing these structures as events or processes. These narratives have familial texts as a primary meaning, even though that meaning may be inverted or displaced in a variety of ways.

The social meaning of *Oedipus*

If we chose only one narrative text for an exemplary analysis in which to explore the relation between narrative text and theories of the family, that text would have to be Sophocles' play *Oedipus Tyrannos*. As narrative, it has been a classic of Western literature since Aristotle privileged it in his *Poetics*, itself a foundation text in the history of Western theories of narrative. His plot provided the inspiration for Freud's 'Oedipus complex', and Lévi-Strauss used the myth to illustrate his method of structural analysis of myth (1963). De Lauretis (1984) has given an important feminist reading of these readings, and of the *Oedipus* narrative itself. As well as being a famous literary text, it is priceless ethnographic data, a narrative of the family produced over two thousand years ago, from a pre-capitalist stage in the development of the family.

The nature of the family in classical Greece is itself of great interest in the history of the family. The 'nuclear' family of modern capitalism, consisting of an autonomous husband, wife and 2.25 children, is by no means a universal form of the family. Exactly when and where and how it arose from earlier forms of extended family and networks of kinship is very much in dispute, but the form of family in classical Athens showed an exceptionally early and crude form of it. It represents an important transitional point in the history of the family, and it has left an exceptionally rich set of documents for later ages – including Sophocles' text, and those of other Greek tragedians. For this reason Engels devoted a great deal of attention to the Greek family in his *The Origin of the Family* (1968), a book which has laid the foundations for Marxist theories of the family. Engels has some strong criticisms of the classical Greek family, all of which are now commonplaces in social histories. He associated these defects with a new form of the monogamous family that arose in patriarchal Greece. 'We meet this new form of the family in all its severity among the Greeks', he comments (Engels 1968: 125). It has two dominating features: the subordination of women to male power and male control of inheritance (patrilinearity), and institutionalized prostitution, which Engels refers to as *hetairism*, a word derived from the Greek word *hetaira*, literally meaning a companion, with the derived meaning of 'courtesan'.

There is no doubt that the wife in classical Greece had a very low status, literally not far removed from that of a slave. The split in the nature of woman, as seen from a patriarchal perspective, is put strongly by Demosthenes, in a famous quotation: 'We have *hetairae* ("courtesans" for physical excitement, *pallakai* ("concubines") to look after our day-to-day bodily comfort; and *gynaikai* ("wives") in order to procreate legitimate children and have a trustworthy custodian for the household' (Demosthenes 1 ix, 122). Demosthenes here confirms Engels's list but adds the *pallakai*, normally female slaves, sometimes translated as 'concubines'. In addition, Greek society was marked by strong separation between men and women, and widespread homosexuality.

Engels makes a more controversial claim about the classical Greek family. Influenced by the American Morgan and the German Bachofen, he postulated an early stage in family structures dominated by what he called *Mutterrecht* ('mother right') – that is, a line of inheritance following the mother's line, within a system organized by clans rather than families. This stage was followed by patrilinear society, which in Engels's view lead inexorably to patriarchy and then monogamy on behalf of men. With slavery and extremes of wealth between rich and poor he saw the emergence of the *polis* or Greek state, a system of power which was opposed to the organization of the household or *oikos* and to the functioning of a clan system, yet also came to determine its form.

The early proponents of 'mother right' overstated the likely extent of matriarchy in such societies, but it is reasonable to suppose that the position of women in matrilinear societies was much better than came to be the case in classical Greece. It is also clear that avunculate systems of the kind Lévi-Strauss studied show traces of matrilinear forms of society, since in matrilinear forms the woman's brother, not her father, is the closest male relative. The play of forces between husband and wife's brother over both the son (especially the son as heir) and the wife/sister is a product of the struggle between two competing principles of power within the family, one of which has virtually disappeared from the modern nuclear family. In this struggle the role of women was crucial, not peripheral as Lévi-Strauss seemed to imply.

We will now turn to Sophocles to see what an analysis of his texts can contribute to an understanding of these issues. He wrote three separate plays about Oedipus and his family: *Antigone* in 440 BC, when he was 55 years of age, *Oedipus at Colonos*, produced after his death by his grandson in 406 BC, and *Oedipus Tyrannos*, produced at some time between those two dates. Sophocles was a citizen of Athens who participated in the public life of the democracy, though he was not of noble birth himself. The plays were produced at festivals of Dionysos, where they competed for prizes, awarded by a panel of male judges. These texts, then, are likely to have the typical bias of the texts that anthropologists normally use: produced by and for adult, male members of a dominant group. The texts, of course, are works of fiction, so we cannot assume that they faithfully reflect Sophoclean social reality (any more than we can assume this of any kind of text). But that is not our goal. We are interested instead in the familial text which is the core meaning of this set of plays, whoever's text it is, and however it may correspond to dominant familial texts in that society.

The most sensational event in the Oedipus story is, as Freud noted, the son who killed his father (Laius) and married his mother (Jocasta), even though he did not do so intentionally. But the father is no innocent. Laius himself had tried to kill Oedipus as an infant by exposing him on a hill top, with his feet shackled together (hence his name 'Oedipus', meaning 'swollen foot'). This was unsuccessful, however, since Jocasta had organized the deed, and entrusted it to a herdsman who relented and spared the child. Oedipus is then brought up by Polybus and Merope, a noble couple in Corinth, whom he believes are his real parents. But warned by an oracle that he will kill his father and sleep with his mother, he leaves Corinth, only to meet and accidentally kill his real father, Laius, at a crossroads. Oedipus having killed his father travels to Thebes, which is under the power of the Sphinx, a female monster, who poses a riddle. The one who answers the riddle of the Sphinx will expel her, marry the Queen and rule the land. Oedipus answers the riddle, marries the Queen, who is also his mother, and becomes ruler of Thebes. He has four children, two sons, Polyneikes and Eteocles, and two daughters, Antigone and Ismene. But Thebes suffers another plague, and again the cure is to answer a question: who killed Laius? When Oedipus's secret is revealed, it is Creon, his mother's brother, who expels him from the city and becomes ruler instead. Jocasta suicides and Oedipus goes into exile with his two daughters, but he curses his sons and his uncle Creon. The two sons battle for possession of Thebes and die. Creon orders the eldest son, Polyneikes, to be left unburied. Antigone dies rather than allow this to happen, refusing to marry Haemon, Creon's son, as Creon wishes. Haemon himself then suicides.

Each event described here is a clear narrative equivalent of a familial relationship, with actions labelled as hostile (killing, sending into exile) or loving (marrying or offering total support). We also note that the role of Creon, the maternal uncle/brother, is important. This, then, is an avunculate, of the kind described by Lévi-Strauss, which Engels saw as a form of continuation of mother right. And Oedipus' claim to the throne of Thebes is based on whom he has married, not on whose son he is. The throne of Thebes goes with the woman and her family, and is possessed by Creon as senior male representative.

If we set out the relationships using anthropological conventions, the pattern in some respects conforms to the Lévi-Strauss avunculate model. In Antigone's case, the brother–sister bond is dramatically stronger than the marital bond (though this is not so clearly the case for her intended groom). In the case of Oedipus, Jocasta addresses him as *anax*, lord, expressing respect not love, but she does not address her brother in the plays, and nor does he express his attitude to her. Her marriage is a political union with whoever rules Thebes, and no one claims any love is at issue, though in her previous marriage, with Laius, she was ready to sacrifice her son on behalf of her husband.

The pattern involving uncles and fathers initially seems to conform less clearly to a Lévi-Straussian pattern. The father–son bond is strongly negative; not only in the case of Laius and Oedipus, but also with Creon and Haemon, and Oedipus and his sons. But this is not balanced by a positive uncle-relationship, even though Oedipus does appeal to

Creon as though expecting help from him. However, not all fathers are repudiated or murdered by their sons, or victims of patricide. Polybus is Oedipus' 'good' father, so respected by Oedipus that he flees Corinth rather than risk killing him. And Oedipus has two significant male others, both slaves: the herdsman who refused to kill him, and his friend who took him to Corinth. Oedipus is saved from murderous parental wrath by a conspiracy of slaves. He is then able to sustain a positive attitude to his father (Polybus), thus conforming to what is clearly spelt out (by Oedipus as by others) as the 'correct' attitude to fathers. From these extracts, we can reconstruct (as figure 7.2) a familial text for Oedipus (constructed by Sophocles on Oedipus' behalf).

The narrative we describe could hardly be good social history. As a way of organizing family relationships it is unreservedly catastrophic. After an infanticide (failed) and a patricide, two fratricides and three suicides (not counting Oedipus' self-mutilation) there is hardly anyone left of the noble house of Thebes. This could not be how the Greeks organized family matters, or they would not have lasted long enough to write tragedies. Even given a convention whereby hostile feelings are signified by murder, positive ones by marriage, this familial text seems to contradict the normative text of patriarchal Greece, which clearly valued the father–son relationship strongly, and said very little about brothers and sisters.

But from another point of view it is precisely this normative text that Sophocles' play sets out to vindicate, by visiting catastrophe on those who offend against the prime directives of patriarchy: love your father,

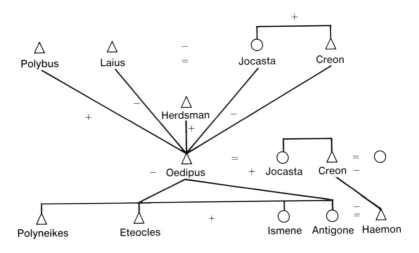

Figure 7.2. A familial text for Sophocles' *Oedipus*

from whom you will inherit, and be indifferent to wife and mother, that you may have power over them. But the play is centred on the text of the son, Oedipus. He is provided with a superabundance of fathers or father-substitutes: a positive father (Polybus) and a negative one (Laius); a positive slave father (the herdsman) and a negative maternal uncle, Creon. Freud's reading of the plot internalizes two of these figures, and treats one (Laius) as the object of unconscious hatred, while the other (Polybus) is the idealized father of the superego. But Sophocles has constructed four not two fathers for Oedipus, and three of these at least have an institutional place in Greek society. One of these coincides with the biological father. The maternal uncle represents the mother's kin. But the slave is also a member of the 'family', the *oikos*, in upper-class Greek society. Precisely because the father–son link was so crucial to the patrilineal structure, the negativity that arose in it had to be displaced and controlled, and the positivity had to be reinforced. The power of the one male (the father) over another must be balanced by one or more father-figures who are either free to be more loving (the slave, or the older homosexual lover) or more punitive (the maternal uncle). But these institutions (homosexuality, slave father and avunculate) are the embodiments of a composite text, produced out of the demands of the patriarchal father to have both love and power in relation to his son, and the counter-demands of the son, to have his own love and power over a slave and over a sister. The result is not an unconscious set of feelings, as in Freud's reading, but an interrelated set of relationships, all conscious, all present in a set of contradictory familial texts which is enshrined imperfectly in a set of institutions.

We will now expand the range of texts to examine, still within the same period of Greek culture, the equally admired cycle of the *Oresteia*, written by Aeschylus. This cycle not only deals with a different noble house, but since its pivotal event is a matricide not a patricide it initially might seem to contradict the Oedipal pattern. Agamemnon, King of Argos, waged war on Troy on behalf of his brother Menelaus, whose wife, Helen, had been stolen by Paris, prince of Troy. On the way to Troy, Agamemnon sacrificed his daughter Iphigenia, reluctantly, on the insistence of the army. When he returned with Cassandra his mistress, his wife Clytemnestra, now having an affair with his cousin Aegistheus, murdered him. His son Orestes, who had been fostered out, returned, accompanied by Pylades, his very good male friend, and with the help of Electra and the female population of Argos he murdered his mother and her lover. Shame at the deed drove him mad, displaying the classic symptoms of schizophrenia (disjointed language, hearing contradictory voices, hallucinating) and he fled Argos, never to marry. So ended the house of Agamemnon: with a total of four murders, one insanity, and

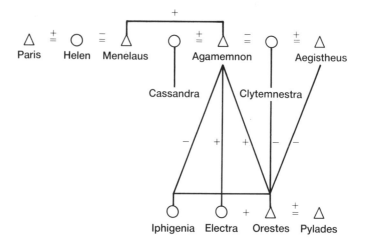

Figure 7.3 A familial text for the *Oresteia* of Aeschylus

no surviving heirs, no more promising than the house of Thebes, but with an entirely different pattern.

In this structure (figure 7.3), a number of patterns emerge. At the upper level, Agamemnon, Clytemnestra and Helen have two mates, one an official relationship, which is negative (−) each time, the other an illegitimate one which is positive (+). At the lower level, Orestes has two 'fathers', one +, the other −. In fact he also has two 'mothers'. Clytemnestra is his natural mother, but when a false report of his death reaches Argos, it is Cilissa, his nurse, who grieves most:

> Never yet did I have to bear a hurt like this.
> I took the other troubles bravely as they came:
> But now, darling Orestes! I wore out my life
> For him. I took him from his mother, brought him up.
>
> (Aeschylus, *Libation Bearers*, 747–50)

In terms of this scheme, we can see how the *Oresteia* in fact repeats the Oedipal pattern. Aegistheus is one aspect of the father, the father as mother's lover; and he is killed by Orestes without remorse. But the mother is split into two also, with the nurse as the loving mother, and Clytemnestra as the powerful mother. It is the second aspect of the mother whom Orestes kills, with great inner reluctance. Sophocles' Oedipus just stopped short of matricide when he found out his wife's true identity, and her suicide was partly a response to his rage. Orestes could kill the transform of his hated father, and love his actual father (or at least, his memory after he was ded). Oedipus killed his actual father but loved the transform. *Oedipus* shows the catastrophic return of the repressed, witness to the difficulty of the required transformation: the *Oresteia* does much the same, disguising it with a simple displacement.

Aeschylus' work explores other dimensions of the problem of marriage in the society of his plays. Agamemnon has two partners (Cassandra and Clytemnestra) and two daughters (Iphigenia and Electra). He kills one daughter, while the other loves him so much that Freud named the Electra complex after her. He is warned by one partner (Cassandra) that the other will kill him. Cassandra, part of the spoils of war, was not his only compensation for a loveless marriage (there were other spoils from time to time), but for the moment she occupies that transformational place. The case of the daughters is a revealing one. Before he killed Iphigenia – at the army's insistence – he had first shown excessive love for her. It was not usual to take a daughter on a military expedition. The army's requirement that she be sacrificed, not simply sent home, declared the punitive sanctions that society exerted on the father–daughter bond, to preserve the existing family structure.

Sophocles does not give us enough detail to begin to constitute the transformations that controlled female sexuality ('What became of the Sphinx after the encounter with Oedipus?' de Lauretis asks pointedly, 1984: 109). Aeschylus' play treats this issue in its study of Clytemnestra, with Helen another instance. Clytemnestra's loveless marriage is counterbalanced by what could be called a love match (she refers to Aegistheus as 'my dearest, dearest of all men' *Agamemnon*, 1654) and she also claims a strong attachment to her daughter Iphigenia. Her positive relationship with Aegistheus is the only compensation for the negative relationships she is surrounded by. In the play, Aegistheus seems a vain, weak, ambitious and selfish man, but that is beside the point for Clytemnestra's construction of him. Whatever he is actually like, Clytemnestra has assigned him a strongly positive affectual value, which is his meaning for her. The particular transformation she used was of course totally illicit (Agamemnon could have twenty concubines, Clytemnestra is not allowed one lover in this society), but without it we can see the barrenness of what this society offered a woman. Clytemnestra's husband is absent from home for ten years, he executes her daughter, and returns with a concubine in tow, but these are only dramatically intensified images of the dominant set of familial relationships in classical Greek society.

Aeschylus was just as male as Sophocles, older and of more aristocratic origins: yet his texts espouse democracy and represent the familial text of women more fully than do Sophocles' texts. He makes his allegiance clear. The *Oresteia* ends with a trial scene in which Orestes is accused of the murder of his mother. The accusers are the

Eumenides, female goddesses, who plead an explicit form of mother's right, in terms of which the mother–son bond is far stronger than that of husband–wife or father–son. In the climax of the play, votes are tied between mother-right and father-right. Only a casting role resolves the issue in favour of Orestes – the vote of a woman, Athena. Aeschylus' work is a classic text to show the currency of theories of mother-right in classical Athens (see, e.g., Thomson 1972). The version of society he represents in his plays shows many traces of female familial texts and the institutions that accommodate them – especially forms of adultery that overtly challenge the patriarchal family at its core. But just as Sophocles exploring the problems of the link with the father needed to project the multiple fathers offered by Greek society, so Aeschylus, exploring the problems of gender links (mother–son and husband–wife) needed to represent something of the familial texts of women.

Thus far we have been attempting to outline the primary social meaning of a set of six narratives, three plays each by two dramatists. It is time to clarify what our reading strategies have been and what they have assumed. The transformations from represented events to synchronic structures may seem *ad hoc* or arbitrary. In practice, the link is so strong and so redundant that we could have drawn a wealth of alternative examples with the same result. Although we have treated the narratives as a set we have not assumed that they are consistent with each other or represent a common meaning. On the contrary, the familial texts presented by each author have areas of overlap and areas of difference. They are both composite texts, signifying the presence of competing familial texts, some of them occluded (especially strongly in the case of Sophocles' narratives). The discrepancies between them and within them do not promise any single ultimate unitary text. There is no universal familial text of classical Greek society. On the contrary, these narratives provide and endorse, to different degrees, familial texts of the silenced, the subordinate, disrupting yet shaping the texts of the dominant. Narratives by the subordinate of their own familial texts no longer exist, but they survive as the necessary completion of the meaning of the texts of the dominant, as rocks to be avoided or trees to cling to.

We chose to analyse these texts because of a series of questions and hypotheses about the family in classical Greek society, and it is proper to return to these questions and hypotheses. Where Freud and Lévi-Strauss were concerned with self-maintaining systems, Sophocles and Aeschylus represented the opposite: a crisis within the family, so catastrophic that the families they represent cannot function and do not reproduce themselves. From macro-histories like that of Engels and from data established by social historians we can sketch in the material conditions which constrained and were incorporated into these familial texts. The material conditions were what these texts made sense of, but the sense they made constitutes the social meaning of those conditions for members of that society. The relationship between material conditions and familial texts is a dialectic, not a one-way causal relationship. Analysis of either on its own will be drastically inadequate, if what we want to understand is precisely this dialectic.

The site of the crisis, for both dramatists, is the *oikos*, the household of the aristocratic and wealthy. The *oikos* was not the only family form in classical Greece. Greece by this period had evolved into a complex structure in which the *polis* – the city/state – was the dominant principle of organization (see Humphreys 1983). As Engels pointed out, class divisions permeated Greek society, breaking the bonds of a society which had previously been organized in terms of tribal and kinship links. The *oikos* was no longer an extended family in the context of kinship networks. But in a slave-owning society, slaves replaced kin in the primary familial text. At the core of the *oikos* was now a nuclear family (husband, wife and children), but the household slaves were also an intrinsic part of it. Aeschylus and Sophocles show the crucial role these others played in the possible affective structures as well as in economic production, as transformational solutions to the problems of the core group. The Greek citizen family was literally unthinkable without its slaves.

These problems stem as Engels argued from the economic and political relationships of the married couple, characterized by a sharp division of functions between men and women and physical separation of the sexes in everyday life. In the interests of male power and a male line of inheritance, the position of the wife was severely diminished. A patriarchal ideology of family life is clearly recorded in moral texts and other documents of the time. What is not so clearly articulated, outside the kind of text we have analysed, is a contemporary sense of the discomforts of this dispensation to all concerned, and the multiplicity of alternative constructions that coexisted with the dominant patriarchal model, and the plenitude of displacements and accommodations which were permitted or even encouraged.

Both Aeschylus and Sophocles were concerned in their different ways with sons as psychic casualties of patriarchy. They trace the transformation by which the sons of the *oikos* were provided with alternative fathers, in order to contain and displace the hostility that would destroy patriarchy, and to reinforce positive attitudes to bind the son to his patriarchal role. The old institution of the avunculate provided one equivocal father-figure, derived from a matrilineal concept of kin, even though the avunculate had seemingly disappeared from Greek social life. The system of slavery provided another class of father, characterized by the reversal of the power inequality. Homosexuality provided a further father-figure, of the same status but outside the *oikos*, though of the two only Aeschylus deals with this Greek institution, and only by implication, in the texts we have looked at.

Corresponding to the construction of a triple father, these texts show the construction of a triple mother-mate, constituted by the same basic categories, the *gyne* (mother/wife as custodian of property), the slave *pallaka* (concubine or nurse, the provider of nurturance and comfort) and the erotic equal (the sister within the *oikos* and the *hetaira* outside it). Women were split by these categories into at least three distinct roles, each an impoverishment of their potential as defined by this very society. Although the role of the *gyne* as official wife and mother was central in the official gender ideology, the other two roles were not accidents, but systemic, just as Engels argued. Because of the ambiguous relationships between love and power, the sons of the powerful demanded a woman they could love because of their own greater power (the slave) and even more strongly someone they could love because their power was neutralized, or not an issue (the *hetaira*, or a homosexual companion).

The familial texts we have examined have some unique features which are specific to one stratum of Greek society, at a specific stage in the development of family and state. In the light of this specificity we need to amend Freud's account of Oedipus' complex. Undoubtedly Sophocles' Oedipus had a profoundly ambivalent attitude to his father, and this was an attitude which society demanded had to be overcome. But the cause of this ambivalence was not his desire for his mother as a psychobiological given, but his response to the hostility of both parents, a hostility conditioned by the social construction of their own relationship. His 'complex' was not an interior psychological fact buried in his unconscious, but a set of specific meanings deployed on a set of significant others from the social framework. Oedipus' problem was not his 'Oedipus complex', but rather the collapse of two kinds of familial text. The extended kin-group had been shrunk to the patriarchal *oikos*, and a barrier had been constructed within the *oikos* between masters and slaves and males and females in an extreme condition of patriarchal power. A framework such as Engels provides allows us to see the specificity of this moment in the development of the modern family. But Engels, like Freud, still sees many close analogies between the patriarchal family in classical Greece and the nuclear family of the nineteenth-century bourgeoisie. Like Freud (and like Lévi-Strauss) he sees patterns of compensatory structures that become intrinsic to the institution itself. And as we examine even a small number of narratives we find a plenitude of contradictory transformations of familial texts which can be best explored in terms of a Freudian theory of transformations, even though it needs a better account than Freud's of the social processes that explain it.

Family photos and familial texts

Familial texts have been represented by a whole range of synchronic narratives from prehistoric carvings (for instance the 'Great Goddess') through various representations of families (genealogies, family portraits, idealized 'holy' families in art or sculpture) to the modern family photo and photo album. Such texts typically do not represent familial texts directly. They are normally decoded as transformations, as specific stages in a diachronic sequence, produced by specific agents, and designed to be inserted into a further chain of discourse. Their synchronicity is a part of their meaning, carrying a message about the permanence and timelessness of family forms. It is also a barrier to their full meaning, since this meaning is intrinsically diachronic, a message about the transformations of love and power that intersect in the static moment of a single text.

To illustrate how this kind of text functions, we will take a photograph (plate 7.1). It was taken about half a century ago, of an American

Plate 7.1 A family photograph as a familial text

Jewish family, and now belongs to the person who was the boy on the extreme right (whom we will refer to as A, and whose interpretations are part of the composite text that we will analyse). It depicts three generations of the boy's mother's family. The grandparents, Larry Sr. and Judith, are seated on the extreme left and right respectively of the front row. Between them are their three daughters: Rachel, the second oldest to the left, Becky the youngest in the middle, and Sarah the eldest to the right. Behind Rachel is her husband, John. Behind Sarah is Larry Jr., her husband. Sarah has three children: A to the extreme right, Lydia, the elder daughter, in front of the grandfather, and Rosie, on Sarah's knee. Rachel's only child, Barry, is on her knee. Becky at this stage is unmarried, and behind her is Sammy, her brother, the youngest of the family.

A made two comments that help us to orientate this text to more basic familial texts. He introduced it as depicting 'the maternal . . . line'. This is his own maternal line, in the first place, but the whole picture is determined by matrilineality, even though he also described the grandfather as a 'patriarch'. This matrilineal basis is indicated by the presence of the sons-in-law immediately behind their wives, with the children distributed in the group without reference to their fathers. A also noted the striking centrality of the youngest daughter, Becky, at the centre of the photo as follows:

A   Well, I'm just thinking that in this picture Becky is. . .the jewel in the lotus. She's the virgin, and she's right there in the centre and the promise that surrounds her is the promise of . . .

G   . . . fecundity?

A   Fecundity, that's right. And . . . there are . . . the . . . the brother . . . and the brothers-in-law . . . flanking him and . . . surrounding this . . . group that needs to be protected. My friend Timna I credit with this insight. She said all the men are in black, and I said my grandmother is, and she said my grandmother is an honorary male, she's stopped being a woman.

From this interpretation we can see some of the main elements of the code. The transparent signifiers of ± close (= ± solidarity) and ± high (= ± power) give equivocal meanings, since the patriarch and matriarch are both seated, like their daughters, while the second-generation males are standing, taller than their wives or sisters. The youngest son, Sammy, towers over both Becky and his brothers-in-law. Since he was only 14 at this time, one might suspect that a box has added to his height, though that was not the case. His height thus seems to signify power or importance, but he is not the patriarch, not even a father. The code that A stresses concerns centres and peripheries, with proximity to the centre a signifier of an object of love, and peripherality the marker of power, a power that exists to protect the object of love.

In fact, there are a number of circular structures which carry this meaning. Becky is the centre of a double circle, as A points out, flanked by her two sisters and by the circle of four senior males (and one honorary male, the grandmother). But 'the son', Sammy, is also flanked and protected by his brothers-in-law, the centre of an epicycle. And the four children form an inner circle whose centre is the camera point-of-view. They are protected by one circle consisting of the three daughters, plus the grandparents, with the grandfather an honorary female, and behind these, the group of three males – although the grandparents could also be constructed as part of this outer group as well.

The ambiguous role of dominant males in this scheme is interesting. This is undoubtedly a patriarchal family (A: 'My grandfather was an important man in his own eyes, and in the eyes of the family'). But the marker of power is peripherality, since power exists for the sake of love, not the other way around, or so the code asserts. Lack of power is the marker of centrality, because lack of power – youth, femininity, virginity – is essential in the object of love. So (to A) the photo seemed to celebrate the youngest daughter, Becky, and the matriarch went through a gender change as she adopted a position of power.

By describing the ages and relationships of the people concerned, we are tacitly accepting that this picture only makes sense in relation to and as a transformation of another picture, which is rendered reasonably transparently by a genogram or family tree of the form that kinship analysts use. A's discourse explaining the picture to us constantly referred to some such map. We can represent the transaction that constitutes the photograph as a transformation, along the lines of figure 7.4.

This transformational process breaks down into a number of component transformations. In the genogram, + close equals + affinity, either by marriage (=) or by blood, within a generation (—) or across generations (|). In the portrait, there is distance added to every marital relationship, with the maximum difference between the patriarch and the matriarch. There is an inverse relationship here between love and power, in that the greater the power of a marital couple, the greater the physical distance (signifying non-love) between them. The young married males do stand behind their wives, but not touching them: not looking at them in fact, in an identical relation to them as 'the son', Sammy, has to the virgin daughter, Becky. The children of Sarah and Larry Jr. likewise are distributed around the significant others of the family group. The elder daughter is assigned, as a surrogate object of love, to the patriarch. The son, A, is assigned to the grim and

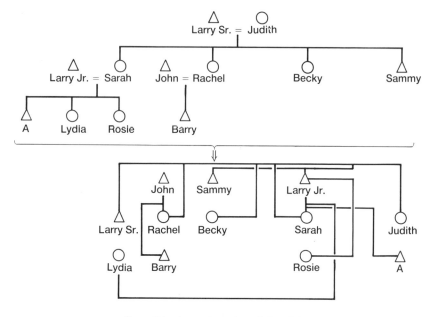

Figure 7.4 A transformation of plate 7.1

unresponsive matriarch. The youngest daughter Rosie (like Barry, Rachel's only son at this stage) is allowed close proximity to the mother, though not the father. In these repositionings we have another transformational rule: when non-close are transformed to close, what is signified is the predominance of love over power. We can set out these two principles as follows:

+ close ⇒ − close signifies power > love
− close ⇒ + close signifies love > power

(i.e., when a known close relationship is represented as a distant one, it signifies that power is the dominant dimension, not love: and the converse, when a known distant relationship is represented as close).

By this principle we can see the complex set of transformations of the marital relationship that exists for Larry Sr. as patriarch. He is closer to his three daughters than to his wife, and closer still to Lydia his granddaughter. Judith his wife has been assigned A, though this is clearly a more ambivalent gift, and her own son is behind and separated by her son-in-law. The marital relationship, then, has one surface transformation into two forms:

$$\text{Larry} = \text{Judith} \Rightarrow \begin{cases} \text{Larry Sr.} = \text{Lydia} \\ \\ \text{A} = \text{Judith} \end{cases}$$

But given the role of the daughters we can reconstruct the three women assigned to the patriarch as threefold:

Matriarch (Judith)
Brides (Becky/Rachel/Sarah)
Nymph (Lydia)

These three roles have a structural resemblance to the three roles of woman in patriarchal Greece: *gyne* (official wife), *hetaira* (courtesan/companion) and *pallaka* (concubine). The resemblance is not fortuitous, and helps to explain how the Jewish Freud was able to understand the Greek Oedipus as well as he did, although the differences between the classical Greek and the Jewish family are also extremely important.

It is clear that different roles are constructed for the three daughters, and the same process is clearly under way in the next generation, with the family of Sarah and Larry Jr. In the photograph, A, 'the son', is assigned to the family of origin, to the matriarch, not to either of his parents. Lydia, the older daughter, is assigned as the object of love to the patriarch, constructed, that is, as lovable to males. Rosie remains the possession of the mother, allied to her and not available to the males of the family. We should not assume, of course, that this is a representation of fixed roles. Barry, for instance, would not have been allowed such proximity to his mother even a year later, according to A, and his position would change with the addition of another son who would be born a year later. The photograph represents only a stage in the familial construction of the personality. But interpreted transformationally, it helps to make.sense of later stages.

In this case, for instance, A reported that his relationships with Lydia were more relaxed than with Rosie, who was always trying to 'make (him) what (he) wasn't', to rule his life. Rosie was the self-appointed upholder of the law of the family: Lydia was the relaxed, non-powerful one who could be liked because she was not feared. The photograph shows her constructed in that role in relation to the patriarch, and it seems that she had it in relation to her brother as well. We can guess that when the patriarchal grandfather was absent she fulfilled this role for her father, too, although in a larger family the transformational possibilities become unpredictably greater. We could ask whether Lydia was 'naturally' nicer, more amenable and less uptight than Rosie, or whether she was formed into the role, and to some extent this is a relevant question, since some people prove intractable in their assigned role. But even so we can see the inexorable demand of the patriarchal familial text for a differentiated set of female options. Far from stamping a single gender stereotype on all boys and all girls, it demands specific differences, and magnifies or creates them as far as it can.

This issue is best understood not as concerned with some 'essential nature' of human beings. The presence or absence of specific genitalia for instance can affect the process of construction of gender, but is not entirely decisive, and cross-gender constructions are possible and not uncommon. It is more a matter of the scope for resistance that individuals can exercise, the degree to which they can produce oppositional familial texts. In this instance, the most obvious site of opposition is the boy, A. A reflected on the meaning of his posture explicitly:

A   I look at the . . . at the pose of this child too, which I think is, I think has something to do with my characteristic relation to . . . er . . . to domestic groups, and maybe to any group. And that is, that I'm partly, moving to be inside it. I'm looking into it . . .

G   You turned that way . . . No, you're actually not . . . your head's a bit turned away . . .

A   Yeah, I'm in and out. I want to be in and I don't want to be in. I'm ambivalent.

A discussed at length the meaning of this posture in straightforward proxemic terms. He agreed that he has disrupted the harmonious pattern of the group by detaching himself so far, and that he could have been positioned in front of Judith. However, he rejected as 'unthinkable' a place in front of Becky, at the vacant centre of the picture. He read the complex twists of his posture as self-cancelled impulses to join the group as much as to leave it. He strongly felt that this ambivalence was one of his dominant characteristics as a social being.

In this picture he is clearly actively involved in constructing this role, the only one to depart from the familial text so markedly. He therefore seems the author of this dissident text, which is included but not assimilated into the overall text. Yet part of the reason he is not incorporated is that no one tries to incorporate him. His grandmother most clearly rejects this role. Asked why he did not stand in front of his grandmother, A replied:

A   That's partly because of her poor sick leg . . . her famous poor sick leg (laughs) so that she . . .

G   But you could have?

A   I could have stood in front of her but I didn't.

In this explanation, A begins by offering as his own a reason that is in fact a buried quotation, the reason of another. He then recognizes its alien origin and laughs, to neutralize it as a reason and reveal its status as a rationalization. 'Famous' indicates that Judith overused this 'poor sick leg' as an excuse for not doing what she did not want to do. In this case, it seems what she doesn't want is having A in front of her, as a permitted substitute male. A's explanation, then, implies a time when he endorsed and repeated the reasons of his grandmother (to repudiate him) and another time when her reliability was put in doubt, though he does not follow up the implication. But it seems that his ambivalent and marginalized position in the photo is co-authored, part of the different familial texts of his grandmother as well as himself. And marginalization, we can see from the position even of the patriarch, is part of being male, in a matrilineal structure of this kind. The grandfather is not only at the extreme edge of the group, he has left a discreet gap between himself and his daughter and his son-in-law. Only the granddaughter and the weight emanating from the other side from his wife keep him seeming in balance as part of the family group. The conflicting pressures on A are undoubtedly experienced strongly by him, and expressed through messages that his own body has constructed, yet they are to some extent pre-given. If the photograph as an official text has accepted his right to inscribe his own dissident meanings into it, his dissidence has worked with and expressed the unacknowledged meaning of others.

A photograph like this does not only record a familial text, it seems to perpetuate its meanings. A talked freely and fluently to us about its implications. He also described something of its discursive history. It had been given him for his 50th birthday by Lydia, on a visit. He mentioned that he had discussed it with friends and with his daughter, and no doubt with others. He even reported a dream he had about it.

A   I had a dream. My sister Lydia sent me this for my 50th birthday. I hadn't seen it for years. And not long after it I had a dream . . . of an Australian hillside in . . . in . . . pleasant sunlight, kind of autumnal sunlight . . . you know the hillside in Tom Roberts's *Bailed up*? You know that painting? *Bailed up*? In the art gallery?

G   Describe it?

A   Um . . . a stagecoach has been stolen . . .

G   Yes, I do.

A   . . . and the bush is behind it. The bush is wonderful, and it's a great masterpiece of Australian landscape. The sun comes through the trees, and it . . . lights this tawny grass. On such a hillside . . . everybody . . . who's been part of my family . . . both . . . both this family . . . and . . . Paula's . . . and Mary . . . and . . . our kids, that is, Paula's and my kids, and also Mary's kids, and maybe other people as well, I'm not sure, for a photograph. It was one of those impossible photographs that can only occur in a dream.

Everybody was on the hillside. Everybody was comfortable and happy. Everybody was doing their characteristically . . . happy . . . thing, they were engaged in an activity. And everybody was ... at the same time that there was enough space between them, that they weren't frozen ... into this unit ... um ... they were all ... in happy relation to each other. That is it, that photo had quite as much structure to it as this one has. And you could see the form ... in it as soon as you looked. That is, it was not ... a tight pattern. And I suppose that's been my dream of ... family, of relations.

Dream analysis takes us into the heartland of Freudian analysis. A explicitly recognized the symbolism of mountain = family, and this all-capacious mountain which can contain infinite families is consistent with a Freudian reading. But it is equally interesting to see this dream as a transformation of the meanings of the photograph, and of A's own body-text within it. Instead of stasis ('they weren't frozen') there is activity. The dream dissolves the paralysing synchronicity of the original, just as anecdotes and other discourses do. The activity is individualized, not lock-stepped into the meanings of others, as in the photographic text. But the scene, he insists, has just as much pattern and order as the photograph, incorporates more not less into the 'family'; including both his wives and their respective children, an acute problem in reality for this family. So the dream expresses the virtues of family and Jewishness as well as the desire for individuation and separation, exactly the same contradiction his 4-year old body had tried to reconcile. Both photograph and dream still function to bond A to his family and to his Jewishness, however much ambivalence they also express.

The familial text which we have tried to reconstruct will underlie later texts which it uses to make sense of relationships, though it will not always remain unchanged. We did not explore A's later emotional relationships. We did however ask him how relevant familial structures were in his work relationships. In response he classified males into three categories: paternal (strongly negative authority figures with whom he came into intense conflict) avuncular (authority figures whom he related to very positively) and fraternal (most male colleagues whom he related to with weak positivity). Women he divided into two categories: those like Rosie, who 'want to reshape me so I make fun of what they say and what they want to make of me', and those like Lydia, whom 'I don't always like or get along with, but they have no wish for me to be other than what I am'. A, it seems, functions best under an avunculate, or a system that he constructs in those terms. However, neither of the models he deploys for women colleagues is entirely positive, and none of them allows him to construct a positive female authority figure.

In this reading, our concern was not the photograph as a self-contained text, but as an important strategic site in a chain of discourses which mediate and derive from familial texts. In recovering these familial texts, the material facts about families as coded in genograms are valuable but not decisive. Familial texts are constructed in response to biologically and socially given groups, but are not identical with such groups. They are texts with multiple authorship, inflected by different sites within the family which are never independent. When in turn these familial texts are employed to make sense of a new group or a new domain, they carry over constraints from their previous history. The different domains will be linked by patterns of opposition and homology, expressed through a new set of relationship texts which will incorporate something from the old. The overall relations in a new domain will ultimately be determined by the forces operating in that domain. If individuals draw on familial texts to make sense of relations in the work-place, for instance, those relations will not themselves be the product of familial relations and familial texts. But the spheres of work and family are ultimately part of a single political and economic system, different but interdependent, and necessarily linked by regular and negotiable transformational routes.

Happy families and narrative order: taking the time out of history

Among the narratives of various kinds which surround everyone, from child to adult, there is one broad class that has peculiar importance: the story. Children demand them from an early age, and endlessly construct and tell their own. Adults know the danger of watching the beginnings of the most banal and clichéd story on television. It takes real effort to get up and leave the story, or to turn it off. What is the attraction of stories, and what is the social work they perform?

In this discussion, it will be noticed, we make a distinction between 'narrative' and 'story'. 'Narrative' in our usage refers to the organization of the world as constructed by a text. 'Story' refers to a generic type of narrative, ordered in particular formal, textual ways, contingent on the social organization of participants in the situation, where or for whom the story functions. 'Narrative', then, is oriented to the mimetic plane. 'Story' incorporates more aspects of the semiosic plane, along with its characteristic mimetic structures. However, in analysing any examples of narrative or story, the essential interrelation of semiosic and mimetic plane can never be ignored. Signs and texts are always socially produced. The structure of signifiers is itself the result of prior social processes of negotiation and contestation, so that the relation of signifiers to signifieds is not arbitrary but signifies the state of social relations at a particular time. In order to uncover this kind of meaning, we need to understand the social relations of the participants involved in the production of story and narrative.

Narrative is a culturally given way of organizing and presenting discourse. The characteristic structures of narrative themselves carry important meanings. Narrative links events into sequential and causal chains, and gives them a beginning and an end. These features are transparent signifiers of coherence, order, and closure. One effect of the use of these persuasive transparent signifiers is to naturalize the content of the narrative itself. By presenting various contingent cultural categories in a narrative frame, the categories themselves take on the appearance of naturalness, and come to seem as inevitable as nature itself.

Another widespread property of narrative serves to signify the stability of the status quo. Aristotle's famous definition of narrative, that it has a beginning, a middle, and an end, seems too banal to be interesting or worth challenging, but as he glossed it it masked an ideologically loaded progression, from an initial state of equilibrium, through complication or disturbance, to a crisis and resolution, leading to a new equilibrium. This gives the formula for the classic narrative of the status quo. Ideologically this structure acknowledges that the state of affairs can be disturbed and unsettled, but it promises that they will return to a state of equilibrium which is prior and natural and therefore inevitable. Narrative is therefore an effective and flexible strategy which particular societies can use to reproduce their value systems. Narrative takes flux, incessant activity, insoluble problems, and turns them into stability, coherence, solution. It puts boundaries around disruptive processes and events, and often breaks them up further into discrete steps or stages, again limiting their disturbing force.

One important class of narrative in contemporary society is history as produced by historians. The incessant activity of historians can be seen as constant attempts to rewrite the past in ways which make the present more secure, discovering moments of closure for every moment of disruption, compartmentalizing history into a vast set of individual narratives, existing as books or articles in a number of individual genres of history. In this way history makes the past at one with the present, as an inexhaustible source of narratives of the ultimate triumph of equilibrium. Thus the discipline of history purveys a narrative form which takes time and process out of history.

Another major form of narrative is what we have called 'story', and this will be our main focus of discussion. The term refers to a class of genres, whose specific forms vary widely at different times or for different occasions. So important is the category 'story' among types of narrative that its features typically seem the 'unmarked' form of narrative, the type which is unremarked and unremarkable, so familiar as to seem the most 'natural' of all. As well as mimetic features, 'story' implies a particular organization of participants, one marked by relatively high levels of informality and solidarity. Types or genres of story vary, by reference either to social occasion (e.g., anecdote, children's story, novel) or to typical mimetic content (e.g., Sci Fi, Western, Fairy Story).

Because 'story' as a category is so directly tied into specific semiosic contexts, it is more liable to change than narrative forms, which tend to respond to semiosic processes at a much slower rate. The logonomically determined conjunction of narrative categories and mimetic categories in specific generic forms therefore presents a structure of great complexity and diversity. It is also, however, more precisely and subtly responsive to immediate social forces. As a result, it is 'story' rather than 'narrative' that offers the best site for analysing specific social meanings as well as continuities of cultural values over time.

The example we will take for purposes of illustration is a children's story *Only One Woof*, by James Herriot (1985), as 'adapted' for children and illustrated by Peter Barrett. The narrative thus exists in a double text, verbal and visual. The relation between the two strands is itself complex, with the visual sometimes subordinate to the verbal as 'illustration' or 'elaboration', sometimes more independent, with a contrapuntal relation to the text structured as like a fugue. In analysing the story we will begin with the verbal narrative. Here it is necessary to proceed at a more local level than the broad progression from equilibrium through disruption to equilibrium, and break the story down into a series of units, which we have numbered for easy reference.

Unit 1   The vet/narrator, James Herriot, sets the scene, introduces us to the relevant world: the country, more specifically a farm(yard). We are introduced to several characters, Mr Wilkin the farmer – the only named character – and two sheepdog puppies. The vet/narrator observes to the farmer 'Those two really love each other, don't they? Mr Wilkin responds: 'Aye, they are great friends. They are never apart.'

Unit 2   The focus is now on Mr Wilkin, a busy farmer, who still has time for his hobby of breeding sheepdogs, at which he has been very successful for many years, winning many trophies. Out of the latest litter he has kept two pups: Sweep and Gyp.

Unit 3   Now the focus moves to the two pups jointly. Both are behaving 'naturally' in the farmer's view as sheepdogs.

Unit 4   Each of the pups is now introduced. One, Sweep, is an ordinary dog. The other, Gyp, is unusual: he has a brown patch, a floppy ear and one ear that always sticks up, and he has never barked.

Unit 5   George Crossley, 'one of Mr Wilkin's oldest friends', wants to buy a dog as his has died. Mr Wilkin sells Sweep. This is odd, because Sweep is more advanced in training than Gyp; perhaps it is because Gyp has 'a lop-sided charm that is difficult to resist'.

Unit 6   Gyp is sad to lose his 'brother and best friend, and there was no doubt that he missed him' but, as he has the other dogs for company he is never 'really lonely'. Gyp is not quite clever enough to compete in the trials.

Unit 7   A year has passed. Gyp is in the fields with the farmer. He remains 'bright-eyed and affectionate. But soundless'.

Unit 8   Another year has passed. There is a sheepdog trial. Groups of men dressed in all sorts of clothing stand in groups in the big field by the river.

Unit 9   The dogs are tied to the fence waiting their turn. There are no growls, no fights. 'It was wonderful to see the long row of waving tails and friendly expressions'.

Unit 10 Mr Wilkin is leaning against his car. Gyp is tied to the bumper, Mrs Wilkin is sitting on a camp stool by his side. Mr Wilkin is not 'running a dog', but has just come to watch.

Unit 11 'George Crossley with Sweep' make their way to the starting post. Gyp stiffens; as the trial starts Gyp slowly rises to his feet.

Unit 12 Sweep understands all the commands of Mr Crossley, gestures, short whistles, long whistles. It is obvious that he is a champion.

Unit 13 Mr Crossley cries out happily 'Good lad', Sweep answers with a quick wag of his tail, Gyp raises his head and gives a single loud bark 'which echoed round the field'.

Unit 14 Mrs Wilkin gasps. Her husbands bursts out, 'Well, I don't believe it!' and looks open-mouthed at his dog.

Unit 15 Gyp is let off his lead. The brothers play, 'chewing playfully at each other as they used to do as pups'.

Unit 16 The vet/narrator and the Wilkins expected that Gyp would now 'bark like any other dog, but it was not to be'.

Unit 17 Six years later. The vet/narrator is at the farm. Mrs Wilkin speaks to Gyp, who is sunning himself outside the kitchen door. Gyp has not barked since the day of the trial. Mrs Wilkin has waited a long time, but doesn't now think that he will ever bark. The vet says 'Ah well, it's not important. But I'll never forget that afternoon at the trial.'

Unit 18 Mrs Wilkin looks at Gyp again. 'Poor old lad. Eight years old and only one woof!'

These are the stages of the verbal text. Of course this account leaves out significant material. If signifiers have a structure which is significant, a full account needs to pay attention to every aspect of the structure of the narrative. For instance, the narrative makes a point of mentioning that the men gathered for the trial are leaning on long crooks 'with the handles carved from ram's horns'. No doubt there is significance in that. From the point of view of this analysis many aspects are left unaccounted for.

The visual text proceeds at its own pace. As we said, at times its function is merely that of illustration. That is important, because it calibrates verbal and visual text at several points, so that readers are encouraged to read the two texts in conjunction: the visual as an illustration, the verbal as an articulation/specification. That calibration (by illustration) also serves to neutralize and naturalize the effects of visual text on one level. If it is merely illustration, then not too much detailed reading/analysis needs to be done, seemingly. But all naturalizations are mystifications, here no less than elsewhere.

Units 1 to 4 of the verbal and the visual texts state the initial equilibrium; units 5–7 state the disturbance; units 8–15 are given over to the resolution; and units 16–18 state the new equilibrium. It is not difficult to see that even the imposition of fixed stages (in the narrative as much as in our description) cannot obscure the essential fluidity of the 'reality' of the processes that are described. Even the very first unit contains evidence of disturbance: the vet, anthropomorphizing the pups, says 'Those two *really love* each other', to which Mr Wilkin responds 'they are *great friends*', and in doing so, shows a contrasting system of classification which will have telling effects. He further says 'They are never apart', a statement to which the narrator/writer has given the syntactic status of a separate sentence. Mr Wilkin's classification system is focused on natural categories – the two pups' behaviour is, for him, entirely a matter of instinct/breeding: in unit 3 he days, 'These little *things* were born wanting to round up chickens, ducks, lambs – anything they see'. Hence the artifice of the larger structures (in the narration and in the analysis) is just that; and a little analysis reveals the constructedness of the stages.

The units do, however, impose a fairly tight and seemingly inexorable grid of sequentiality on this reality. That sequence carries or pushes the reader, in its 'natural' momentum. Each unit both introduces particular cultural categories, and sets them in motion in the narrative with a particular dynamic. Unit 1 introduces the reader to the relevant world and some of its classificatory terms: the 'country', nature in its cultivated form; domestic(ated) animals; animals both as commodities, and as pets, distinct and proximate to humans; the humans who control this world – and whose classifications count, or who may challenge the classifications; youth (the puppies) versus age, both in the form of older animals and older humans. Associated categories, essential to the support and underpinning of these larger ones, are also introduced: love (human) versus friendship (human and animal), the concept of 'play' (appropriate to young animals or humans). In unit 2 'play' for instance is transformed to 'hobby', 'sport' and 'competition': all adult activities, which can be shown to have affinity to 'work', the ostensible legitimation of many other categories as processes. Unit 3 links 'play' and 'work' as natural, inborn, biological categories: from a happy playful wrestling match the two pups turn without noticeable transition to work, rounding up ducklings, an activity they are 'born wanting to engage in'. 'Work' has thus been naturalized, with all the consequences of that: for instance, the sale of objects in unit 3, linked to the sale of Sweep as labour/labourer in unit 5. Unit 4 introduces another crucial cultural construct, one which suggests the entire classificatory system, namely that of usualness/normalness and unusualness/non-normalness. Sweep is usual, Gyp is not, in appearance and in behaviour. It is around the resolution of this problem that the narrative is constructed, and it is pivotal to the valuation and re-evaluation of all the other categories.

These are the categories and the contradictions which provide the dynamic: how do old and young, parent and child, human and animal, relate in this world? There are attributes – happiness, sadness, friendship, love – to be distributed, and what are the consequences of any particular system of distribution? What at the end of the day will count as usual/normal and what will count as unusual/non-normal?

One of the fundamental set of categories absent – and therefore seemingly not at issue – is that of male/female. Mrs Wilkin does not appear until unit 10, right in the centre of the structural stage of disturbance. This points to an interesting structural division in the narrative. The initial section is marked by the absence of the category female, as though gender were not an issue in this world. The last section of the narrative is marked by the presence (nearly the dominance) of the category female, as though no resolution/equilibrium is possible without that category. Interestingly, this presence is much more strongly marked in the visual than in the verbal text. In the second half, the visual text is dominated by Mrs Wilkin, both by her presence, and by her positioning in the images. It is as though the visual text is used to articulate meanings which cannot be written or spoken in the verbal text.

The disturbance in the narrative can therefore be seen to be brought about by the inherent contradictions in the categories introduced in the early stages, and the unsaid suppression of the female. The resolution solves some though not all of these problems. Sweep, the usual dog, becomes unusual, as a mature dog, by becoming a champion. Gyp, the unusual dog, becomes usual by not being a champion, and by demonstrating his quintessential dog-likeness in barking. To some extent the narration relativizes these values: what is usual/ordinary for Sweep – barking, normal ears, being a champion – is unusual/ extraordinary for Gyp. What is usual/extraordinary for Gyp – no bark, lopsided ears, a brown patch, 'charm difficult to resist' – is unusual/ extraordinary for Sweep. Nevertheless, some attempt has to be made to bring Gyp into the realm of the generally normal.

The contradictions or difficulties at issue at the point of climax are the more intractable ones: the categorizations of animal/human, of love/friendship, of youth/adult, of male/female. And they are not resolved in the verbal text. In the visual text however some resolution of these problems seems to be suggested. When we first meet Mrs Wilkin, in unit 10, she sits in front of her husband. He stands behind her, leaning on the car. Gyp is in the foreground, slightly to the right. It is not the traditional 'family snap' though it has elements of that. Were the image presented from the front, it would show Mrs Wilkins in front of and lower than her husband. This would suggest a difference in generation: (grand)father and (married) daughter, rather than husband and wife. Gyp, as pet (or child) should be in front of Mrs Wilkin. This ambivalence is both revealed and glossed over in this image: glossed over because it is not constructed as a 'family snap', and motivated by a reason other than posing as a family; revealed because the asymmetries are so apparent. Mr Wilkin looks to be in his late fifties/early sixties; Mrs Wilkin looks in her early forties.

Unit 11 shows this same view from behind, at an angle of 45°. If anything this exposes the problems more: the distance between Mr Wilkin and his wife is enhanced: they seem unconnected, as is Gyp. They are represented as three individuals, who have no motivating connection. This is not true of unit 14, when Mr and Mrs Wilkin are side by side, united in their astonishment at Gyp. This, however, is the last time we see Mr Wilkin. The next time we meet a male, it is the vet, who has now intruded into the story (the only mark of Mr Wilkin is an empty tractor seat). Mrs Wilkin looks youthful, as does the vet. In units 16/17 of the visual text Mrs Wilkin and the vet are in intense conversation: she is leaning towards him, his hands and gestures indicate some close urging of her. He looks worried; she looks slightly assured and expectant. In unit 18 (see plate 7.3) that tension is resolved. They stand, relaxed, side by side, smiling at Gyp, who is sitting in front of them. Apart from the house door, the nearby stone wall and gate and the hills beyond, there is nothing else in this world.

According to our reading, this story establishes a 'normal' family structure, passing from the dissolution of a 'happy' family, displacing the 'father' who sells one of his children because the categories he uses do not permit him to solve the tensions, and finally re-establishing

It was over a year since he had seen his
brother and it seemed unlikely, I
thought, that he would remember him.
But he was obviously *very* interested and,
as the judge waved his white
handkerchief to begin the trial and the
three sheep were released from the far
corner of the field, Gyp rose slowly to his feet.

Plate 7.2   Fragmented families

a family unit whose members hold to a classificatory system that makes
such a solution possible – transcending the boundaries of animal/
human, youth/age, and valuing/acknowledging the necessity of gender
categories and the role of women.

The question of course is: to what extent can this be the meaning
of the writer, or, perhaps even more importantly, the reading of the
child reader? Perhaps there are two things to say. The story is clearly
an 'adaptation', written for a child reader. Hence its form and content,

"Nor will I!" Mrs Wilkin looked at Gyp again, and she smiled as she remembered. "Poor old lad. Eight years old and only one woof!"

Plate 7.3 A family unit re-established

both the cultural classifications which are deployed, and their expression in language and image, are constructed with the child reader in mind. The writer's notions of childhood, of its anxieties and concerns, of its potent and relevant classification transmuted by the writer's and illustrator's own more or less concealed concerns, make up what the writer/illustrator's text is finally about.

In other words, the notion of adaptation is highly complex. Structural elements are introduced, in stages, and their sequences gives them a momentum and a particular tension. The visual and the verbal text interact, contrast, contradict and modalize each other in particular ways. These structures are there to be read, but they do not *determine* the child reader's reading. This is further reinforced by the fact that the 'unspeakable' meanings are carried in the visual text. Child readers will respond to them in particular ways, not unpredictably but in ways that respond to their prior experience as a social being of these categories and of their working out. The child reader is not a cultural or social *tabula rasa*, and does not come naïvely to the text. The child reader (even if as a 'read-to' reader) is located in complex sets of social relations, and already has a social and cultural history.

Only One Woof is not simply a children's book, a story for children to read. It is also published, as a book to be bought. It is, as such, a commodity that is produced, sold and bought, consumed. It exists in a market, with advertising and promotion. This process constructs its own set of texts which mediate the narrative. Here, for instance, is the text from the back cover of the book:

> ONLY ONE WOOF is a charming story which first appeared in VET IN HARNESS, and follows on the success of James Herriot's first book for children, MOSES THE KITTEN. BEAUTIFULLY ILLUS-TRATED BY PETER BARRETT, IT IS SURE TO BECOME A FIRM FAVOURITE WITH CHILDREN EVERYWHERE.
>
> ALSO IN PICCOLO: Moses the Kitten:
>
> 'YOU HAVE TO LIKE THIS WHOLLY AGREEABLE BOOK'
> – *The Times Educational Supplement*
>
> 'THE ILLUSTRATIONS BY PETER BARRETT ARE FIRST-CLASS'
> – *Daily Telegraph*

The publisher's blurb addresses a reader who is not, (or who is most likely not) the child reader. This is an adult reader, who buys books on behalf of child readers, according to notions of what is good for child readers, and what child readers like to read. In this, buyers are guided by institutionalized advice, the advice of professionals. Hence the extracts from the reviews in places which lend authority to reviewers (who, in this market, unlike others, remain unnamed).

At this level we can see the cultural determinations of narrative working at the semiosic plane of genre. An industry, in itself complex, which (re)produces culturally acceptable versions of society for those who are to be acculturated; the publishing industry supported by the industry of reviewing, itself sustained by the disciplines/professions/industries of education, literary criticism, psychology. This genre is additionally formed by notions of pleasure and entertainment, for just as Sweep and Gyp are shown at their happiest when they are at (biologically) determined play, so children are happiest at play – which can lead unnoticed into notions of work.

This text is further complicated by the fact that James Herriot's tales have a much wider circulation. They have been constructed for adults as a television series (suitable for children) and as novels. In some of his publications James Herriot acts as a guide to nature, to his native Yorkshire, for instance in coffee-table picture books, so that this text itself is complicated by the various versions of these narratives, by the characterization of the country vet in these various places. All of them give expression to an overall ideology, of the individual's place in the scheme of things, of country values, a conservative web of values sustained both by the forms of the narrative, and by the web of generic forms in which it appears. A child can grow happily from *Only One Woof* to the coffee-table versions of England without needing to change ideologies.

8

Entering Semiosis: Training Subjects for Culture

From the moment children are born, perhaps from a time before then, they are subject to the effects of semiosis and culture. The new-born enter at once into a semiotic relationship with other humans around them and, in a process which ceases only at death, they construct a world of meaning, and are constructed by an already semioticized world. That process is constantly interactive and dynamic; children are not simply *tabulae rasae* to be inscribed by culture. Children are active participants in their own cultural formation, neither simply inscribed by culture, nor simply assimilating cultural forms, values and processes. The notion of 'assimilation' is ubiquitous in discussions of education, but that fact only points to its ideological potency. The process described as being 'assimilated' into a culture, whether it is used of a child or an adult immigrant into a society, covers over a multiplicity of complex processes of reaction, resistance, subversion, acquiescence and acceptance. The process described by many teachers as assimilating knowledge – 'They seem to have no problem in assimilating this stuff . . .' – equally obscures complex dynamic interactive processes between an individual semiotic agent and aspects of the larger semiotic system. 'Assimilating knowledge' is not like stacking a new delivery of firewood up against the pile that is already there in the backyard.

'Look, those are the instructions': early steps into gender and power

In this chapter we wish to explore some aspects of that complex process. The education system is the major state institution that presides over this process in contemporary Western societies, but the scope of the educational process goes outside the classroom. The education system enters at a later stage in the transformational processes that produce social beings for society. For this reason our analysis will begin with a text that comes from a home setting, in the domain of the family. The text is a 'cooking lesson'. The participants are 3-year-old Timothy, his mother, and her friend Doris. It is a middle-class academic household.

DORIS	Has Mummy just done that do you think?
MOTHER	No darling you don't spit on the spoon
	Shall I do a bit now ...
	Oh dear if only I had a ...
TIMOTHY	Can I read the instructions?
MOTHER	Just a minute love (*inaudible*)
TIMOTHY	... butter honey ... what have we got up to ... now what do we do
	... are we doing it
MOTHER	That bit have we done pet ... look those are the instructions ... and what did that tell us to do?
TIMOTHY	Crack the eggs?
MOTHER	
DORIS	} Yes (*approvingly*)
DORIS	We have cracked the eggs and what's that one?
TIMOTHY	Mix it
DORIS	Whisking it all up ... yes ... that's where we got up to .. good .. yes
TIMOTHY	Number three
DORIS	What's that one do you think ..
	number four?
TIMOTHY	(*inaudible*)
DORIS	And Mummy's just done that hasn't she

This seems an innocuous exchange, in a relaxed family situation. Some overt learning has evidently occurred: Timothy has learnt a little about cooking, and he has been reinforced in both reading and counting. But this, we will see, is not all that he has learnt or had reinforced. We will start with the setting. This is a kitchen, within a home. Thus it is a specific domain, with attributed gender, as women's space, and opposed to the public spaces of school and work. Yet within this space, 'Mummy' and Doris engage in working (cooking). Mother is also child-minding, carrying out a role as teacher, a different kind of work. She is also relaxing and socializing with her friend Doris. Doris herself adopts a range of roles and functions. She instructs Timothy, even though the setting is in 'Mummy's' home and kitchen, while declaring her solidarity as friend. What Timothy is faced with, in this situation, is a fluid set of transformations of basic logonomic systems – so fluid that it would not seem easy for him to grasp the system itself.

The same is true of the gendered nature of the task itself. Overtly it seems that Timothy is (at his own request) being instructed in cooking, a traditionally female task but one which many 'progressive' couples today try to redefine in a non-sexist way. Timothy, it seems, is being socialized into this transformed gender system, not into the traditional one. However, it isn't the case that Timothy actually engages in cooking. What he does (after the food preparation has been done) is to repeat the instructions which his mother has obeyed. His mother's instructions to him contains a double message which specifies a double gender role: 'Learn to cook' (transform your male gender role); or 'Learn to give instructions to women/cooks' (i.e., learn your male gender role).

A similar complexity and ambiguity characterizes the language used in the exchange. The process of learning to cook furnishes the occasion for deploying forms of language that express and negotiate the intimate linkages of knowledge and power. The three major modes of linguistic interaction are all used here: interrogative: 'Has Mummy just done that?'; declarative: 'you don't spit on the spoon'; and imperative: 'look (those are the instructions)'. Of these Timothy uses only two: five interrogatives and the rest declarative. Doris also uses interrogatives and declaratives. But whereas Timothy uses five interrogatives (out of six (or seven) clauses), Doris uses them with equal frequency (twelve clauses – counting 'yes' as a 'restated clause'). Timothy's mother uses more declaratives (five) than interrogatives (two), and she uses the one imperative.

There is thus a significant skewing in terms of the distribution of the social/linguistic roles implied in these forms. That however becomes even more apparent when we look at the matching of syntactic form and pragmatic deployment. Take Doris' first interrogative 'Has Mummy just done that do you think?' Pragmatically, this is clearly not a question. Doris is telling Timothy that his mother *has* just done that, so there is no need for him to do whatever he is doing, and therefore he should stop doing what he is doing. In other words, the interrogative functions not as a question, but as a command. Take Mother's first declaration. 'No darling you don't spit on the spoon'. Uttered in the context where Timothy has just spat on the spoon this is either counterfactual or indeed another command, 'Do not spit on the spoon (again)'. Her next interrogative, 'Shall I do a bit now' also does not function as a question (it does not expect the reply 'Yes, if you want to') but as a statement, 'I will do a bit now', and hence possibly even as a command: 'Move over and let me . . . .'

These shifts also have effects on modality. The interrogative form, for instance, signifies a lower modality than the declarative. But the questions asked by Mother and Doris are asked after the event. When Doris asks 'Has Mummy just done that do you think', Timothy's eyes can tell him that she has. So the uncertainty must concern the semiosic not the mimetic plane, expressing lack of power not lack of knowledge.

But this is a catechistic question of the kind much used in classrooms, where the teacher knows the answer but tests children for their competence. So the lack of power signified by the interrogative form is Timothy's not Doris's, though Doris's power is masquerading as a lack of it in the interests of solidarity. And Timothy is given the opportunity to acquire power, the power to affirm the rightness of the system itself.

What Timothy is learning therefore is about the interrelation of meaning and power on the semiosic plane. Apart from the specific knowledge about a skew between syntactic form and pragmatic deployment (interrogative to statement and perhaps to command, declarative – concerning the child's action – to command) which are a part of the semiosic rules of Timothy's social group, he is learning one meaning of those roles: 'Do not directly assert the power that you have.' Direct negation or prohibitions on Timothy's actions do not occur. We've mentioned how 'Don't do that' is presented as 'Has Mummy just done that do you think'. That extends even as far as the refusal or unwillingness outrightly to deny anything that Timothy says. His mother, for instance, responds to his question 'Can I read the instructions' with 'Just a minute, love'. Doris, instead of saying 'No, not mixing, whisking' to Timothy's 'Mix it' says 'Whisking it all up . . . yes'. Timothy is therefore learning about indirectness, about the disguising or obscuring of power in certain circumstances by those who hold it.

The strategy which is being used here is one of 'involvement' (or perhaps 'recruitment'). The indirection that is at play in these rules may seem to have no real function. If the power is successfully read off in the end, why bother to disguise it? One answer seems to be that this use of forms demands of the hearer/reader a greater effort in the reconstruction of the meaning. Consider the steps involved in the reading of the various forms. 'Has Mummy just done that do you think?' 'Mummy has just done that, can't you see?', and 'Stop doing that, I've already done it!' The last, which articulates most directly what is 'being meant' also makes least demand on hearers in their reconstruction. They cease the action because they are commanded to do so. (Note that in many social dialects 'I was told to' means 'I was commanded to'.) With the second form, hearers are positioned as 'recipients of information'. Nevertheless they are required to make some inferences: 'If the action is completed that must mean that there is no need for it to be done again by me. The evidence is before my eyes'. The first utterance requires most reconstruction. Here the hearer is addressed as 'supplier of information'. He (in this case) is asked to supply information to himself, as there is no plausible other recipient of this answer. (At an earlier age Timothy might have answered 'yes' to this question.) By giving himself an answer, and then by engaging in the further inferences from there, Timothy is positioned very differently. The processes that lead to his eventual course of action went on in his own head, he gave himself the answer, as the result of his own thinking/action. Assent to external power is here therefore reconstructed by the individual for himself as assent on the basis of his own action and volition.

The use of pronouns in this little extract supports that mechanism. The most obvious instance is the 'you' in 'you don't spit on the spoon'. Given that Timothy has spat on the spoon, he does not seem the proper addressee of this 'you'. The very clash between reality and his mother's reconstruction of that reality forces him to attempt an interpretation that makes sense. That involves a complex series of steps, in which he will arrive at the conclusion that his action had been an aberration from what is known to be true of him by his mother. That 'you' is therefore not a specific but an ideal 'you' which conforms to a statement of the kind made by his mother. That ideal 'you' is also a highly general one, which for now covers 'all good little boys' and later of course will cover all members of a particular social group – 'you don't/can't wear that sort of thing any more . . .' His mother's and Doris's 'we' and 'us' function similarly, though in the reverse direction, from the general to the individual: 'what did that tell *us* to do?' and '*We* have cracked the eggs . . .' Here the plural pronouns seem to refer to the whole group, but are used to address one individual. The meaning that Timothy might derive from this is that in his social group everyone is similarly placed, has similar knowledge, values and histories, so that it is entirely possible to refer to an individual by naming the collectivity: there are no significant differences.

The striking thing about all this is the sheer complexity and ambiguity that surrounds this ideological episode for young Timothy. In some respects he has learnt a system of norms which specify in the manner of rules the forms and limits of appropriate and permissible behaviour. Since Timothy is a 'good' boy who copes adequately with the cooking lesson, he has clearly learnt well. But at the core of what he has learnt must therefore be the endemic pressure of double message, contradiction and mystification in the discourses of power and control, along with an underlying system which disambiguates its meanings and identifies the rules which will have real sanctions and force. Mother and Doris help him to translate the cooking instructions but make no concessions over ideology, yet Timothy operates more effectively with ideological complexities than with cooking. He is already better equipped to cope with the discursive complexities of a school than with the demands of a kitchen. And he is still only 3.

Teeth or pimples: enculturation or resistance

Timothy is skilful and active in threading his way through the semiotic minefield of discourse. But equally clearly there are different, non-adult rules applied to his performance. It is as though childhood itself constitutes a broad domain area, in which error is tolerated and forms of resistance can be developed. Even though domains are instituted as strategies for control, they are also sites where real concessions are made to the power or interests of the subordinate. In this section we will look at a text produced in one such sub-domain, the child-care centre as it functions in Australia.

The form of child-care centres is unstable even within Australia, and other closely related cultures such as Britain and America have different forms again. This inconsistency is what is to be expected with sub-domains that are situated on the boundary between two such major domains as home and school, operating with subjects whose classification within the culture is indeterminate (educable or not). The child-minder (usually female) is therefore faced with an ambiguous task. On the one hand 'good' child-care centres are tied in with quite formal educational processes. But the contrary need to relax their prescriptions leads to 'slack' child-care centres where children are allowed 'to run riot' or 'to vegetate'. There is a demand from the culture for action which is controlled and directed, yet the energy and activity of the children is intrinsic to their role as active agents in social life, and it cannot be simply quashed. Children need to be offered (within limits which aren't always fixed) the opportunity to explore the margins of rule systems, or even deliberately contravene them, which may amount to the same thing. The child-minder, then, must have a cultural agenda which shapes or frames activities which do not however always arise from within its bounds. The example text which we use to explore this question comes from a pre-school day-care centre. Sarah and Aaron are about $3\frac{1}{2}$ years old.

TEACHER	Look at this (*pointing to picture of mother and young rhino*)
SARAH	His mothers a lot of toothes
TEACHER	How many teeth? How many have they got?
SARAH	one two three four
TEACHER	What are they up the top?
SARAH	One two three four five
TEACHER	Five at the top and four at the bottom
AARON	No they're pimples
TEACHER	Do you think they're pimples?
AARON	Yeah

TEACHER	But they're where his teeth should be ... do you think they're just a different colour?
AARON	Well ... that ... those are pimples cos those are pink
TEACHER	Um ... could be too ... and what do you call those things there?
SARAH	Whiskers
TEACHER	You do too and what's that Sarah?
SARAH	A ear
TEACHER	It's a funny looking ear isn't it?
AARON	Yes ... a little ear
SARAH	That's got two ... one two ... two ears
TEACHER	Do you think they'd be friendly? ... these rhinoceroses?
AARON / SARAH	No
TEACHER	Why not?
AARON	Cos they'll eat people
TEACHER	How do you know? What makes them look unfriendly?
AARON	Their teeth ... they can eat people
TEACHER	They *are* big ... what about this animal?
SARAH	That hasn't got any teeth
TEACHER	Hasn't he?
SARAH	No
TEACHER	Do you think he'd be friendly?
SARAH	Yes
TEACHER / AARON	Look what he *has* got
SARAH	He's got little claws
TEACHER	Claws
SARAH	See ... but that ... but he's still our friendly ...
TEACHER	He's still friendly even if he's got claws?
SARAH	Look ... they're not flendry
AARON	Yes they are
TEACHER	Do you think lions are friendly Aaron?
AARON	Yeah ... because ... if they ... if people hurt them they hurt them back.
TEACHER	And it's quite safe you think if you don't hurt them?
AARON	Yes
TEACHER	I don't know.

The child-minder/teacher begins by setting up an agenda of 'difference' between herself and the children. She pins up a poster that shows some African animals. Power and knowledge are entirely fused in that action: the right and ability to put up the poster coincide with the right and ability to determine what area of the cultural domain will be explored. The teacher has control of both. In terms of the logonomic rule system that (perhaps only momentary) identity of the mimetic and the semiosic planes is crucial. The teacher controls who puts up the poster, and where, and she has control over what is to count as relevant knowledge. Ostensibly what is at issue here is learning about the mimetic plane: about rhinos and lions, and their characteristics. But it quickly becomes apparent that what is really at issue is not so much the teacher's knowledge, but the teacher's power. The teacher's direction to the children to 'Look at this' is reconstructed by Sarah as 'Tell me about this'. Obligingly, she offers the comment that 'His mother's a lot of toothes'. This offers the teacher the substance that she needs and on which she is able to work. Sarah's co-operative mode, attempting to demonstrate solidarity with the teacher, is shattered by Aaron's challenge 'No they're pimples'. Aaron rejects solidarity via a contradiction of Sarah's and the teacher's classification. That is, he uses the mimetic plane to express his challenge to the teacher's power on the semiosic plane. However, Aaron's challenge goes somewhat further, for not only does he challenge the classification, he also challenges the teacher's control of this whole situation. She had signalled the end to this particular conversational sequence by restating/correcting Sarah's last comment. That restatement functions as a signal both of conclusion, closure of one textual episode, and of her intention to initiate a new one. Aaron's challenge is therefore shrewdly timed. Had he chosen to interrupt after Sarah's first comment the teacher would have been entirely unchallenged; had he interrupted after the teacher's 'How many have they got?' his challenge would have been on the mimetic plane alone, as the teacher's closure had not yet been attempted.

In response to this move, the teacher's strategy is to pretend that this is a 'sincere' comment, within the logonomic system that she herself is operating in. She re-labels the challenge as being one about the mimetic plane alone, and indicates that she believes in Aaron's sincerity. 'Do you think they're pimples?' This then becomes refocused as a difference about classification, where Aaron's 'thinks' is opposed to the teacher's 'knows'. By the simple strategy of 'mishearing' Aaron's challenge, the teacher maintains her power. She could of course have played this differently: 'Aaron, you *are* a naughty boy, always trying to disrupt'. That however would simply have acknowledged Aaron's success, and prevented her from scoring the victory in this insurrection.

The teacher's closing 'Um . . . could be too . . . and what do you call . . .' goes unchallenged here. Nor is she conceding anything to Aaron's counter-classification. The children will by now have learned to recognize a supportive positively evaluative closure ('Good, right' or 'Yes, good girl') from one which is not supportive. In that context lack of support will signal the teacher's lack of agreement, that is, her disagreement. Throughout this brief text she adopts very similar strategies to those adopted by Timothy's mother and her friend Doris

in the 'cookery' text: she avoids direct disagreement, preferring to let
the children infer – construct for themselves – her disagreement/
disapproval. Other instances of this are her 'How do you know?'; 'They
are big" (i.e., this could be a relevant criterion but happens not to be
in this case); 'Look what he *has* got' (that is, 'Attend to the *relevant*
characteristics'); and 'I don't know (i.e., if it's outside the teacher's
range of knowledge it can't be right).

In this text there is a systematic difference between Aaron's and
Sarah's responses to the situation. Over the three instances of difference
– teeth versus pimples; eating people versus being friendly; dangerous
claws versus friendly animal – Aaron opposes the teacher's classification.
Sarah twice starts in disagreement with the teacher. On the first
occasion she simply leaves it to Aaron to oppose; her perception of the
teacher's disagreement ('Why not?') silences her. On the second
occasion she again starts on the opposite side to the teacher. However
after three challenges from the teacher – 'Look what he *has* got',
'Claws', 'He's still friendly even if he's got claws?' – she caves in to
the pressure. Aaron maintains his opposition on both occasions, each
time supporting his challenge with his own set of criteria. Only on one
occasion does Aaron go along with the (female) teacher's argument
and even here he shifts from the teacher's 'It's a funny looking ear' to
'Yes . . . a little ear'. Aaron's overt mode is to reject the possibility of
solidarity, which, given that it is solidarity with the powerful, is essentially
the possibility of submission and acquiescence. Sarah's overt mode is
to seek the possibility of solidarity, and of acquiescence. Of course it
is dangerous to speculate from this brief textual example; moreover
Sarah's hesitancy, especially her 'See . . . but that . . . but he's still
our friendly . . .' suggests that there is more than a residue of
disagreement, and some possibility of opposition.

Nevertheless, there is a clear difference which may point, even at
this relatively early age, to a difference of gender-specific behaviour.
Ultimately, both Sarah and Aaron will enter fully into the semiotic
systems of their culture. It does seem, however, as though the paths
by which they reach the same end point may be fundamentally different:
Sarah by seeking solidarity, Aaron by constant opposition. That
difference in routes may indeed leave them differently positioned at
the end. While both are fully competent users of the semiotic system,
it may be that the possibility of resistance will have quite receded for
Sarah, while for Aaron it may remain a possibility. Aaron's opposition/
subversion has the additional advantage of gaining him the attention of
the teacher, of the powerful. Just so long as he chooses to remain
within the rules of the game, it may be that for him that will always
be the reward; whereas for Sarah acquiescence may simply produce
the expectation of more acquiescence, delivered ever more readily.

Our point here, sketchily developed at best, is that entry into semiosis seems to have gender-specific aspects. It may be that access to both the mimetic and the semiosic planes tends to be differently structured for male and female children. Of course, the differential treatment by teachers of male and female students has often been commented on, and is well demonstrated. Similarly, the differing curricular paths laid out for children of either gender are also well documented. Our point is that this is a process that is established very early, and proceeds always simultaneously on both of the axes of mimesis and semiosis, of knowledge and power. Further, the differential entry of men and of women into language and into semiosis has a real history, a history of specific experiences in particular social institutions – such as the preschool day-care centre, or the school – a history which may also be a significantly differentiated one for different individuals from differing social origins. At any rate it is not the pseudohistory posited in asocial, ahistorical psychoanalytic accounts. The entry into semiosis has that institutional specificity, a specificity which attends to class, gender, ethnicity. Children's construction of meaning, their reconstruction of texts, their construction of their semiotic systems always takes place in contexts of this kind, not in some decontextualized or contextless fantasy of 'childhood'.

Production and reproduction of meaning

In both the texts we have looked at, the orientation has been towards reception regimes, although these are necessarily realized through semiotic production. Both texts touch on the discourses of the school, for which they are a kind of preparation. But school as a site for semiotic processing of subjects is distinguished by its attention to production regimes, by its meticulous control over 'correct' forms of the production and reproduction of cultural meaning. The relations between production and reproduction and the regimes that support the process vary with different stages of schooling and with different categories of child and curriculum.

We will begin our analysis with a text from a genre which plays an important role in the primary school curriculum, the 'school project'. The project, as a genre, demands that children attend to sets of relevance constructed by a powerful other, the teacher (although the teacher functions as mediator for the classifications of a larger 'discipline'). The project demands the assemblage of a text that brings together the relevant materials in the relevant order. Often teachers hand out lists of topics and questions which are to be 'covered'. The project is therefore for the child text-makers always an excursion into

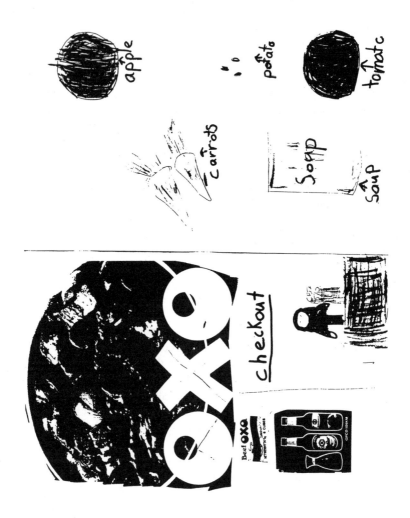

apple

potato

tomato

carrots

Soup

Soup

OXO

Beef OXO

checkout

Plate 8.1 A project-text: 'What Supermarkets Have'

semiotically uncertain or unknown territory. It presents the difficulties and problems of everyday text-making in a heightened form, particularly around the question of the control of signs.

Plate 8.1 is a reproduction of the second and third pages of an (18-page) project, 'Supermarkets', done by an 8-year-old Australian schoolgirl. This project demanded a range of things from the children: to indicate what supermarkets 'have' and how they function; to show their connection with the 'chain of production', and so on. Here the child illustrates something of the 'range' of commodities sold in the supermarket. At the same time she reveals a growing awareness of semiotic processes themselves through an interesting error she makes. She calls these labels 'pictures of labels' although they are in fact the labels themselves. Presumably for her they turn from 'label' to 'picture of label' through the process of display in the project book. The shift from 'object' to 'representation of the object' seems to involve for her the cutting-off or cutting-out of the label, that is, taking the object out of its usual context, and using it 'decontextualized', in a quotational manner, as 'example' in the project. This metaphor of 'quotation' may serve to illustrate the child's relation to semiotic systems generally. On the one hand the child is always in the position of taking existing signs from semiotic systems and 'quoting' them in her own semiotic uses; on the other hand, she is therefore also in the position of 'reproducing' signs when she uses them in their 'own' text. The text constructed by the child on these two pages is 'her' text; indeed it is an appropriate symbol for the mode in which children are positioned as makers of texts in relation to existing semiotic systems: drawing on the inventory of signs (of which they are reproducers) from systems of signs which they do not fully know.

The problem is particularly compounded for the child as these signs are at a great 'distance' from her own semiotic experience. The mode of production of these labels/signs is remote from her in every way; it is a process known to those who have power. At the same time therefore the use of these ready-made signs promises to confer power to her text. Bringing signs of that complexity into her text promises both some control and power for her text. That is of course quite like the use of powerful indexical words in certain domains in the speech or writing of those who wish to gain power by indicating their membership of particular groups. In many other ways this text is like all texts: it draws, intertextually, on existing texts in relevant and appropriate domains, and constructs a new text out of the assemblage of such fragments in accordance with the demands of particular genres. The child-writer's explanatory text provides the principle which gives coherence to this text.

The teacher/reader's comments on this text is a single tick. The second page which is in many ways comparable gets a two-tick comment. It is the page below where the child has herself drawn commodities for sale in the supermarket. The drawings are done with coloured pencils: this is a black-and-white reproduction. What seems to have led the teacher to the higher evaluation is the fact that these are the child's 'own' signs: they are produced by her, not merely reproduced. For this teacher at any rate, and we assume that her judgement is typical, this evaluation signifies the much higher value attaching to production than to reproduction. At a later stage in the curriculum, 'production' equates with notions such as control, 'mastery', spontaneity, authenticity, sincerity; all of them values highly esteemed in our society.

But a valuation in these terms overlooks the fact that the project-text as a whole is primarily an attempt to get the child to reproduce a set of conventions, operating through codes of various kinds. The apparent openness of the project format is offset by the fact that it is constituted in the school curriculum as a genre, governed by a genre-regime that is not always known by the pupil, or even known to exist. The genre of project is highly constrained, as we mentioned, by the teacher's set of instructions as well as by the demands of a number of disciplines, 'the (social) sciences'. So at that level what is rewarded is the ability to reproduce generic schemata of different kinds.

The teacher's final comment on this 18-page project said: 'What a pity you didn't finish your project, Elizabeth. You have barely done half of what was on the sheet. Why?' Clearly a well-articulated aspect of a larger logonomic rule system is operating here, and what is expected of the child by the teacher (/discipline) is conformity with that system. On another level, the child's drawn pictures of vegetables and the tin of soup are highly conventionalized/stylized, so that again it seems not to be 'originativeness' which is at issue. Or take the page below (plate 8.3) from a project on motor cars (from a later year in primary school, done by a male child). Certainly what is displayed here is not 'inventiveness' or 'originativeness', but rather a careful attention to the pre-existing structure of a particular object. It may be that growing into culture and semiosis is making demands of this kind much more often than demands of an originative kind. Indeed, the motor-car project may be thought to be entirely characteristic of what is at issue in the officially enforced processes of entering semiosis. That is, what is really demanded and rewarded is an accurate grasp of specific complex signs from a pre-given repertoire, as shown by an ability to reproduce those signs in a competent manner. In the case of Elizabeth's project, the teacher's highest valuations are attached to pages (plate 8.2) where the child has produced an extended written text. The comments here are: two ticks and 'Good girl', and two ticks and 'Well done'. Both pages are characterized by a well-developed sense of the sentence as the criterial unit. What is rewarded is not complexity or originality of thought, nor even sophisticated language forms. What she knows and is praised for is a highly developed and apparently spontaneous need to write in complete sentences. Again the teacher's high valuation seems to attach to a reproductive rather than to a productive/originative process.

The teacher's valuation scale thus ranges from a single tick for the 'merely reproductive', to a double tick for visual with textual production by the child, to double tick plus comment for extended textual production. This scale may reveal the real principle of evaluation: verbal code over visual code. Beyond that, and at a more ideological level, it seems to be a valuation of reproduction based on internalization over reproduction as mere quote or collage. But whatever 'internalization' may mean, it does in fact represent a much more stringent notion of control, one where the child/subject has become a part of the reproductive device.

This then is the paradox. The pages which are least valued by the teacher show the child text-maker as most active, free and productive. The pages which are most valued by the teacher show the child text-maker as most constrained, confined to the reproductive. Yet this is not how the education system represents itself, especially at the primary level. Our point is not that these constraints should be cast aside in the name of a romantic belief in children's unfettered creativity. It is rather that the semiotic strategy of education works substantially through a double message about creativity and constraint, in which the extent and elaboration of the constraints is often mystified. We can begin to understand, then, why Timothy's lesson in cooking and double talk will be so useful a preparation for later academic success, and why Aaron might run into some problems if he continues to assume that he has a real right to his own opinions.

Codes and subjects: the case of writing

The semiotic conditions in education differ from those of other pre-educational contexts in one decisive respect: the dominance of the written code. The transition from an oral to a literate cultural system is a major achievement of the education process. Proponents of literacy talk of it as an indispensable tool to be acquired, but much more than a set of skills is involved in the entry into literary semiosis. The code of writing allows the development of production and reception regimes that are significantly different from oral codes. These regimes and the practices that they control project new kinds of semiotic agents, new

WHERE THE SUPERMARKET GETS IT'S THINGS FROM.

The Supermarket gets it's things from the whare house. A big truck gets the things from the whare house. Some Strong men put the things on the truck. Then the truck goes to the Supermarket The whare house ᴧ gets it's things from the factory. **The** factory gets raw materials to make the things for the Supermarket. When the Supermarket gets it's things it buys it quite abit cheaper than the price we buy it for. at the Supermarket. This is how it makes money.

Well done

warehouse

Plate 8.2 Extended writing for the supermarket project

HOW THE SUPERMARKET WORKS

When you go to the Supermarket
you park your car in the car
park. You get your shopping list
out and take a trolley from outside and go in. You walk a-
round the shelves and get the
things you want. Then you go
to the checkout and the lady
will **tell** you the price of
them then you give her
the money.

                                              //

                              Good girl

kinds of language and meaning, new forms of subjectivity. The practice of writing, then, is a key stage in the ideological formation of all individuals in contemporary society. That is not, of course, to say that the ideological contents and effects are consistent, or the same for everyone. There are different degrees and kinds of literacy, and this has the further function of helping to mark membership of dominant groups.

The supermarket project we have been looking at comes from a relatively early stage in this child's entry into the semiotic code of written language. By this time, at about 8 years of age, children tend to be proficient though not yet fully accomplished users of the semiotic code of spoken language. The transition from the one code to the other, for that is how the process is constructed by the school system, involves a slow redefinition for the child of itself. That redefinition has to do with a more deliberate and deliberately constructed positioning of self in relation to others, in a set of complex ways. In speaking the role of the 'self', the positioning of the self as speaker or hearer, is not at that stage an issue. Spoken texts are constructed interactively, and for children very often the other participants are adults, who take an initiating and directing role in the formation of the text. So, by virtue of their lesser power, children are 'relieved' of responsibilities for initiating and maintaining the formation of texts. In interactions with their peers, self-consciousness is also not an issue.

In writing, the 'position' of writers is immediately problematic. They are responsible for the construction of the text; they have to construct a text for a particular audience, and in doing so, reciprocally construct a particular position for the writer. These are major problems in learning to write, quite apart from the different organization of the two codes of verbal language, in the modes of speech and writing. Those organizations are themselves closely interconnected with the problems we just mentioned, as well as with the question of the writer's relation to the topic of writing. Take the page reproduced on the left-hand side of plate 8.2, one of the two pieces of extended writing in the project.

The reader is directly addressed as 'you', as he or she might be in spoken language. This 'you' has some overtones of the generalized, universal 'you' of Timothy's mother's 'you don't spit on the spoon'. That is, although the child is imagining one reader, that reader could be nearly anyone. This is reinforced by the use of the definite articles in 'the car park', 'the checkout', 'the lady', 'the money'. Notice the difference that replacing 'the' by 'a' would have: 'you go to a supermarket . . .'

The child's task is to describe 'How the supermarket works'. If she was telling her mother or father or brother, these are the forms she would use, and they would be perfectly usual in that situation, in the immediate presence of the addressee: they would attract no attention. Here in a written text they do, and what does attract attention is that the child has transferred not just grammatical forms but modes of relating to other language-users from the spoken to the written form. At this stage her notion of herself is still constructed within the classifications and notions made available in speech. So instead of describing 'How the supermarket works', she describes what *you*, a particular person, would do in the supermarket. She deals with the demand for abstraction and generality in the mode that she is most familiar with.

Note that in doing so, she too remains an involved participant: '*I* am telling *you*; *I* vouch for this.' In the other lengthy text 'Where the supermarket gets its things from' her positioning is different. Here she is a detached observer. The strategy she uses for this is to give agency to inanimate entities: 'A big truck gets the things . . . the truck goes to the supermarket. The warehouse gets its things from the factory. The factory . . . make(s) the things . . .' So by a fairly consistently applied 'writing out' of human agency, the picture does take on a character of generality; with the disappearance of human agency comes a lack of specificity so that the description becomes universalized. In the process the child writer assumes a position of detached observer/ recorder.

The possibility of assuming that position has important consequences for the writer as a subject, who need not be involved, who can be and is 'objective' and distanced. The requirements of the topic, the issue at hand, have become foremost. This kind of impersonality is what is demanded by science and the scientific mode. Although the forms in which this writer expresses distance and objectivity are not those of fully fledged scientific writing (though the attribution of agency/ animateness to inanimate/non-agentive objects is quite typical of scientific writing as it turns out) the strategies are there, and clear enough. What is perhaps even more astonishing is that the child knows these strategies and meanings already, and that she attempts to reproduce them in terms which her own knowledge of this semiotic code permits.

The motor-car project, written by an 11-year-old male child, shows a much greater development of the code of writing. Although this project is in the social science area, it points very clearly to technical/ scientific areas of the curriculum. In plate 8.3, the page we have previously discussed, the child manages to achieve the effects of distance and objectivity by a number of linguistic/textual devices which are entirely typical of scientific writing. The hypothetical modality 'If . . ., (then) it would be . . .' marks hypothesis off from 'actuality'. The numerous agentless passives ('when heavily loaded', 'can be timed',

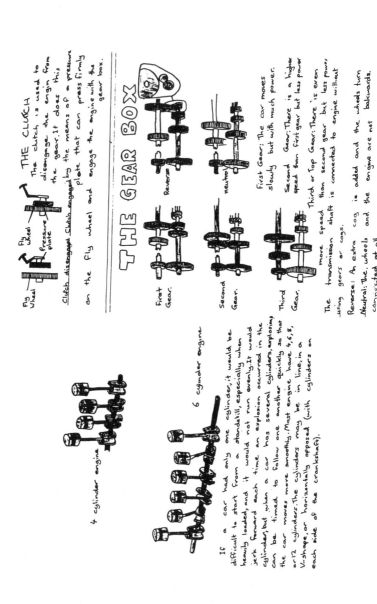

Plate 8.3 A motor-car project: an exercise in objectivity

'horizontally opposed') as well as agentless verb forms such as 'difficult to start' serve to remove human agency from the surface of the text and to focus on process rather than on cause, thus again conveying the impression of objectivity – constructed here as the absence of human subjects and therefore, literally, a focus on the objects under attention. This text is marked too by the use of the technical terms of that domain.

The writer's place is extremely carefully constructed as a non-existent place. That is, the text is written in a manner which indicates that *anyone* could have been the author, so that no particular writer is either needed or involved; consequently, the reader is, as in the supermarket project, reciprocally positioned as absent.

A process such as this clearly has fundamental effects on the user of this code, especially if the use of the code becomes habitual. The subject position of writers in texts of this kind is complex. They learn to efface themselves from the text. The text/object is the all-important thing. It may be that many writers actually come to see that as the reality of their position and of texts: that is the instance of the mindless bureaucrat. Even as mindless bureaucrat, a writer wields the power inherent in this kind of text. Other writers will be aware of the artifice of their constructed absence, and of the increased power that this device gives them. That is the instance of the skilled, manipulating politician. But growing into semiosis also entails not just production, but, most frequently, consumption of semiotic commodities. Here it is essential to understand how consumers/readers are positioned as the result of their entry into semiosis: ranging from fully aware readers who are able to (re)construct texts for their own purposes, to readers who are relatively at the mercy of the text's positioning of its readers.

The process of entering semiosis is surrounded by myth and mystification. Theories of ideology tend to treat ideology as a once-for-all category whose immutable forms confront pre-ideological individuals, assigning them the only social roles and meanings they can have, allowing no space or time in which negotiation or divergence or resistance could occur. Psychoanalysis, especially as expounded by the French theorist Jaques Lacan (1977) proposes a kind of history, a sequence of three stages as a progression through three orders of discourse, the 'real', the 'imaginary' and the 'symbolic'. But this history has the characteristics of myth, since the three stages complete their work shrouded in the mists of a world of infancy, unexaminable and unvariable yet providing a potent charter for explanations of the present. Against these views, which either eliminate history or turn it into myth, we argue that the process of entering semiosis is for everyone a real and complex historical event, or rather a series of histories. These histories contribute different ideological traces to the overall set that comprises the adult ideological repertoire, with different routes that open or close different possibilities for effective action. The determination of the relevant histories is often difficult in practice, and our own account is certainly schematic and full of gaps. However, the main point still stands: semiosis and the processes of social and ideological formation necessarily take place in time, and only a theory with a strong diachronic component can hope to provide an adequate explanatory framework.

Appendix

Key Concepts in a Theory of Social Semiotics

1 Scope of subject

1.1 *Semiotics* is the general study of *semiosis*, that is, the processes and effects of the production and reproduction, reception and circulation of meaning in all forms, used by all kinds of agent of communication. ('Semiotic' as an adjective thus refers to the range of objects of this study while 'semiosis' refers specifically to the process itself.)

1.2 Social semiotics is primarily concerned with human semiosis as an inherently social phenomenon in its sources, functions, contexts and effects. It is also concerned with the social meanings constructed through the full range of semiotic forms, through semiotic texts and semiotic practices, in all kinds of human society at all periods of human history.

1.3 Social semiotics studies all human semiotic systems, since all these are intrinsically social in their conditions and content. Semiotics outside social semiotics would include communication entirely between non-animate entities (e.g., the study of genetic codes, or exchanges of energies within a physical system). However, communication exchanges between machines (e.g., computer–computer communication) would come within the scope of social semiotics, since machines are products of human intentionality and serve social functions.

2 Elements

2.1 Semiotic phenomena always have both social and referential dimensions, and must therefore be described in terms of both the *mimetic plane*, implying some version(s) of reality as a possible referent, and also the *semiosic plane*, implying some semiotic event(s), linking producers and receivers and signifiers and signifieds into a significant relationship.

2.2 The semiosic plane is the indispensable context for the mimetic plane, and the mimetic plane is an indispensable constituent of the semiosic plane. The interaction of both is necessary for the social production of meaning to occur. They are constituted by homologous structures and processes, though capable of producing conflicting or contradictory meanings.

2.3 The smallest unit of meaning that can have an independent material existence is a *message*. A message must have a material existence in which at least two units of meaning, that is *signs*, are organized into a *syntagmatic structure* or syntagm. A syntagm is a significant combination of signs in space–time.

2.4 A sign is a portion of the syntagmatic plane that is treated as a unity. It is fixed by the interaction of both a syntagmatic structure and a paradigmatic structure (or classification system). Paradigmatic structures are organized sets of choices, and the paradigmatic meaning of a sign is derived from the sets of signs that are affirmed or negated by the act of choice in the context of that structure.

2.5 The material realization of a sign in a message is its *signifier*, and the referent it constructs is its *signified*. The structures of message systems are linked to the structures of referents via *codes* which organize signifieds and signifiers through compatible paradigmatic structures.

2.6 Sign systems function most economically in producing meaning if there is a clear link perceived between signifiers and signified by all users of the signs. However, negative and hostile relationships within the semiosic plane motivate the opposite tendency, an inaccessible link between signifiers and signifieds, leading to systematic distortion of such links. Signs can therefore be ranged on a continuum between *transparent* and *opaque*, in terms of how clearly the link between signifier and signified is perceived by a class of semiotic participant.

2.7 Messages are normally organized in relation to the conditions of semiosis by a class of signs called *metasigns*. Metasigns signal different aspects of the semiosic plane in order to constrain the semiotic behaviour of participants. Metasigns are frequently pervasive in the construction of messages, and usually composed of transparent signs as *markers*.

3 Principles of semiotic structure

3.1 Semiotic structures are built up by the two basic acts of joining and separating, producing a play of unities and differences. These acts are complementary and interdependent as they function in semiosis. So acts of separation imply a prior unity, and acts of joining act on a prior stage of greater disunity.

3.2 Some important semiotic operations derived from these two basic acts include kinds of expansion and kinds of contraction, with one major kind of contraction the act of *negation*, and another the act of *choice*. Negation is only meaningful in terms of the positive that it rejects, so that forms of negation (including full and partial negation and inversion) signify the possibility of a positive term. Choice is a type of negative (affirming one term and negating another in a system of differences). It is a major class of operations on paradigmatic systems in the process of constructing syntagms and texts. In so far as choice is a species of negation, an act of choice is only meaningful in relation to the fuller structure of what is chosen and what is rejected.

3.3 Semiotic structures can be described in terms of relations of *cohesion* (fusion/separation, identity/difference) and *order* (vertical and horizontal, involving degrees of complexity and subordination). Two important kinds of order are *hypotaxis* (involving subordination and hierarchy) and *parataxis* (involving parallelism and sequence).

3.4 Structures exist on different *levels*, which can be labelled in relation to the point of semiotic entry as *macro-structures* (structures so large in space or time as to be difficult to perceive directly), *meso-structures* (structures of a scale that makes them accessible to direct inspection) and *micro-structures* (structures too small to be easily perceived). These terms are relative to specific problems and specific semiotic positions. This relativity and specificity is not a disadvantage from the point of view of semiotic analysis. On the contrary, to recognize it is itself an important contribution to effective analysis. Structures at different levels can be related by similarity of patterning, i.e. *homology*, or by contiguity or causality, i.e. *determination*. Semiotic movement between levels can be termed either *stretching* (movements upwards) or *diving* (movements downwards).

3.5 In the syntagmatic plane, an important site of analysis is the *text*. A text is a string of messages which is ascribed a semiosic unity. Texts often contain messages by more than one producer, in more than one code. These messages typically include both mimetic content and series of metasigns, which together project both a version of reality and a version of the semiosic conditions of the text.

3.6 In the semiosic plane, an important site of analysis is the *discourse*. A discourse refers to the process of semiosis rather than its product (i.e. text). It is always realized through texts and is inseparable from them. Since a discourse is a major signified of any text, the semiotic analysis of text must defer to an analysis of discourse.

3.7 Paradigmatic structures consist of items (the materials they organize) and classifiers (principles of classification, differentiating features, identifying labels). Paradigmatic structures exist only in so far as they can be realized materially in texts, either through relational syntagms (syntagms whose meaning is a paradigmatic relationship) or through *markers* (signifiers of classifiers and classifications). Paradigmatic structures are not intrinsically any more abstract or immaterial than syntagmatic structures: in both cases, semiosic acts can project elaborate structures which have no other material existence, but which have semiosic force in so far as they are thought to exist.

3.8 A decisive determinant of the semiosic effect of a message is its *modality*, that is, the presumed relation of its mimetic content to a world of referents. This relationship is situated on a continuum between affirmation (high affinity, high modality) and negation (weak or zero affinity/modality). Modality judgements are conveyed through *modality markers* but interpreted through *modality cues*, through which receivers assess the status of a message by reference to modality markers and also to any or all constituents and relationships of the semiosic plane. Where there is a large amount of modalizing activity in the semiosic plane, the text can be said to be densely modalized, as opposed to lightly modalized. Because modality judgements are based on the semiosic context considered as a unity, modality judgements typically express and are expressed by other major relationships in the semiosic plane, so that modality markers and definitions of 'truth' and 'reality' are used to express or construct specific social relationships.

4 Semiosis and time

4.1 Semiosis as a material event always exists in both space and time, so that all syntagms have a *diachronic* dimension. However, where for purposes of interpretation the passage of time in production or reception of messages is thought to be negligible or irrelevant, syntagms can be treated as *synchronic*.

4.2   Diachronic structures are constituted by either contiguity (identity/ opposition over time, either continuous or discontinuous) or by change or *transformation*.

4.3   Change involves both relatively continuous and relatively discontinuous aspects. Where the discontinuous aspects are emphasized, the process is constructed (and construed) as a *transformation*, that is a discontinuous progression from one structure to another. Where continuity is emphasized, the process is constructed as a *slide*. But every slide can be analysed in structural terms as a transformation, by isolating initial, intermediary and final states, and every transformation can be analysed as composed of slides and patterns of continuous rapid changes. The choice by an interpreter of either model (slide or transformation) is itself ideologically significant.

4.4   Transformational analysis involves minimally an initial and a final structure, and a process, a force and an agent producing the change. Transformations can be attributed to the mimetic plane (*mimetic transformations*) or to the semiosic plane (*semiosic transformations*).

4.5   Mimetic transformations act on syntagmatic and paradigmatic structures of the mimetic plane to produce both *syntagmatic* and *paradigmatic transformations*. Explanation of mimetic transformations must always refer to the semiosic plane for an account of the forces producing the change and its social meaning.

4.6   Semiosic transformations organize the flow of discourse in all media. Explanation of semiosic transformations must always refer to the social relationships of the participants for an account of its social meaning and the forces producing it.

4.7   The meaning of a transformational analysis is the sequence of material structures and the material agents it projects, even though in many cases those structures and agents are not fully accessible to the analyst or never existed in that form. Producers of texts may imply pseudo histories which are, however, part of the meaning of their text; receivers construct their own versions of history, as part of the interpretative process, by reference to the text itself and to other texts that they may invoke. Conversely, producers of texts may deliberately obscure the material history of the text and make transformations that are irreversible: or a class of receivers may find a set of transformations irreversible or even invisible. The status of a transformational analysis, then, is never absolute, but always refers to a particular semiosic event or state.

5 Semiosis and social process

5.1 Social relations in semiotic acts and in social formations are constituted by relations of power (order and subordination) and solidarity (cohesion and antagonism), with these dimensions typically both complementary and opposed. As a result, every social group is characterized by processes of conflict and struggle, and by mechanisms for resolution and mediation, between different social categories based on class, race, gender, age and other aspects of group formation.

5.2 Opposing groups in society express their social relations and negotiate their interests through motivated versions of social reality called *ideological schemas*. Since specific groups may attempt to both express and control conflict through semiotic activity, asserting power and creating solidarity, the ideological content of texts is typically characterized by contradiction and inconsistency, and the functional unit for analysis is not the ideological schema but the *ideological complex*, a set of different and contradictory ideological schemas which serve and express the interests of a single group.

5.3 Ideological complexes are expressed through the mimetic plane. They are also inscribed in the conditions of semiosis as *logonomic systems*. Logonomic systems constrain social behaviour through rules prescribing semiotic production: who is able/forbidden to produce or receive what meanings under what circumstances and in what codes. Logonomic systems at any specific time are social facts. To function they must rely on known categories and rules and active enforcers with means of communication and enforcement.

5.4 Logonomic systems can be specified and transmitted by reference to any of the main elements of the plane of semiosis, although in practice each mode of transmission will be part of an interlocking system. They focus on: (i) producers, through *production regimes*, rules oriented to producers, specifying what meanings they can produce, how and to whom; (ii) receivers, through *reception regimes*, rules oriented to constrain the semiosic potential of receivers; (iii) texts, through *genre regimes*, which use categorizations of texts to enforce constraints on the possibilities of meaning, and production and reception relationships; (iv) referents, through *regimes of knowledge*, or categorizations of possible topics of semiosis in terms of specific versions of reality and social constraints concerning who can properly claim to know or understand them.

5.5 Logonomic systems are realized through syntagmatic forms, which link particular kinds of agent, action, object and circumstances, and through paradigmatic forms, classifications of people, objects, actions and circumstances covered by the rules. At the core of a logonomic system is its kernel, giving the major options of the major classes of agent and object. But logonomic systems are sites of struggle. Logonomic imperialism acts through the syntagmatic plane, extending the strength and scope of syntagmatic bonds, and through the paradigmatic plane, classifying and reclassifying agents, objects, actions and circumstances.

5.6 Logonomic systems can also be resisted and subverted. The kernel can be attacked directly, in its syntagmatic or paradigmatic structures and rules. Or domains of exceptions can be constructed where the structures and rules of the dominant form are weakened or inverted, to create antisocieties, antilanguages and antiworlds.

6 Principles of analysis

6.1 *Semiosic determination* Conditions of the semiosic plane, logonomic systems and sites of opposition, need to be fixed before analysis of the mimetic plane, since semiosic structures determine mimetic structures.

6.2 *Mimetic anchorage* The world of referents needs to be specified independently of the mimetic content of the text.

6.3 *Ideological content* The competing versions of social reality implied by texts and discourses need to be explicated for every text.

6.4 *Analytic anchorage* Analysts need to position themselves in a semiosic structure which incorporates the text, with its discursive processes, in order to make decisions about their own level of analysis, its orientations and implications.

6.5 *Homology* Possible homologies should be investigated, between mimetic and semiosic structures; syntagmatic and paradigmatic structures; synchronic and diachronic structures; micro-, macro- and meso-structures; and verbal and non-verbal structures.

6.6 *Redundancy and absence* Patterns of redundancy should be investigated; messages repeated at different levels, in different codes and media; and also specific absences; motivated suppressions on the mimetic plane.

6.7 *Contradictions*　With every dominant ideological message, the presence of opposing messages and meanings needs to be investigated, in the mimetic and the semiosic plane, in different codes, media and levels.

Annotated Bibliography

What we have called social semiotics is in some respects a particular route through a diverse set of readings from many different disciplines. In order to help readers to use our book more effectively as a point of departure for their own purposes, we list some of the more important authors and texts that we have drawn on or reacted against. These should also enable readers to place our argument in a broader context of debate. We have limited ourselves as far as possible to texts which are readily available, including some introductory texts where appropriate.

Semiotics and discourse

On Saussure, some major theorists have written commentaries, including E. Benveniste, 'Saussure after half a century' (1971), R. Jakobson, 'Sign and system of language' (1980), and J. Derrida in *Of Grammatology* (1976). J. Culler's *Saussure* (1976) is a useful short introduction.

Other influential exponents of semiotics who have developed some of the themes of social semiotics include R. Barthes, especially in *Mythologies* (1973) and the essays in *Image–Music–Text* (1977), and U. Eco, especially in *The Role of the Reader* (1978).

Post-structuralist theorists tend to be difficult, precisely because they seek to emphasize the difficulties and instabilities of structures and structuralism. Some important and challenging works along these lines include J. Derrida, *Writing and Difference* (1978), J. Lyotard, *The Postmodern Condition* (1984), and J. Kristeva, *Desire in Language* (1980). C. Norris, *Deconstruction* (1982), R. Coward and J. Ellis, *Language and Materialism* (1977), and C. Belsey, *Critical Practice* (1980) provide useful introductions to different aspects of this tradition.

There are a number of distinct versions of discourse analysis. Foucault's fullest exposition of his methods is *The Archeology of Knowledge* (1972). Our use of his work draws most directly on his 'Orders of Discourse' (1971). A recent though critical introduction to his work is J. G. Merquior, *Foucault* (1986). See also M. Poster, *Foucault, Marxism and History* (1984).

M. Pêcheux in *Language, Semantics, Ideology* (1982) attempted to link the categories of discourse and ideology (in an Althusserian version of the term) with formal methods of linguistic analysis, in an ambitious contribution to social semiotics. J. Habermas, in such works as *Theory and Practice* (1974) has developed a sophisticated framework for a critical practice of discourse analysis. One critical account of types of discourse analysis is J. B. Thompson *Studies in the Theory of Ideology* (1984).

A number of philosophers of language have contributed useful insights to a theory of social semiotics. Apart from Peirce (1940/65) and Wittgenstein, *Philosophical Investigations* (1967), some important works are A. Schütz, *Collected Papers* (1970–3), G. Mead, *Mind, Self and Society* (1934), and J. L. Austin, *How to Do Things with Words* (1962). Voloshinov's ideas on language and ideology are most forcefully put in his *Marxism and the Philosophy of Language* (1973). D. Silverman and B. Torode, *The Material Word* (1980) provides a number of provocative critical readings of influential texts in sociology and the philosophy of language.

Much work in contemporary linguistic theory can be safely ignored by anyone interested in language or social semiotics. One major exception is Michael Halliday, best approached through the essays in *Learning How to Mean* (1971) and *Language as Social Semiotic* (1978), which have had a profound influence on our own theory. In sociolinguistics, major works and figures are B. Bernstein, *Class, Codes and Control* (1971), Dell Hymes, particularly his 'Models of the interaction of language and social life' (1972) and *Foundations in Sociolinguistics: an Ethnographic Approach* (1974), and W. Labov *Sociolinguistic Patterns* (1978). A useful introduction to sociolinguistics is W. Downes, *Language and Society* (1984).

Other helpful texts include A. Cicourel, *Cognitive Sociology* (1973) and J. Gumperz (ed.), *Language and Social Identity* (1982).

The theory of language of the critical linguistics approach has its fullest expression in G. R. Kress and R. Hodge, *Language As Ideology* (1979). R. Fowler et al., *Language and Control* (1979) also contains useful statements and analyses, while P. Chilton (ed.), *Language and the Nuclear Arms Debate* (1985) includes a range of recent applications and criticisms of the approach.

Society, culture, ideology

There is a very large and diverse body of work in social and political theory that is relevant to social semiotics. Our work is within the tradition deriving from the classics of European sociology, Marx, Weber and Durkheim, as represented by such contemporary works as A. Giddens, *New Rules of Sociological Method* (1976). Among contemporary sociologists, particularly significant is the work of P. Bourdieu: *Distinction* (1984) and *Language and Symbolic Power* (1988).

Anthropology has contributed many works that have been important for social semiotics. B. Malinowski in 'The problem of meaning in primitive languages' (1923) is the most relevant for social semiotics. C. Lévi-Strauss is best approached through the essays collected in *Structural Anthropology* (1963) and *Structural Anthropology II* (1976). G. Bateson, *Steps to an Ecology of Mind*

(1973) covers the main contributions to social semiotics of this important theorist. M. Douglas, *Purity and Danger* (1970) and the essays collected in *Rules and Meanings* (1973) are useful exercises in structural analysis. E. Leach, *Genesis as Myth* (1969) contains a number of exemplary structuralist analyses. Two elegant and stimulating theorists of symbolic structures in non-Western societies are C. Geertz, *The Interpretation of Cultures* (1973) and V. Turner, *The Forest of Symbols* (1967).

For the study of semiotic systems in individual and group interaction, the most important theorist is E. Goffman in his *The Presentation of Self in Everyday Life* (1959), *Asylums* (1961) and other works. See also P. Berger and T. Luckmann, *The Social Construction of Reality* (1966) for the exemplary exposition of the argument of their title.

Theories of counselling and therapy have developed some illuminating insights into the dynamics of language and group interaction, though with some unexamined and contentious ideological assumptions behind their therapeutic practices. Most derive from the work of Freud and/or Bateson. See Watzlawick, Beavin, and Jackson, *Pragmatics of Human Communication* (1967), E. Berne, *Games People Play* (1967), M. Selvini Palazzoli et al., *Paradox and Counterparadox* (1978) and R. Bandler and J. Grinder, *Frogs into Princes* (1979). For a more critical approach to therapeutic discursive practices see R. D. Laing, *The Divided Self* (1969), *The Politics of the Family* (1971) and *Knots* (1972).

Theories of ideology are as important as they are numerous. Marx and Engels' fullest treatment is in *The German Ideology* (1970), on which we draw heavily. Important later contributions to a theory of ideology are L. Althusser in 'Ideology and ideological state apparatuses' (1971) and A. Gramsci's concept of hegemony in *Prison Notebooks* (1971). R. Williams discusses the term usefully in *Keywords* (1976).

A recent and productive synthesis of social and political theory with an account of media and the social production of meaning is found in the work of the Birmingham cultural studies group. One of the best introductions to the approach is the collection of essays in S. Hall et al. (eds), *Culture, Media, Language* (1980).

A number of feminists have theorized the issue of gender so powerfully as to have altered the scope and terrain of contemporary social analysis. Among the most significant works for social semiotics are J. Kristeva, *Desire in Language* (1980) and L. Irigaray, *Divine Women* (1986). A helpful commentary on the work of Irigaray is E. Grosz *Irigaray and the Divine* (1986). A. Cranny-Francis has examined the question of gender and genre in 'Gender and genre' (1987) and 'Sexual politics and political repression in Bram Stoker's Dracula' (1987). A linguistic version of the questions around gender and language is Cate Poynton, *Language and Gender* (1985). A most useful survey is B. Thorne et al., *Language, Gender and Society* (1983).

Mind, meaning and consciousness

Freud's work is a major influence in semiotics as in psychiatry. His own expositions of his ideas are so lucid and comprehensive as to need no popularization: see, for example, his *Introductory Lectures on Psychoanalysis* (1971).

Lacan's influential attempt to synthesize Freud and a version of semiotics is to be found in his *Écrits: a Selection* (1977). This approach has been influential in cinema studies (see, e.g., S. Heath, *Questions of Cinema* (1981) and feminism (see, e.g. J. Mitchell and J. Rose (eds), *Lacan: Feminine Sexuality* (1982)). Another post-structuralist development of Freud is G. Deleuze and F. Guattari, *Anti-Oedipus* (1977).

There have been many critiques of Freud's social theory, in particular from a Marxist perspective. Of particular value for social semiotics has been H. Marcuse, *One Dimensional Man* (1964), which attempts a synthesis of Frankfurt Marxism with Freud and a theory of discourse.

The anthropological–linguistic tradition of Boas, Sapir and Whorf developed its own account of the relation between language, culture and consciousness, though the social and political theory of this school is not strong. Whorf is best approached through the essays collected in *Language, Thought and Reality* (1956), and Sapir in *Selected Writings* (1949).

On the relation between code and culture, H. McLuhan in *Understanding Media* (1964) and other works has been a source of provocative generalizations. More scholarly, with special emphasis on oralcy, is W. Ong, *Orality and Literacy* (1982). W. Benjamin, 'The work of art in an age of mechanical reproduction' (1973) has proved an influential essay on this theme.

Applications/connections

Social semiotics grows out of distinct disciplines, many of them oriented to specific codes and practices. Typically these have fed into social semiotics, rather than being the applications of that theory. The following texts are only a small proportion of those that might be included under this heading.

In literary criticism and cultural studies, a major figure is R. Williams, in *Marxism and Literature* (1977), *Culture and Society 1780–1950* (1958), and *Television: Technology and Cultural Form* (1974). Other significant work is F. Jameson, *The Political Unconscious* (1981) and, in a more structuralist tradition, T. Hawkes, *Structuralism and Semiotics* (1977).

Film and media studies provided a fertile ground for the development of social semiotics. Eisenstein's *The Film Sense* (1968) was an important early work. J. Fiske and J. Hartley, *Reading Television* (1978) is a useful introduction to TV. The Glasgow University Media Group's *Bad News* (1976/80) is a polemical set of studies whose aims have much in common with our own. A. Dorfman and A. Mattelart, *How to Read Donald Duck* (1975) focuses on the issue of cultural imperialism. In the USA, Gerbner's 'cultivation hypothesis' has been a productive focus for research on ideological effects of the media – see, e.g., G. Gerbner, 'Comparative cultural indicators' (1977). On popular song, see R. Barthes in *Image – Music – Text* (1977), R. Hodge, 'Song' (1985) and T. van Leeuwen, 'Music and ideology' (1987).

In art, J. Berger's *Ways of Seeing* (1972) has proved popular and provocative in presenting a critical form of art history which develops many of the same principles as social semiotics.

References

Aers, D. and Kress, G. R. 1981. 'The language of social order: Individual, society and historical process in *King Lear*'. In Aers, D., Hodge, R. and Kress, G. R., *Literature, Language and Society in England, 1580–1680*, Dublin: Gill Macmillan.

Aeschylus 1963. *The Orestes Plays* (trans. P. Roche). New York: Mentor Books.

Althusser, L. 1971. 'Ideology and Ideological State Apparatuses'. In *Lenin and Philosophy and Other Essays*. London: New Left Books.

Althusser, L. and Balibar, E. 1977. *Reading Capital*. London: New Left Books.

Arieti, S. 1981. *Understanding and Helping the Schizophrenic*. Harmondsworth: Penguin.

Arnold, M. 1869. *Culture and Anarchy*. London: Smith, Elder.

Austin, J. L. 1962. *How to Do Things with Words* (2nd ed., 1975). London: Oxford University Press.

Bakhtin, M. 1968. *Rabelais and his World* (trans. H. Iswolsky). Cambridge, Mass.: MIT Press.

Bandler, R. and Grinder, J. 1979. *Frogs into Princes*. Moab, Utah: Real People's Press.

Barthes, R. 1973. *Mythologies* (trans. A. Lavers). London: Paladin.

Barthes, R. 1977. *Image–Music–Text* (trans. S. Heath). London: Fontana.

Bateson, G. 1973. *Steps to an Ecology of Mind*. London: Granada.

Belsey, C. 1980. *Critical Practice*. London: Methuen.

Benjamin, W. 1973. *Illuminations* (trans. H. Zohn). London: Fontana.

Benveniste, E. 1971. *Problems in General Linguistics* (trans. M. Meek). Coral Gables: University of Miami Press.

Berger, J. 1972. *Ways of Seeing*. Harmondsworth: Penguin.

Berger, P. and Luckmann, T. 1966. *The Social Construction of Reality*. New York: Doubleday.

Berne, E. 1967. *Games People Play*. Harmondsworth: Penguin.

Bernstein, B. 1971. *Class, Codes and Control*, vol. 1. London: Routledge and Kegan Paul.

Bourdieu, P. 1971. 'The Berber house or the world reversed'. In *Échanges et Communications: mélanges offerts à Claude Lévi-Strauss à l'occasion de son 60ᵉ anniversaire*, The Hague: Mouton.

Bourdieu, P. 1984. *Distinction: a Social Critique of the Judgement of Taste* (trans. R. Nice). London: Routledge and Kegan Paul.

Bourdieu, P. 1988. *Language and Symbolic Power* (ed. J. B. Thompson). Cambridge: Polity Press.

Bourdieu, P. and Passeron, J.-C. 1977. *Reproduction in Education, Society and Culture* (trans. R. Nice). London: Sage.

Brown, R. and Gilman, A. 1960. 'Pronouns of power and solidarity'. In Sebeok, T. (ed.), *Style in Language*, Cambridge, Mass.: MIT Press.

Brown, R. and Ford, M. 1961. 'Address in American English'. *Journal of Abnormal Psychology*, 62.

Chilton, P. (ed.) 1985. *Language and the Nuclear Arms Debate*. London: Frances Pinter.

Chomsky, N. 1957. *Syntactic Structures*. The Hague: Mouton.

Chomsky, N. 1965. *Aspects of the Theory of Syntax*. Cambridge, Mass.: MIT Press.

Chomsky, N. 1976. *Reflections on Language*. New York: Pantheon Books.

Cicourel, A. 1973. *Cognitive Sociology*. Harmondsworth: Penguin.

Clark, K. 1969. *Civilization*. London: BBC Publications.

Coward, R. 1984. *Female Desire: Women's Sexuality Today*. London: Granada.

Coward, R. and Ellis, J. 1977. *Language and Materialism*. London: Routledge and Kegan Paul.

Cranny-Francis, A. 1987(a). 'Gender and genre: feminist rewritings of detective fiction'. In *Women's Studies International Forum*.

Cranny-Francis, A. 1987(b). 'Sexual politics and political repression in Bram Stoker's *Dracula*'. In C. S. Bloom (ed.), *Masters of Nineteenth-century Suspense*. London: Macmillan.

Culler, J. 1976. *Saussure*. London: Fontana.

Davis, J. 1982. *Kullark/The Dreamers*. Sydney: Currency Press.

de Lauretis, T. 1984. *Alice Doesn't*. Bloomington, Indiana: Indiana University Press.

Deleuze, G. and Guattari, F. 1977. *Anti-Oedipus: Capitalism and Schizophrenia* (trans. R. Hurley, M. Seem and H. Lane). New York: Viking.

Demosthenes 1889. *The Orations* (trans. C. Kennedy). London: Bell.

Derrida, J. 1976. *Of Grammatology* (trans. G. Spivak). Baltimore: Johns Hopkins University Press.

Derrida, J. 1978. *Writing and Difference*. (trans. A. Bass). Chicago: Chicago University Press.

Dorfman, A. and Mattelart, A. 1975. *How to Read Donald Duck* (trans. D. Kunzle). New York: International General.

Douglas, M. 1970. *Purity and Danger*. Harmondsworth: Penguin.

Douglas, M. (ed.) 1973. *Rules and Meanings*. Harmondsworth: Penguin.

Downes, W. 1984. *Language and Society*. London: Fontana.

Durkheim, E. 1970. *Suicide* (trans. J. Spaulding and G. Simpson). London: Routledge and Kegan Paul.

Eaton, T. 1972. *Theoretical Semics*. The Hague: Mouton.

Eaton, T. 1978. 'Literary semantics: modality and style'. *Journal of Literary Semantics*, vii. 1.

Eco, U. 1976. *A Theory of Semiotics*. Bloomington, Indiana: Indiana University Press.

Eco, U. 1978. *The Role of the Reader: Explorations in the Semiotics of Texts*. Bloomington, Indiana: Indiana University Press.

Eisenstein, S. 1968. *The Film Sense* (trans. J. Layda). London: Faber and Faber.

Engels, F. 1884. 'The origin of the family'. In K. Marx and F. Engels (1968), *Selected Works*. London: Lawrence and Wishart.

Everett, M., Waddell, J. and Heath, D. (eds) 1976. *Cross-cultural Approaches to the Study of Alcohol*. The Hague: Mouton.

Faris, J. 1968. 'Validation in ethnographical description: the lexicon of "occasions" in Cat Harbour'. *Man*, n.s., 3, 1.

Fergusson, C. 1959. 'Diglossia'. *Word*, 15, 325–40.

Fiske, J. and Hartley, J. 1978. *Reading Television*. London: Methuen.

Fiske, J., Hodge, R. and Turner, G. 1987. *Myths of Oz: Readings in Australian Popular Culture*. Sydney: Allen and Unwin.

Foucault, M. 1967. *Madness and Civilization* (trans. R. Howard). London: Tavistock.

Foucault, M. 1971. 'Orders of discourse'. *Social Science Information*, 10 (2), 7–30.

Foucault, M. 1972. *The Archaeology of Knowledge* (trans. M. Sheridan Smith). London: Tavistock.

Fowler, R., Hodge, R., Kress, G. R. and Trew, A. 1979. *Language and Control*. London: Routledge and Kegan Paul.

Freud, S. 1965. *The Interpretation of Dreams* (trans. J. Strachey). New York: Avon Books.

Freud, S. 1971. *Introductory Lectures on Psychoanalysis* (trans. J. Strachey). Harmondsworth: Penguin.

Game, A. and Pringle, R. 1983. *Gender at Work*. Sydney: Allen and Unwin.

Geertz, C. 1973. *Interpretation of Cultures*. New York: Basic Books.

Gerbner, G. 1977. 'Comparative cultural indicators' in G. Gerbner (ed.), *Mass Media Policies in Changing Cultures*, New York: John Wiley.

Giddens, A. 1976. *New Rules of Sociological Method*. London: Hutchinson.

Glasgow University Media Group 1976/80. *Bad News* (2 vols). London: Routledge and Kegan Paul.

Goffman, E. 1959. *The Presentation of Self in Everyday Life*, New York: Doubleday.

Goffman, E. 1961. *Asylums*. New York: Doubleday.

Gramsci, A. 1971. *Prison Notebooks* (ed. and trans. Q. Hoare and G. Nowell-Smith). London: Lawrence and Wishart.

Grosz, E. 1986. *Irigaray and the Divine*. Sydney: Local Consumption Publications.

Gumperz, J. (ed.) 1982. *Language and Social Identity*. Harmondsworth: Penguin.

Habermas, J. 1974. *Theory and Practice* (trans. J. Viertel). London: Heinemann.

Habermas, J. 1976. *Legitimation Crisis* (trans. T. McCarthy). London: Heinemann.

Hall, E. 1966. *The Hidden Dimension*. New York: Doubleday.

Hall, S. et al. (eds) 1980. *Culture, Media, Language*. London: Hutchinson.

Halliday, M. A. K. 1971. *Learning How to Mean: Explorations in the Functions of Language*. London: Edward Arnold.

Halliday, M. A. K. 1976. *System and Function in Language* (ed. G.R. Kress). London: Oxford University Press.

Halliday, M. A. K. 1978. *Language as Social Semiotic*. London: Edward Arnold.

Halliday, M. A. K. 1985. *An Introduction to Functional Grammar*. London: Edward Arnold.

Halliday, M. A. K. and Hasan, R. 1976. *Cohesion in English*. London: Longmans.

Hawkes, T. 1977. *Structuralism and Semiotics*. London: Methuen.

Heath, S. 1981. *Questions of Cinema*. Bloomington, Indiana: Indiana University Press.

Heider, F. 1958. *The Psychology of Interpersonal Relations*. New York: Wiley.

Herriot, J. 1985. *Only One Woof*. London: Piccolo Books.

Hjelmslev, L. 1953. *Prolegomena to a Theory of Language*. Bloomington, Indiana: Indiana University Press.

Hodge, R. 1984. 'Historical semantics and the meaning of "discourse"'. *Australian Journal of Cultural Studies*, 2, 2.

Hodge, R. 1985. 'Song'. In *Discourse and Literature* (ed. T. van Dijk). Amsterdam: John Benjamin.

Hodge, R. and Kress, G. R. 1982. 'Semiotics of love and power: *King Lear* and a new stylistics'. *Southern Review*, 15, 2.

Hodge, R. and Kress, G. R. 1986. 'Rereading as exorcism: semiotics and the ghost of Saussure'. *Southern Review*, 19, 1.

Hodge, R. and Tripp, D. 1986. *Children and Television*. Cambridge: Polity Press.

Hoggart, R. 1958. *The Uses of Literacy*. Harmondsworth: Penguin.

Humphreys, S. 1983. *The Family, Women and Death*. London: Routledge and Kegan Paul.

Hymes, D. 1972. 'Models of the interaction of language and social life'. In J. Gumperz and D. Hymes (eds), *Directions in Sociolinguistics: the Ethnography of Communication*, New York: Holt, Rinehart and Winston.

Hymes, D. 1974. *Foundations in Sociolinguistics: an Ethnographic Approach*. Philadelphia: University of Pennsylvania Press.

Irigaray, L. 1986. *Divine Women*. Sydney: Local Consumption Press.

Jakobson, R. 1968. *Child Language, Aphasia and Phonological Universals*. The Hague: Mouton.

Jakobson, R. 1980. 'Sign and system of language: a reassessment of Saussure's doctrine'. *Poetics Today*, 2: 1a, 33–8.

Jakobson, R. and Waugh, L. 1979. *The Sound Shape of Language*. Brighton: Harvester Press.

Jameson, F. 1981. *The Political Unconscious: Narrative as a Socially Symbolic Act*. London: Methuen.

Kress, G. R. 1982. *Learning to Write*. London: Routledge and Kegan Paul.

Kress, G. R. 1985. *Linguistic Processes in Socio-cultural Practice*. Geelong: Deakin University Press.

Kress, G. R. (ed.) 1987. *Communication and Culture*. Sydney: N.S.W. University Press.

Kress, G. R. 1987. 'Textual matters: the social effectiveness of style'. In D. Birch and M. O'Toole (eds), *Functions of Style*, London: Francis Pinter.

Kress, G. R. 1988. *Writing as Social Process*. London: Routledge.

Kress, G. R. and Hodge, R. 1979. *Language as Ideology*. London: Routledge and Kegan Paul.

Kristeva, J. 1980. *Desire in Language* (trans. T. Gora, A. Jardine, L. Roudiez). New York: Columbia University Press.

Kuhn, T. S. 1970. *The Structure of Scientific Revolutions*. Chicago: Chicago University Press.

Labov, W. 1978. *Sociolinguistic Patterns*. Oxford: Blackwell.

Lacan, J. 1977. *Écrits: a Selection* (trans. A. Sheridan). New York: Norton.

Laing, R. D. 1969. *The Divided Self*. New York: Pantheon Books.

Laing, R. D. 1971. *The Politics of the Family*. New York: Pantheon Books.

Laing, R. D. 1972. *Knots*. Harmondsworth: Penguin.

Leach, E. (ed.) 1969. *Genesis as Myth*. London: Jonathan Cape.

Leach, E. 1970. *Claude Lévi-Strauss*. London: Fontana.

Lévi-Strauss, C. 1963. *Structural Anthropology* (trans. C. Jakobson and B. Schoepf). New York: Basic Books.

Lévi-Strauss, C. 1969(a). *The Raw and the Cooked* (trans. J. and D. Weightman). London: Jonathan Cape.

Lévi-Strauss, C. 1969(b). *The Elementary Structures of Kinship* (trans. J. Belle and J. von Sturmer). London: Jonathan Cape.

Lévi-Strauss, C. 1976. *Structural Anthropology II* (trans. M. Layton). Harmondsworth: Penguin.

Lukacs, G. 1963. *The Meaning of Contemporary Realism*. London: Merlin.

Lyotard, J. 1984. *The Postmodern Condition* (trans. G. Bennington and B. Massumi). Minneapolis: University of Minnesota Press.

Malinowski, B. 1923. 'The problem of meaning in primitive languages'. In C. K. Ogden and G. A. Richards, *The Meaning of Meaning*, London: Routledge and Kegan Paul.

Malinowski, B. 1965. *Coral Gardens and Their Magic*. Bloomington, Indiana: Indiana University Press.

Marcuse, H. 1964. *One Dimensional Man*. London: Routledge and Kegan Paul.

Marx, K. 1971. *Early Texts* (trans. D. McLellan). Oxford: Blackwell.

Marx, K. and Engels, F. 1970. *The German Ideology* (trans. C. Arthur). London: Lawrence and Wishart.

McLuhan, M. 1964. *Understanding Media: the Extensions of Man*. New York: McGraw Hill.

Mead, G. 1934. *Mind, Self and Society* (ed. C. Morris). Chicago: Chicago University Press.

Mead, M. 1962. *Male and Female*. Harmondsworth: Penguin.

Merquior, J. G. 1986. *Foucault*. London: Fontana.

Mitchell, J. 1975. *Psychoanalysis and Feminism*. New York: Vintage Books.

Mitchell, J. and Rose, J. (eds) 1982. *Lacan: Feminine Sexuality* (trans J. Rose). New York: Norton.

Morris, C. 1971. *Writings on the General Theory of Signs*. The Hague: Mouton.

Muecke, S. 1982. 'Language as a series of statements'. *Southern Review*, 17, 4.

Muecke, S. 1984. *Reading the Country*. Perth: Fremantle Arts Centre Press.

Namba, M. and Kaiya, H. 1982. *Psychobiology of Schizophrenia*. Oxford: Pergamon.

278 REFERENCES

Newcomb, H. 1974. *TV: the Most Popular Art*. New York: Doubleday.
Norris, C. 1982. *Deconstruction: Theory and Practice*. London: Methuen.
Ong, W. 1982. *Orality and Literacy*. London: Methuen.
Orwell, G. 1954. *1984*. Harmondsworth: Penguin.
Palazzoli, M. Selvini, Boscolo, G., Cecchin, G. and Prata, G. 1978. *Paradox and Counterparadox* (trans. E. Burt). New York: Jason Aronson.
Pêcheux, M. 1982. *Language, Semantics, Ideology*. London: Macmillan.
Peirce, C. S. 1940/65. *Collected Papers*. Cambridge, Mass.: Belknap Press.
Poster, M. 1978. *Critical Theory of the Family*. London: Pluto Press.
Poster, M. 1984. *Foucault, Marxism and History*. Cambridge: Polity Press.
Poynton, C. 1985. *Language and Gender: Making the Difference*. Geelong: Deakin University Press.
Price, R. and Paisley, W. (eds) 1981. *Public Communication Campaigns*. Beverley Hills: Sage.
Quant, M. 1984. *Colour by Quant*. London: Octopus Books.
Rochester, S. and Martin, J. 1979. *Crazy Talk*. London: Plenum.
Sansom, B. 1980. *Camp at Wallaby Cross*. Canberra: Australian Institute of Aboriginal Studies.
Sapir, E. 1949. *Selected Writings* (ed. D. Mandelbaum). Berkeley: University of California Press.
Saussure, F. de 1974. *Course in General Linguistics* (ed. J. Culler, trans. W. Baskin). London: Fontana.
Schütz, A. 1970–3. *Collected Papers*. The Hague: Martinus Nijhof.
Silverman, D. and Torode, B. 1980. *The Material Word*. London: Routledge and Kegan Paul.
Sophocles, 1947. *The Theban Plays* (trans. E. F. Watling). Harmondsworth: Penguin.
Spender, D. 1980. *Man Made Language*. London: Routledge and Kegan Paul.
Thompson, J. B. 1984. *Studies in the Theory of Ideology*. Cambridge: Polity Press.
Thomson, G. 1972. *Aeschylus and Athens*. New York: Haskell House.
Thorne, B., Kramerae, C. H. and Henley, N. 1983. *Language, Gender and Society*. Rowley, Mass.: Newbury House.
Turner, V. 1967. *The Forest of Symbols*. New York: Cornell University Press.
Tylor, E. 1971. *Primitive Culture*. London.
Van Gennep, A. 1960. *Rites of Passage*. London: Routledge and Kegan Paul.
van Leeuwen, T. 1987. 'Music and ideology: notes towards a sociosemiotics of mass-media music'. *SASSC* (Sydney Association for Studies in Society and Culture), Sydney: Sydney University Press.
Voloshinov, V. N. 1973. *Marxism and the Philosophy of Language*. New York: Seminar Press.
Vygotsky, L. 1962. *Thought and Language*. Cambridge, Mass.: MIT Press.
Watzlawick, P., Beavin, J. and Jackson, D. 1967. *Pragmatics of Human Communication*. New York: Norton.
Whorf, B. 1956. *Language, Thought and Reality* (ed. J. Carroll). Cambridge, Mass.: MIT Press.
Williams, R. 1958. *Culture and Society 1780–1950*. London: Chatto and Windus.
Williams, R. 1974. *Television: Technology and Cultural Form*. London: Fontana.

Williams, R. 1976. *Keywords*. London: Fontana.

Williams, R. 1977. *Marxism and Literature*. London: Oxford University Press.

Withnell, E. 1984. 'Spatial determinations of the criminal's existential world'. *Australian Journal of Cultural Studies*, 2, 2.

Wittgenstein, L. 1967. *Philosophical Investigations*. Oxford: Blackwell.

Wittgenstein, L. 1971. *Tractatus Logico-Philosphicus* (2nd edn). London: Routledge and Kegan Paul.

Index

Italic page numbers indicate major, definitional entries.